# HAMLYN
# ALL COLOUR
# KITCHEN
# GARDENING

# HAMLYN
# ALL COLOUR
# KITCHEN
# GARDENING

## BCA
LONDON · NEW YORK · SYDNEY · TORONTO

Where necessary, varieties of vegetables and fruits have been given.

## Key to vegetable and herb symbols

| Container | Suitable for a small plot (under 100m²/ 120 sq yd) | Suitable for a large plot (over 100m²/ 120 sq yd) | Suitable for greenhouse cultivation | Sun | *Preferred situation* Semi-shade | Shade | Sowing or planting depth | Distance between rows | Distance between plants | Growing time from sowing or planting |

## Key to fruit symbols

| Container | Suitable for a small plot (under 100m²/ 120 sq yd) | Suitable for a large plot (over 100m²/ 120 sq yd) | *Preferred situation* Sun | Semi-shade | Degree of pruning necessary | Type of training recommended | Distance between bushes or trees | Harvest time |

### Acknowledgements

This book has been compiled with material previously published by Octopus Illustrated Publishing. Additional text by Suzy Powling, Jenny Plucknett and Stella Vayne.

Line drawings by Sandra Pond and Will Giles
Colour illustrations by Jim Robins and Rod Sutterby

The publishers would like to thank the following organizations and individuals for their kind permission to reproduce the photographs on the jacket and inside of this book.
*Jacket* Octopus Publishing Group Ltd/Jerry Harpur: FC right, BC top left; Neil Holmes: FC left, FC centre; George Wright: BC top right, BC below left. Harry Smith Collection: BC top centre, BC below right.
*Inside* A-Z Botanical Collection; Eric Crichton; Brian Furner; Garden Picture Library; the Octopus Illustrated Publishing Picture Library/Rex Bamber, Michael Boys, Melvin Grey, Jerry Harpur, Neil Holmes, Andrew Lawson, George Wright; Photos Horticultural/Michael Warren; Harry Smith Horticultural Collection; Sue Stickland/Henry Doubleday Research Association; Thompson and Morgan.

This edition published 1992 by BCA
by arrangement with
Hamlyn which is an imprint of Octopus Illustrated Publishing,
part of Reed International Books Limited,
Michelin House, 81 Fulham Road, London SW3 6RB

CN 3512

A catalogue record for this book is available from the British Library

Typeset by Dorchester Typesetting Group Ltd, Dorchester
Produced by Mandarin Offset – printed in Hong Kong

# CONTENTS

# INTRODUCTION

To grow fruit and vegetables successfully it is important to care for the soil and to raise healthy plants that can resist pests and diseases.

## SOIL

Soil is produced over many millions of years by rock breaking up. Each type of rock produces a different type of soil. There are five main soil types: clay, sand, silt, peat and chalk. All have different characteristics with some advantages and some disadvantages so it is important to understand your soil in order to build on its good points and improve its poor points. All types of soil can be improved by adding organic matter.

**CLAY**  This is a cold and heavy soil made up of tiny particles which pack tightly together holding the water in, rather than allowing it to drain away. Clay feels sticky when wet, making it hard to work, and goes hard when dry. The drainage can be improved by adding lime and digging in organic matter. Both help to aerate the soil, allowing water and roots to pass through it more easily. Dig it over roughly in the autumn and leave for winter frosts to break it up. Clay usually contains reserves of plant nutrients and when improved will grow good crops of most fruit and vegetables. Root vegetables are the likely exception but digging deep beds should improve the chances of success.

**SAND**  Sandy soil is light and gritty, made up of larger uneven particles with space between them. This makes sandy soil easy to work, and quick to heat up in the spring. However, because it is free draining, there is little reserve of moisture for plants in dry weather and nutrients can be quickly leached out of the soil. Replace lost nutrients in the spring, shortly before planting, by spreading organic matter on top of the soil or by digging it into only a shallow top level – it will soon sink deeper. You will need to provide extra plant food with fertilizers. Mulch well with well-rotted compost to minimize evaporation of water and to further build up a fertile layer of top soil. A sandy soil improved in this way should grow peas, beans, cauliflowers, potatoes and fruit well.

**SILT**  This very fine soil packs down when wet in the same way as clay and so does not drain well either. Use the same methods as for clay to improve the drainage. Dig over roughly in the autumn and add lots of organic matter plus coarse grit to open up the soil. A well-cultivated silt soil will grow most vegetables and fruit well. Dig special deep beds if you intend to grow root vegetables, which will not otherwise do well on silt.

**CHALK**  This pale coloured soil, which is often stony, is free draining like sand but contains high levels of calcium, which combines with iron, boron, manganese and zinc to make these nutrients unavailable to plants. It is often too alkaline for growing vegetables, which prefer a slightly acid soil. To counteract chalky soil's high level of lime dig in plenty of organic matter. In an improved chalk soil brassicas, peas and beans and fruit will grow particularly well.

**PEAT**  This dark brown or grey soil is derived from decayed plants rather than rock. It is usually acid and badly drained so you will need to improve drainage by digging deeply and incorporating plenty of bulky organic matter. Fork over regularly to improve aeration. Adding lime will lower the acidity. Many vegetables will flourish in a well-cultivated peaty soil, especially potatoes, celery and the onion family. Fruit is less likely to be successful.

**ANALYZING YOUR SOIL**  To find out what your soil is lacking and therefore enable you to improve it efficiently, send off a sample for professional analysis. Companies who offer this service advertise in gardening magazines. They will be able to tell you the chemical make-up of your soil, and what type of fertilizer and how much you need to use to correct it. If you intend to garden organically ask for information about organic fertilizers only.

**ACID OR ALKALINE SOILS** How well plants grow also depends on how acid or alkaline the soil is. In a slightly acid soil, ideal for vegetables, most nutrients dissolve slowly and can be taken up by the roots. If the soil is too acid, nutrients can be washed away altogether or lie in toxic quantities in the soil water while vital phosphorus becomes unavailable to plants. Earthworms, so important for improving the structure of the soil, will move out of a very acid soil. If the soil is alkaline, trace elements become insoluble and cannot be taken up by plants.

Use one of the widely available testing kits to check the pH of your soil. A neutral soil has a pH of 7; anything below that is acid, anything above is alkaline. Most vegetables grow best on a soil with a pH value of 6-6.5. If your soil is too acid, adding lime will help. The quantity needed will depend on your soil type: clay will take more than a sandy soil. Be cautious when using lime, as over-liming can be very harmful, and only apply lime every three to four years. Adding calcified seaweed will also make the soil less acid. To increase the acidity of an alkaline soil, add large quantities of well-rotted organic matter.

**IMPROVING YOUR SOIL** In the wild a plant grows, taking nutrients from the soil, then dies back, and aided by worms, insects, and bacteria the rotted plant returns those nutrients to the soil so that they can be used again by other plants. In cultivation, and especially in the vegetable and fruit garden, this balanced cycle is broken because we harvest the plants and tidy up the garden by removing dead material. We therefore need to replace the naturally rotted organic matter each year by digging in manure or garden compost.

Apart from supplying food for the growing plants, digging in organic matter improves the soil's structure. Worms, insects and beneficial bacteria are attracted by the supply of food and multiply. Worms and insects improve the aeration of the soil by burrowing; in addition, worms provide fertilizer in the form of worm casts. Some bacteria help in the process of decay while others fix nitrogen from the air into the soil.

Bulky organic matter also helps to turn clay particles into larger crumbs and holds these crumbs apart so that drainage will be improved. It also coats the particles of sand so that the water drains less easily.

*Animal manure* The manure provided by herbivores is an excellent soil conditioner. Contact local stables for supplies of horse manure, which is better if it is based on straw bedding rather than wood shavings. Cow manure is not as readily available as it used to be as a result of current cattle-rearing methods. If you live in the country look for a local farmer who turns out his cattle in the summer in the hope that he has supplies to spare at the end of the winter. Sheep manure is high in nutrients so if you live near a sheep farm ask the farmer if you can collect it off the fields. Pig manure is also high in nutrients and chicken manure is very rich.

Do not use fresh animal manure on the garden. It needs to rot down completely first as in the fresh state it can burn plant leaves and stems, and the decomposing straw it contains will use up nitrogen in the soil.

*Mustard is a quick-growing green manure, which is dug into the soil before flowering to provide nutrients and improve the soil's structure.*

**Three-part compost bin**
*Where space permits, it is best to have a compost heap with three compartments: one for filling with recent waste; one for the compost in the process of decomposing; and the last for the compost ready for using in the garden. Forking the compost from one bin to another has the advantage of aerating it. The heap can be built on either soil or concrete.*

Leave it to decay for at least two to three months, longer if possible. If you can only get small quantities, add it to the compost heap where it will speed up decomposition. Larger quantities should be stacked and covered, especially through winter to protect the heap from bad weather. If you are worried about hormones fed to cattle or chickens, or pesticides that may remain in the straw, it is wiser to leave the manure for at least a year before using it.

*Green manure* Green manure is a quick growing crop that is dug back into the soil, while still young and green, to improve the soil's structure. If you have an empty bed, especially if your soil is light and free draining, it is better to sow a green manure like mustard, winter tare or red clover than leave the soil bare when rain can destroy the structure, nutrients drain away and weeds start to grow. Although the growing plants remove some nutrients, when dug back they provide more. As an alternative to digging the plants back into the soil they can be chopped off and left on the surface to be incorporated when they have decayed.

*Garden compost* A very good source of bulky organic material, free to us all, is household and garden vegetable waste. This again needs to decompose before it can be added to the soil. A compost container not only looks tidy but it speeds up decomposition by keeping the material warm. You can simply pile the material in a heap but it will take longer to rot down.

Waste material shrinks considerably when decomposing and the house and garden waste from one family results in a depressingly small heap, too small to provide all the bulk that a vegetable garden will need. You can increase the quantity by collecting waste from local vegetable shops or market stalls.

*Tips on creating good compost* Make the size of the container as large as you can: 1sq m/3sq ft is the minimum practical size. If your garden is very small, purpose-built compost bins are available.

Use good insulating materials for the container to help maintain the heat in the heap. Line the base of the container with a 15-cm/6-in layer of coarse material like straw or tough stalks or use wire mesh laid over widely spaced bricks to allow air to circulate.

Add about 20cm/8in of fresh mixed material to the container at any one time. The easiest way of doing this is to place waste materials first into a black dustbin liner, mix up, then add the contents when full. By adding a mixture of materials, the heap remains well aerated and doesn't pack down.

Include any fresh or cooked plant or vegetable waste from the house or garden, including lawn mowings. Slightly woody stems will need shredding or chopping.

Do not include animal waste which may attract vermin, woody material such as hedge clippings or rose prunings which will take a long time to break down, any diseased or infected plant material, weeds that have gone to seed or roots of perennial weeds like ground elder, couch grass or creeping buttercup.

The bacteria which act to decompose the material put on the heap need air, moisture and nitrogen. The water is mainly obtained from the leaves put on the heap but you should water dry materials like straw before adding them. Including animal manure in the heap will help to provide nitrogen, as will seaweed or seaweed extract or a proprietary compost activator. Adding lime helps to neutralize the natural acidity. The bacteria prefer a less acid environment so this will also help to speed up decomposition.

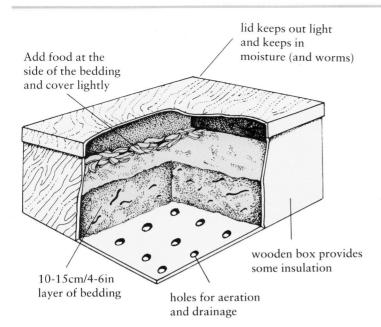

Add food at the side of the bedding and cover lightly

lid keeps out light and keeps in moisture (and worms)

10-15cm/4-6in layer of bedding

holes for aeration and drainage

wooden box provides some insulation

**Worm box** *Moist compost, shredded newspaper or leaves make up the bedding in the base. The worms are fed with vegetable and kitchen waste.*

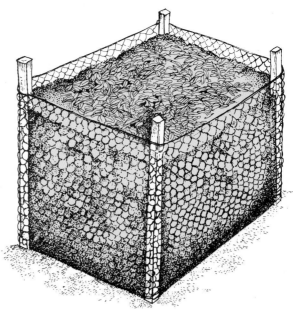

**Leaf enclosure** *Fill a simple, rectangular structure with leaves, watering them if dry. In 3 years, the resulting mould may be used for potting compost.*

Compost needs to be covered to keep the heat in and to prevent the material becoming too wet. An old piece of carpet or black plastic is suitable. In summer a heap should be ready for use in about three months, in winter it will take more like nine months.

**MAKING A COMPOST BIN** If you have the room make the compost bin with three separate compartments, one in which to put fresh waste material, one which has been filled up then left to rot down and one of compost ready for use. The sections can be made from timber planks or breeze blocks on three sides of the square with removable wooden boards on the fourth side so that the compost is easy to get at.

*Worm compost* Worm casts are very rich in nutrients in a form that is readily available to plants, so the compost produced in a worm box is closer to a fertilizer than a compost. The worms used are brandlings which are used by fishermen, and are available from fishing shops. In the base of the box (see illustration above), place a layer of moist compost, shredded newspaper or leaves. Feed the worms with a mixture of chopped-up vegetable and kitchen waste; include some protein which they also need. Animal manure is also suitable. Do not add huge quantities of material, no more than a 7.5-cm/3-in layer per week. Add some calcified seaweed because the worms do not like acid conditions. The worms will work best between 13-25C/55-77F and will die in freezing weather so cover the box with old carpet to insulate it. Some of the compost can be removed after 2 months.

*Leaf mould* Autumn leaves take a long time to rot down but are well worth collecting and making into leaf mould. In a dry, shady area make a simple frame from four posts pushed into the ground and with wire-netting stretched around them. Fill with leaves, pressing down each layer as you add it, and allow about two to three years for the leaves to decompose. Then use for potting compost or, sieved, for seed compost.

*Seaweed* A valuable source of organic material for the soil, seaweed can be added directly to the soil but leave it to stand for a few days for some of the salt to evaporate before using it.

*Mushroom compost* Mushroom compost is a dark, crumbly material. It is the growing medium for commercially cultivated mushrooms, which having been used once is discarded because mushrooms are extremely vulnerable to soil-borne diseases and each crop is grown on fresh, sterilized compost. It is good for improving the texture of the soil but as it contains lime it is more suitable for use on acid soils. Spent mushroom compost usually contains residues of chemicals as well as the fungus gnats they are used to destroy, so it is best to let it stand for 12 months before use.

**CARING FOR PLANTS AND GARDEN**

In most years it is only necessary to dig the soil, or fork it, to the depth of a spade blade. However, every three to four years it is a good idea to dig more deeply. This stops a compressed layer forming below the cultivated section which will impede drainage and it allows compost or manure to be included at a deeper level. The deeper cultivated soil encourages plant roots to go downwards, drawing nutrients from a greater depth, and this means that they are also more able to withstand drought. Plants can also be grown closer together.

**DIGGING** Double digging is done in a similar way to single digging (see illustrations below) except that the soil at the bottom of the trench is loosened to a further blade's depth with a fork. A good layer of manure or compost is put into the bottom of the trench, then the soil from the second trench is spread over the manure in the first and soil and compost are forked to mix them. The last trench is filled with the soil from the first.

Heavy soils are usually dug in autumn. The surface is left rough so that frost will help to break up the heavy clods. The surface is forked lightly in the spring, before sowing or planting. The soil in a narrow bed can be formed into a long ridge and covered in manure. This helps drainage and still allows the weather to break up the soil. With light soils it is better to cover the surface with compost or manure through the winter but leave any digging until the spring.

Once the soil has been dug it is important to keep off it. The structure of the soil is easily destroyed so it is wise to keep beds to a size that allows you to attend to growing plants without going on to the soil. Lay a plank on the surface if you have to walk on it.

**WEEDING** Perennial weeds with creeping root systems, like ground elder, or deep tap roots, like dandelions, need to be dug out and burned. Include even the smallest piece of root.

Annual weeds will gradually decrease over the years if you make sure that you never allow them to flower or seed and remove them as soon as you see them, or even better hoe to remove them before they reach the light. Mulching will help considerably by cutting off the light from emerging weeds but this cannot be done until vegetable seedlings are through.

**WATERING** In dry weather it is better to water less often but thoroughly than frequently and lightly. Light watering simply encourages roots to grow near to the surface and these will immediately suffer in dry weather whereas deeper roots have a reserve to draw on. It takes time for water to sink through the soil. Check by pushing a finger into the ground: it can look very wet on the top and feel bone dry only a short way below the surface. It is at a deeper level that roots need water.

The exception to the above rule is when watering seedlings which have just been planted out, as they can take up only a little water at a time and will need daily but light watering. Leafy vegetables need a lot of water throughout growth. Fruiting vegetables like tomatoes and cucumbers benefit most if they are watered well when flowering and when the fruits start to swell. Root vegetables should need little watering in the early stages unless it is very dry when, if they are not watered, subsequent heavy rain could result in the roots splitting.

**MULCHING** Mulching is adding a layer of material on top of the soil to stop the soil from drying out. It can also have a number of other benefits, including warming up the soil, but these depend on what material is

**How to dig correctly**
*First, chop at right angles to the trench, marking out only a small bite at a time.*

*Holding the spade vertically, and placing one foot on the tread, cut down parallel to the trench.*

*Slipping one hand down to the base of the handle, turn the clod over into the previous trench.*

## Some methods of conserving water

○ Dig in organic matter, which helps to conserve water in the soil.

○ Mulch plants to stop the top layers of soil from drying out.

○ Water around plants, but not on any surrounding bare soil. This simply encourages weeds to grow.

○ Use a length of special flat watering hose with small holes in it. Where possible keep this in place beneath the mulch.

○ Protect plants from wind which quickly dries out the soil's surface.

used. Some materials, black polythene, biodegradable paper, or newspaper for example, will also act as a weed control because they cut out the light from growing weeds. The papers can be dug into the soil at the end of the season. Compost and manure mulches will eventually be drawn into the soil surface by worms and so continue to feed the soil and improve the structure but weeds, like the vegetables, will flourish. They are, however, more easily removed from a mulch. White plastic reflects on to plants and aids growing and ripening fruit, but does not suppress weeds.

Lay plastic mulches when planting out, either between rows of plants or cut crosses in the plastic and plant through them. The easiest way to water plants grown in this way is to lay a length of flat seep hose beneath the plastic and leave it there. Less water will be necessary as the plastic stops evaporation. Any sheet material and especially plastic needs to be held down securely or it can easily blow away. Place it on the soil and with a trowel make 10cm/4in slits in the soil along the edges. Feed the edges of the sheet into the slits and push the soil back over the top to hold the edges in place.

If you are using loose material, allow seedlings to come through before you spread it. Use enough material to make a layer at least 5cm/2in in depth. This can be put down in advance when planting out seedlings and simply be pushed to one side while planting, then moved back into place around the plants afterwards.

**FEEDING PLANTS** Fertilizers are used to supply extra nutrients to growing plants when needed. They are applied in two ways, either before planting or

sowing as a base dressing, which is raked or forked into the soil, or as a top dressing, which is sprinkled around the growing plants, or, if in liquid form, applied with a watering can around the base of a plant.

Plants need the following nutrients plus some trace elements to grow.

NITROGEN – N This is important for leaf growth, so brassicas require large amounts of nitrogen.

PHOSPHATE – P This is necessary for root growth and for young plants and new shoots.

POTASH – K This aids the production of flowers and fruit and keeps plants healthy.

To provide supplies of one or all of these nutrients you can use a chemical or organic fertilizer.

*Chemical fertilizers* These can contain one major nutrient or are a compound, a balance of all three. They are easy to use, produce quick results and promote high yields but organic growers would argue that flavour suffers and plants are more prone to pests and diseases. Furthermore, artificial fertilizers do not put anything back into the soil itself for the next generation of plants.

*Organic fertilizers* These are usually gentler in action and so there is no danger of giving plants too much, which can occur with a chemical fertilizer.

**CROP ROTATION** The few perennial vegetables and a number of herbs require a permanent position but most vegetables are grown as annuals. Those of a similar type have similar requirements of the soil and therefore need to be grown together. They also attract the same pests and diseases, however, which, if the plants were continually grown in the same spot, would build up in the soil. Annually grown crops are therefore moved to a new spot and this is usually done – because of lack of space – on a 3-year rotation. This means that the same plants are only grown every third year in the same spot. In Victorian times a 7-year rotation was used.

Crop rotation also helps to care for the soil as one type of vegetable will remove more of certain nutrients, so the time lapse allows these to be replaced. Peas and beans add nitrogen to the soil which can then be utilized by the next crop and the rotation of shallow and deep rooting vegetables helps the soil structure. Unfortunately, moving the position of a crop does not guarantee that you will have no pests or diseases. Airborne pests will not be deterred and pests in the soil may attack any crop. However, rotation is a valuable

# Organic fertilizers, ground minerals and liquid feeds

## DRY ORGANIC FERTILIZERS

**Dried blood** A very quick-acting source of nitrogen.

**Fishmeal** A useful source of nitrogen and phosphorus, fairly quick acting.

**Bonemeal** Rich in phosphorus and also contains a little nitrogen. Fairly slow acting, depending partly on how finely it is ground.

**Blood, fish and bone** Supplies phosphorus and some nitrogen but scarcely any potassium – any brand listing a %K will almost certainly have it added in chemical form.

**Hoof and horn** Supplies mainly nitrogen; slow action, depending on how finely it is ground.

**Seaweed meal** One of the few organic fertilizers containing a significant amount of potassium; also supplies nitrogen and a small amount of phosphorus, so is near to being a complete fertilizer like the chemical Growmore.

**Calcified seaweed** Contains a very wide range of minerals, particularly calcium and magnesium, but none in large quantities, though it is said to help release phosphorus and potash locked up in the soil. It is valuable for poor soils needing trace elements and it can also be used instead of lime to increase alkalinity. It is claimed to work as a compost activator, not because it has a high nitrogen content but because its porous particles provide a good breeding ground for bacteria. This also helps its action in the soil.

**Dried animal manures** There are several brands of dried animal manure on the market, providing all the nutritional benefits of farmyard manure without the constraints of its bulk. The problem is that some come from intensive farms and contain contaminants. If in doubt about a particular product, contact an organization concerned with organic growing.

**Worm casts** A concentrated and balanced source of plant foods which you can produce at home (see page 9). The same reservations as for manures apply to products in the shops, as the worms may be fed on the output from intensive farms.

## GROUND MINERALS

**Rock potash** From natural rock containing about 10 per cent potassium, ground to a fine dust; some is available fairly quickly, but it will last in the soil for up to five years.

**Rock phosphate** A natural ground rock providing a more lasting source of phosphorus than bonemeal.

**Dolomite** A ground rock similar to limestone, but containing magnesium as well as calcium. Use instead of lime for increasing the alkalinity of the soil, and for correcting magnesium shortage.

**Gypsum** A ground rock made up mostly of calcium sulphate, which supplies sulphur to the soil. However, it is most often mixed with dolomite and used as a 'soil conditioner' for clays, as it gradually helps the small clay particles to stick together and let water drain through.

## LIQUID FERTILIZERS

**Seaweed solutions** Like calcified seaweed, liquid seaweed contains a wide range of minerals (the main plant foods and trace elements) but in small quantities. It is very useful as a foliar feed to correct deficiencies and to increase general plant health, especially of seedlings. It does not contain sufficient nutrients to feed plants in pots or high yielding greenhouse crops, though its effects are greater than a simple chemical analysis would indicate. Liquid seaweed also contains plant growth hormones; this supports claims that it helps rooting, gives plants some resistance to pests and diseases, improves fruit set, and extends the storage life of fruit and vegetables.

**Liquid manures** Proprietary liquid manures are available, or you can make your own by suspending a sack of well-rotted manure in a water butt. These liquids contain significant amounts of the main plant foods (although not as much as most chemical liquid feeds) and a range of trace elements.

**Comfrey liquid** This has a high concentration of potassium, and is therefore particularly useful for feeding fruiting crops such as tomatoes and courgettes. It is also the best feed for greenhouse plants in pots and houseplants. It contains concentrations of nutrients of the same order of magnitude as chemical tomato feeds.

## VEGETABLE GROUPS FOR CROP ROTATION

| Root crops | Brassicas | Legumes and salad vegetables | Permanent and specialist vegetables |
|---|---|---|---|
| Beetroot | Broccoli | Beans, broad, kidney and runner | Asparagus |
| Carrot | Brussels sprout | Celeriac | Aubergine |
| Chicory | Cabbage | Celery | Cucumber |
| Jerusalem artichoke | Calabrese | Endive | Florence fennel |
| Parsnip | Cauliflower | Land cress | Globe artichoke |
| Potato | Kale | Leek | Herbs |
| Swede | Kohl rabi | Lettuce | Marrow, courgette, pumpkin and squash |
| Turnip | Radish | Mustard and cress | Pepper |
| | | Onion and shallot | Rhubarb |
| | | Pea, asparagus and mangetout | Tomato |
| | | Spinach, spinach beet and leaf beet | |
| | | Sweet corn | |

deterrent to those pests that are specific to one type of crop and move little – like the minute eelworms which affect potatoes and cabbages – or to the build-up of diseases caused by fungus such as club root. A good working plan is illustrated below.

It is not possible to be absolutely strict about rotation, because some crops require more space than others or have a specific requirement as regards position, or preferred harvesting time – but it helps to keep to it as closely as you can.

**Crop rotation plan**

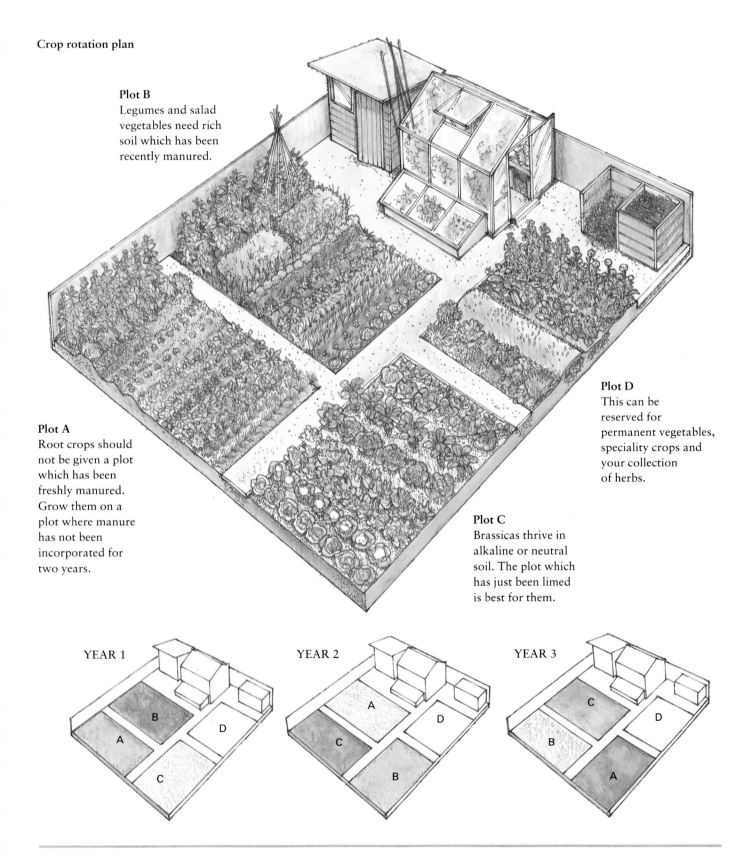

**Plot B**
Legumes and salad vegetables need rich soil which has been recently manured.

**Plot A**
Root crops should not be given a plot which has been freshly manured. Grow them on a plot where manure has not been incorporated for two years.

**Plot D**
This can be reserved for permanent vegetables, speciality crops and your collection of herbs.

**Plot C**
Brassicas thrive in alkaline or neutral soil. The plot which has just been limed is best for them.

YEAR 1

YEAR 2

YEAR 3

## GROWING FROM SEED

The most economic method of growing annual vegetables is to raise them from seed – you will also be able to try less usual varieties.

**SOWING OUTDOORS** The best seeds for sowing outdoors are those of hardy crops like peas and beans, those which germinate easily and those which dislike being transplanted, such as endive. Check under each specific vegetable for sowing time. Using cloches allows you to sow seeds up to a month earlier. Position the cloches two weeks before sowing so that the soil can warm up.

*Preparing the bed* A bed dug over in autumn, then left rough over winter, will need levelling with a rake before it is prepared. If it has been dug in spring leave it to settle before preparation. Don't work the soil if it is so damp it sticks to your boots. When it is dry, tread it firm, rake to a fine tilth and follow the steps illustrated on page 16.

*Tips for successful germination* Don't use old seed, especially if it has been stored at high temperatures or in damp conditions.

Sow at the time recommended, bearing in mind the weather conditions. Seed sown too early may not germinate unless given protection.

Place seeds at the recommended depth, no more (see symbols with each vegetable). If necessary water the drill before sowing, not afterwards, then cover with dry soil. If conditions are very wet, line and cover the drill with dry seed compost.

Thinly sown seeds, which do not have to compete for light, are less likely to be spindly. They are more resistant to diseases and will need less thinning.

*Thinning and transplanting seedlings* Before thinning or transplanting seedlings grown outdoors, water the plants well. To thin, pull up weak seedlings so that those left are spaced at the required distance. Discard spindly seedlings. If you have to pull up some healthy seedlings, to achieve the right spacings, and wish to transplant them, take them out with care (treat as for Pricking out seedlings – *see below*).

**SOWING INDOORS** Use fine lump-free seed compost for sowing in trays indoors and sieve if necessary. Fill seed trays almost to the top with compost, pushing it well into the corners. Firm with a flat piece of wood. Stand trays in water until the compost is thoroughly wetted. Sow the seeds thinly on top spacing them 1-2cm/½-1in apart. The easiest method is to pick them up individually on a wetted knife blade or place the seeds on a sheet of paper and push one off at a time. Lightly cover with a little dry compost, then gently press down the surface. Cover with a sheet of glass or put in a polythene bag. Remove the cover for a short time each day to prevent damping off and check to see if the seeds have germinated. As soon as the first true leaves have appeared, bring the tray into full light.

*Tips for successful sowing indoors* If you keep your trays on a windowsill, rather than in a greenhouse, place them in a box on its side lined with aluminium foil. This helps light to be reflected back on the seedlings ensuring more even growth.

Don't leave trays by a window at night when there is danger of frost nor in scorching sunlight.

Seed trays can be placed in the airing cupboard as long as the temperature is that required by the seeds for germination. Remove as soon as the first seedlings appear.

**Pricking out seedlings**
*When young seedlings are large enough to handle, loosen their roots with a stick, and prick them out holding by the leaf, not stem.*

*Fill new trays with John Innes potting compost No. 1 and, making holes large enough to take the seedling roots, plant them up to their necks.*

*Place a fine rose on a watering can and gently water in the seedlings. Make sure that you keep them out of direct sunlight for a few days.*

## BEATING PESTS AND DISEASES

Healthy plants are much more resistant to pests and diseases than unhealthy ones which have been starved, forced or grown in overcrowded conditions; see the *Tips on maintaining a healthy garden* below on general prevention. Act as soon as a problem occurs.

**ORGANIC CONTROL** Attract predators into your garden so that they will do the work for you.

*Birds* eat grubs, caterpillars, slugs and aphids. Attract them with bird baths and nesting boxes.

*Bats* come out at dusk to feed on aphids, cutworm moths, craneflies and other insects.

*Frogs and toads* eat slugs, woodlice and other small insects. A garden pond will encourage them and will also appeal to another slug-eater, the slow worm.

*Hedgehogs* will remove slugs, cutworms, millipedes, wireworms and woodlice for you. Give them an undisturbed wild corner with a pile of rotting logs, leaves and a tree stump where they can hibernate.

*Hoverflies,* which look like slim wasps, lay their eggs in colonies of aphids on which the larvae feed. They are attracted to bright, open flowers like marigolds.

*Ladybirds* and their grey larvae devour aphids. Grow a wide selection of plants to attract them.

*Lacewing* larvae eat aphids in large quantities. They lay their eggs on the undersides of leaves.

*Ground beetles* hide under leaves during the day. At night they eat eelworms, cutworms, leather jackets, insect eggs and larvae. Ground cover plants, dense vegetation and organic mulch will all attract them.

*Centipedes* feed on small insects and slugs and, like ground beetles, need ground cover.

Organic control starts with physically removing any pests you find. When digging, look out for the fat, creamy coloured *leatherjacket* and squash it. Check plants for *grey mould or powdery mildew* and remove and burn any infected leaves or shoots. Remove *aphids* by hand or by spraying with a jet of water. Use an insecticidal soap to spray badly infected plants. Remove *caterpillars* by hand and drop into paraffin. Remove eggs laid by *moths* and *butterflies* on plants, especially cabbages.

Large *slugs* will not harm living plants – it is the small black and brown slugs that attack growing plants. Protect small plants with cut-off plastic bottles pushed into the ground. Surround larger plants with lime or soot, which slugs don't like. Collect slugs and snails at night, and drop into paraffin.

In late summer and autumn *millipedes* tunnel into potatoes and other root crops. A healthy soil with deep dug beds and plenty of manure will help to keep them at bay. During the day *cutworms* eat through the base of a plant and cut it off. Weed to reduce the risk of infestation and hoe around the plant searching for the grubs, as they live just below the soil. Drown in paraffin. *Wireworms* will be attracted by a potato, carrot or split cabbage stalk pushed into the ground. Fix on the end of a stick, then periodically remove the stick and bait and destroy the worms.

Sticky traps can be used to catch *flea beetles and whitefly.* Coat one side of a small piece of wood with heavy grease. Pass the board, grease side down, just over the top of infested plants. The flea beetles will jump up and stick to it. Hang up a grease-coated piece of yellow card to trap whitefly.

**CHEMICAL CONTROL** If you have a major pest or disease problem you may have to use chemicals. Choose the less toxic plant-based insecticides such as insecticidal soap, pyrethrum, derris, quassia and copper fungicide and follow the manufacturer's instructions closely. Spray on a windless evening when pollinating insects are no longer around.

---

### Tips on maintaining a healthy garden

○ Improve your soil (see page 7), and continue to dig and feed it well. A healthy soil will grow disease-resistant plants.

○ Crop rotation helps to prevent the build-up of some soil-based pests and diseases.

○ Remove rotting plants and weeds, which attract pests. Burn diseased vegetation.

○ Sow seeds thinly and thin early. Over-crowding encourages disease.

○ Harden plants off completely by placing outside for gradually longer periods before planting out.

○ Plants that grow steadily are much more healthy than those that have a setback. Water when necessary, feed regularly and mulch to retain moisture.

○ Damaged plants attract pests and disease so handle gently and hoe with care.

○ Protect fragile plants from wind with a shield of larger more robust varieties.

○ Act fast to remove aphids as these may be carrying virus diseases.

# PEAS AND BEANS

Following the crop rotation plan on page 13, peas and beans come under Plot B. They need plenty of organic matter dug in to keep their roots moist. Taller varieties of peas and beans are not suitable for deep dug beds as the soil is unlikely to hold stakes rigid enough. Because legumes make their own nitrogen they need little extra fertilizer. Taller pea and bean varieties can be used to shade summer grown lettuce, land cress or Chinese greens that would otherwise go to seed in hot weather.

**STAKING CLIMBERS** Most taller varieties of peas and beans need some support. Choosing the particular form of support, whether utilitarian or decorative, adds to the enjoyment of growing these vegetables.

*Asparagus peas* These do not grow very high, about 45cm/18in, but will still need some support. Use a short twiggy stick for each plant to cling to.

*Broad beans* Taller varieties of broad beans need supporting. Use stakes that when hammered into the ground stand 90-120cm/3-4ft above the soil and place on each corner of each short double row. You will need extra stakes in long rows. Tie twine from one stake to the next about 30cm/12in above the soil and across row ends. When the plants are about twice this height tie in a second row of twine higher up the posts and a third if necessary.

*French beans* Dwarf varieties will not need staking but climbing French beans which grow to about 2m/6-7ft need strings, canes or nets to climb up.

*Runner beans* The traditional support for runner beans is to use two 2.4m/8ft poles or canes, crossed and tied at the top, to form an inverted V. A row of these is placed with one pole at each point where a bean is planted and the row is held rigid by a horizontal cane at the cross points. Alternatively, a length of twine can be used pegged into the ground at each end of the row and attached where each pair of canes crosses. Another method is to use a T-shaped support with twine pegged into the ground at each plant point, then up and over the top of the T to form the inverted V.

If you want to grow the plants up a wall, fix two horizontal battens to the wall one just above the soil, one about 3m/10ft from the ground. Position nails at plant-spaced intervals along the battens and tie vertical lengths of twine between the two. Instead of using a soil height batten you can anchor one end of the string with the plant's root ball itself.

In the flower garden, beans are often grown up wigwam shapes constructed from canes but beans are ornamental enough to clothe a pergola, or surround an arch, particularly if you are waiting for a rose to climb around either.

**Sowing seed outdoors**
*Rake ground previously dug over. Stretch a line down the rows and make straight, shallow drills, using a pointed stick.*

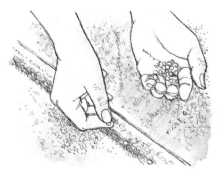

*Water the drill lightly. Sow the seeds as evenly and thinly as possible to prevent wastage and reduce the need for thinning out later on.*

*Cover the seeds by shuffling along the rows, pushing the soil back over the drill. Write labels to indicate crop name and sowing date.*

Dwarf varieties are also available or you can pinch out the growing tip of runner beans when they reach a height of about 30cm/12in to produce your own dwarf plants.

*Peas* Depending on variety, peas can grow from 45-120cm/18in-4ft. Although they can be grown without support, a system of posts with wires or netting stretched between them will keep the plants off the ground. Twiggy sticks about 120cm/4ft long are the traditional supports for peas, if you can find them. Place one beside each plant. Whatever supports are used, make certain they are sufficiently thin for the tendrils to grasp and as tall as the expected height of the variety grown.

In deep beds use a leafless variety and plant every 5cm/2in in rows 15cm/6in apart. Here the plants will support each other.

*Mangetout and asparagus* These can grow up to 2m/7ft tall depending on variety. Support tall varieties in the same way as runner beans. Dwarf varieties are also available.

**AFTER HARVESTING** In warmer areas, after harvesting early crops you can cut broad bean plants back to 5cm/2in above the ground and they will grow again to provide a second crop. Peas and beans and broad beans in particular have nitrogen-fixing bacteria in their roots which will improve soil fertility for future crops, so when beans are harvested cut off the stems just above soil level, cut them up and add to the compost heap. Dig in the stem bases and roots. If you have any seeds left after planting use these up in any spare plot of ground later in the season for a late harvest and to provide nitrogen for future crops.

**PESTS, PROBLEMS AND DISEASES**
*Aphids* Greenfly and blackfly group on plant stems, especially at new growth tips, and suck the sap. Broad beans are specially vulnerable to blackfly in early to mid summer. Remove the insects by hand or hose them off leaves and shoots. Use an insecticidal soap to spray badly infected plants. Attract ladybirds, lacewings and hoverflies, who eat quantities of these pests.

*Chocolate spot* Brown, chocolate-colour blotches on leaves and stems of broad beans are symptoms of chocolate spot fungus. Pull up and burn badly affected plants. This is a sign of overcrowding and lack of feeding. Prevent it in the future by following instructions for growing healthy plants and feed plants adequately.

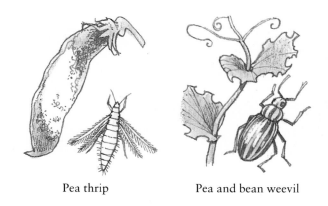

Pea thrip     Pea and bean weevil

*Flowers don't set* This usually occurs when the plant roots are dry. The flowers wilt and bees and other pollinating insects cannot reach the pollen. Water plants well in dry weather. Dig in plenty of organic matter before you plant beans so that moisture will be retained around the roots.

*Halo blight* A problem of French and runner beans, the leaves have dark spots surrounded with a lighter colour halo. Spray diseased plants with a copper fungicide. In future check seeds and reject those that are blistered as this is a seed-borne disease. Buy only from a reputable seed supplier and replace your own if they caused the problem.

Chocolate spot     Halo blight

*Pea and bean weevil* This beetle eats pea and bean leaves, leaving serrated edges. If young plants are attacked dust with derris; older plants will be little harmed.

*Pea moth* Maggots inside the pods are the tiny caterpillars of the pea moth which lays its eggs on the flowers. In a severe attack use derris but as this is also harmful to beneficial insects it is not an ideal answer. Look out for pheromone traps which commercial growers use.

*Pea thrips* These live on pea foliage and leave a silvery trace behind.

*Slugs* Young plants are prone to attack by slugs. Protect with cut-off plastic bottles pushed into the ground around the plant.

## CLIMBING FRENCH BEAN

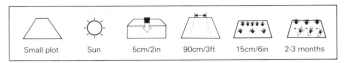

| Small plot | Sun | 5cm/2in | 90cm/3ft | 15cm/6in | 2-3 months |

Climbing French beans are half-hardy annuals which cannot be sown in the open until all danger of frost has passed. This type of bean is most popular in France – hence its common name.

**GROWING**  Light, well-drained soils are required, while it helps if organic manure/compost has been worked in during the autumn preparations. Acid soils will not be tolerated. Incorporate a good general base fertilizer dressing during the final preparations before sowing: 25-50g/m²/1-2oz per sq yd of something like fish and bone meal will be suitable, provided that soft growth is not induced by too much nitrogen. Sow seeds 7.5cm/3in apart and 4-5cm/1½-2in deep from late spring onwards in single rows, spaced 90cm/3ft apart. Thin to 15cm/6in apart in the rows after the first leaves emerge. They are easily damaged by wind buffeting, so grow them in a sheltered spot. The beans can climb as high as 1.5m/5ft, so support with tall pea sticks.

**HARVESTING**  Pick the beans when they are young and tender. Any delay will tend to cause stringiness, even though 'stringless' varieties are available. Regular picking will encourage more pods to develop. Small pods that snap easily and which have no sign of the beans showing through the skin are the tastiest.

**POSSIBLE PROBLEMS**  Aphids may damage the pods.

## DWARF FRENCH BEAN

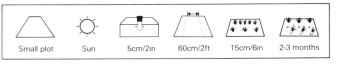

| Small plot | Sun | 5cm/2in | 60cm/2ft | 15cm/6in | 2-3 months |

Dwarf French beans are half-hardy annuals which cannot be sown in the open until all danger of frost has passed. They are grown for their edible pods, which are usually sliced before cooking. The traditional French bean varieties produce flat pods but cylindrical or 'pencil'-podded varieties are now available.

**GROWING**  Light, well-drained soils are required, while it helps if organic manure/compost has been worked in during the autumn preparations. Acid soils will not be tolerated. Incorporate a good general base fertilizer dressing during the final preparations before sowing: 25-50g/m²/1-2oz per sq yd, of something like fish and bone meal will be suitable, provided that soft growth is not induced by too much nitrogen. Sow seeds 7.5cm/3in apart and 4-5cm/1½-2in deep from late spring onwards in single rows, spaced 45-60cm/1ft 6in-2ft apart. Thin after the first leaves emerge.

**HARVESTING**  Pick the beans when they are young and tender. Regular picking will encourage more pods to develop. The beans are in prime condition for picking when the pods can be snapped cleanly. At the end of the crop, remove the visible parts of the plants and dig in the roots to provide valuable nitrogen.

**POSSIBLE PROBLEMS**  Look out for slugs and aphids. Weeds may swamp young plants; hoe carefully, for they are very easily chopped off at ground level.

### ■ GARDENER'S TIP

*Train climbing vegetables up a tepee of canes. Then while the plants are still small you can use the space beneath for a fast-growing crop like garden cress or lettuces.*

### ■ COOK'S TIP

*Use French beans when they are young, then you only need to top and tail them. Steam them for a short time so that they are still crunchy, then eat them on their own with butter and freshly ground black pepper or sprinkle with chopped, toasted almonds.*

*For a delicious salad, make a French dressing, mix with a tablespoon of Greek yoghurt and toss the beans in this. Chop up tomatoes, sprinkle with freshly chopped basil and add to the bean salad.*

## PURPLE-PODDED FRENCH BEAN

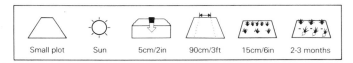

| Small plot | Sun | 5cm/2in | 90cm/3ft | 15cm/6in | 2-3 months |

Purple-podded French beans are half-hardy annuals which cannot be sown in the open until frosts are over. They lose the purple colour during cooking and compare well with other French beans for flavour.

**GROWING** Light, well-drained soils are required, while it helps if organic manure/compost has been worked in during the autumn preparations. Acid soils will not be tolerated. Incorporate a good general base fertilizer dressing during the final preparations before sowing: 25-50g/m²/1-2oz per sq yd of something like fish and bone meal will be suitable, provided that soft growth is not induced by too much nitrogen. Sow seeds 7.5cm/3in apart and 4-5cm/1½-2in deep from late spring onwards in single rows, spaced 90cm/3ft apart. Thin after the first leaves emerge. They are easily damaged by wind buffeting, so grow them in a sheltered spot. The beans can climb as high as 1.5m/5ft, so support with tall pea sticks, bamboo canes or strings.

**HARVESTING** Pick the beans when they are young and tender. Purple-podded French beans are stringless and remain tender longer than other types. Regular picking will encourage more pods to develop.

**POSSIBLE PROBLEMS** Aphids may damage the pods.

## SCARLET RUNNER BEAN

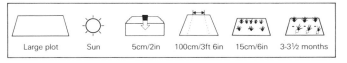

| Large plot | Sun | 5cm/2in | 100cm/3ft 6in | 15cm/6in | 3-3½ months |

A perennial, usually grown as an annual, the scarlet runner bean is a very tender plant and will be killed by very slight frosts either at the beginning or end of the season. By nature it is a climber and most crops reach a height of 1.5-1.8m/5-6ft when grown on supports. As well as producing quantities of beans both for fresh consumption and freezing, runner bean plants form very attractive living screens in summer.

**GROWING** The best results are obtained in fertile, well-drained land which has been deeply dug in the autumn and had liberal dressings of organic manure incorporated. This helps to improve soil structure as well as retaining moisture. Maincrop runner beans are sown outside from late spring onwards. Sow the seeds 5cm/2in deep and 15cm/6in apart in double rows, leaving 60cm/2ft between the two lines of plants and 100cm/3ft 6in between each double row. As soon as the young plants emerge, push 2.5m/9ft long poles or bamboo canes into the ground and when the plants are tall enough, train them on to the supports. Water regularly and very thoroughly in dry weather.

**HARVESTING** Pick before the seeds become obvious through the pod wall. Regular picking will ensure continuous flowering and fruiting.

**POSSIBLE PROBLEMS** Look out for aphids in summer.

---

■ DECORATIVE TIP

*Grow the variety Purple Tepee up bamboo canes to form a wigwam shape. Pods are held above the foliage forming the shape of a North American Indian tepee. The pods have an excellent flavour. They are also suitable for late planting.*

---

■ DECORATIVE TIP

*While waiting for newly bought climbing roses or clematis to make their way around an arch or arbour, let runner beans clothe it with their decorative flowers and pods.*

## BROAD BEAN

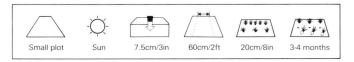

| | | | | | |
|---|---|---|---|---|---|
| Small plot | Sun | 7.5cm/3in | 60cm/2ft | 20cm/8in | 3-4 months |

Broad beans are the hardiest of the legumes that we grow. They are usually shelled from the pods when they are almost fully grown, although young pods may be cooked whole or sliced like French or runner beans.

GROWING The earliest of the successful sowings in the spring will need to be made into light, open-textured soils. In common with many other legumes, broad beans do not grow well in acid soils. On soils which are reasonably fertile and have had organic material worked into them, it should be possible to apply base fertilizers which just provide phosphate and potassium. You can grow broad beans in double rows, allowing 20cm/8in between the two lines and from 60-90cm/2-3ft, according to variety, between the double rows. Alternatively they can be grown in single rows spaced 60cm/2ft apart. Put each individual seed into a 5-7.5cm/2-3in deep hole made with a dibber.

HARVESTING Pick beans for slicing or cooking whole when they are 7.5cm/3in long. Those for shelling are ready when the seeds are about 2cm/³⁄₄in across.

POSSIBLE PROBLEMS Blackfly may attack from late spring onwards but the damage can be reduced by pinching out the tops of the plants when they are in full flower. Give support to large plants by knocking in stakes at each corner of the growing area and encircling the crop with string.

## ASPARAGUS PEA

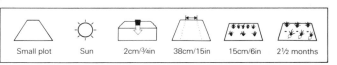

| | | | | | |
|---|---|---|---|---|---|
| Small plot | Sun | 2cm/³⁄₄in | 38cm/15in | 15cm/6in | 2½ months |

The asparagus pea is a half-hardy annual, grown for its curiously ribbed pods, which are eaten whole like a mangetout pea. The pods have a slight flavour of asparagus. This legume is not a true pea, but a type of vetch. Only the species *Tetragonolobus purpureus* is available.

GROWING Asparagus peas grow best in deep, rich soils which are moisture retentive. Sow in late spring, when the danger of frost is almost past. With its low-growing, bushy habit, the asparagus pea should be grown in a single, narrow drill with seeds sown 10-15cm/4-6in apart and 1-2cm/³⁄₄in deep. In dry weather, the bottom of the drill should be well watered and then allowed to drain before sowing. After sowing, rake the soil back over the seeds. Like ordinary garden peas, asparagus peas need pea sticks for support.

HARVESTING Pick as soon as the peas are 2.5cm/1in long or they will become stringy. Regular picking encourages the plants to go on cropping over a period of several weeks.

POSSIBLE PROBLEMS The asparagus pea tends to crop far less than peas but, by way of compensation, has fewer ailments.

### ■ ORGANIC TIP

*If you cut plants down to 5cm/2in after harvesting they should regrow to give you a second crop. The roots of bean plants take nitrogen from the air and fix it in the soil so plant any leftover seeds, then dig in the young plants as manure.*

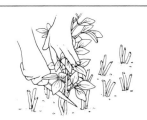

### ■ DECORATIVE TIP

*Asparagus peas, which grow to about 45cm/18in, make an ornamental addition to the flower garden with their clover-like foliage and unusual pods preceded by deep rusty-red flowers. They also make an attractive addition to the table and can be eaten raw*

*in salads when very small, or steamed for about 5 minutes, seasoned and tossed in butter.*

# MANGETOUT

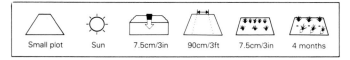

| Small plot | Sun | 7.5cm/3in | 90cm/3ft | 7.5cm/3in | 4 months |
|---|---|---|---|---|---|

Sugar pea is another name for the mangetout pea. The whole pod, complete with the young, immature seeds, is eaten, after topping and tailing and cooking.

**GROWING** Like all peas, mangetout grow best in deep, rich soils which are moisture retentive. Sow at intervals from early to mid spring in flat-bottomed drills which are 10-15cm/4-6in wide and 5-7.5cm/2-3in deep. Scatter the peas evenly in the bottom of the drill to leave the individual seeds 5-7.5cm/2-3in apart. Rake the soil back over the seeds. Distances between rows will vary from 60cm-1.2m/2-4ft and should be roughly equivalent to the expected height of the varieties being sown. When the seedlings are 5-7.5cm/2-3in high, provide support with well-branched and twiggy pea sticks.

**HARVESTING** Pick the pods while flat and immature – before you can see the seeds from the outside and when they are 7.5cm/3in long. Pick – regularly to encourage yield – from the bottom of the plant upwards.

**POSSIBLE PROBLEMS** Birds and mice may cause damage by eating or removing the germinating seeds. Two or three single strands of black cotton, not nylon thread, above the seed row will hinder birds. Shaking the seed in a little powdered seed dressing before sowing, or stretching a renardine-soaked string along the soil surface, will both deter mice.

# PEA

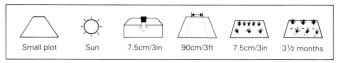

| Small plot | Sun | 7.5cm/3in | 90cm/3ft | 7.5cm/3in | 3½ months |
|---|---|---|---|---|---|

The early types of pea were round-seeded, but the less hardy, wrinkle-seeded or marrowfat peas have a much higher sugar content and, as a result, a better flavour. Round-seeded peas are now mainly used for winter and early spring sowings because of their greater hardiness.

**GROWING** Peas grow best in deep, rich soils which are moisture retentive. It is most important that the roots are always able to obtain enough water. Sow at intervals from early to mid spring in flat-bottomed drills which are 10-15cm/4-6in wide and 5-7.5cm/2-3in deep. Scatter the peas evenly in the bottom of the drill to leave the individual seeds 5-7.5cm/2-3in apart. Rake the soil back over the seeds. Distances between rows will vary from 60-1.2m/2-4ft and should be roughly equivalent to the expected height of the varieties being grown. When the seedlings are 5-7.5cm/2-3in high, provide support with twiggy pea sticks. Make certain that they are thin enough for the tendrils to grasp and as tall as the expected height of the variety being grown.

**HARVESTING** First early, second early and maincrop peas sown at intervals during early and mid spring will produce mature crops through early and mid summer. Your crop should be ready for picking to start about 3 weeks after flowering. Pick while young and tender, at 2 to 3 day intervals.

**POSSIBLE PROBLEMS** A serious pest is the pea moth.

## ▦ DECORATIVE TIP

*Tall varieties, which grow to about 1.5m/5ft, can be grown in the smallest garden if you train the plants on wires or up climbers on the walls. Or use them in place of sweet peas as a decorative barrier between flower and vegetable garden.*

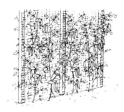

## ▦ ORGANIC TIP

*Planting can sometimes be planned to miss the worst period of attack by a particular pest. Peas that are sown early or late will miss most of the damage caused by pea moth larvae. Alternatively, see if you can procure pheromone traps.*

*Pheromone is a chemical secreted by the female moth to attract males and is available on a sticky tab. The attracted male sticks fast so is unable to mate with the female and reproduction is prevented.*

# SALAD VEGETABLES

Like many other vegetables the majority of salad plants require fertile soil, good drainage and some sun and shelter. Improvements can be made to your soil, whatever type it is (see pages 6-9), and the regular addition of organic matter will then ensure that plants receive their necessary supply of nutrients.

Waterlogging proves fatal to most salad plants, so check that the soil drains well and correct any problem before you start to prepare your salad garden.

**WHERE TO GROW SALAD PLANTS** Plants will grow far more sturdily if they are sheltered from wind. If your site is exposed then it pays to erect windbreaks. Vegetables such as runner beans or Jerusalem artichokes will provide shelter.

As the structure of the soil can be damaged if you walk on it, particularly in wet weather, it is a good idea to plan beds to a width that is comfortable for you to work on from a path on either side. The width is a personal choice but somewhere between 1-1.5m/3-5ft should allow you to do any work on the plants without treading on the bed. If you don't have the space for a separate vegetable or salad garden this need not stop you from growing a range of salad ingredients.

**IN THE FLOWER GARDEN** Some of the colourful varieties of loose-leaf lettuces, lemon-shaped cucumbers and purple-leaved beetroot are all decorative enough to earn a space in the flower garden.

However, vegetables require a more fertile soil than ornamental plants so if you want them to flourish, fork in compost where you are to plant them and mulch well afterwards. Allow small plants plenty of space in which to grow. Group them rather than dot individual plants around the space.

*In containers* Growing bags, boxes and pots can all be used to grow salad plants where space is very limited. The yield will not, however, be as great as from those planted directly into the ground.

Different plants require different soil depths. Lettuces need about 15cm/6in, larger plants like cucumbers, tomatoes and peppers need at least 23cm/9in. Tall plants that need staking must be sheltered from winds as they so easily become top heavy. Growing bags are probably the best containers to use. Because containers are exposed to all-round heat they dry out very fast in hot weather and need daily watering. Lining with plastic helps, but provide a few drainage holes first. Cutting out small crosses or slits in the tops of growing bags where plants are positioned, rather than cutting a larger opening, also helps moisture retention.

**RESTRICTED SPACE** Where space is restricted there are some useful techniques that can be put into operation to get the best possible value from the land.
*Using the block system* Many more plants can be raised if plants are grown in blocks or staggered rows rather than in the traditional straight single or double rows. Each plant is provided with a circle of space which it will fill when fully grown. Plants protect each other equally on all sides, and, because each one is provided with exactly the right amount of space to grow well, there is little room available for weeds to flourish.
*Deep digging* The block system can be used in conjunction with deep digging. The roots of plants grown in a deeply dug area will grow downwards, taking up less surrounding soil and thus allowing plants to be placed closer together. See page 10 for deep digging techniques.
*Training plants vertically* Trailing plants like cucumbers take up much less space, as well as looking decorative if they are grown up a wigwam or ridge tent shape of canes (see Tip on page 27). Where there are alternative forms and space is at a premium, choose varieties that will climb rather than bush out.

Grow trailing nasturtiums in hanging baskets or window boxes.

**A CONTINUOUS SUPPLY** There are a number of methods you can use to extend the growing season and to spread out the time when plants are in peak condition.

*Mixing varieties* By mixing varieties of one type of plant and by growing a wide range of salad plants suited to different weather conditions, the season when plants are available is greatly extended.

For instance, if you grow both globe and long beetroot, the round beetroot will provide a supply through the summer and the long varieties, which store well, will come into use through the winter. Young beetroot leaves can also be used in salads, either freshly chopped or cooked lightly.

Endive comes into its own when summer lettuce supplies die out. Curled-leaved endive can be used for salads from early to late autumn. Winter radishes, sown in late summer, are ready about 3 months later. Leave the crop in the ground during winter, lifting as needed.

The slow-growing corn salad, or lamb's lettuce, is a hardy plant that can survive low temperatures outside, although it will do better if protected. It therefore provides another useful winter or early spring crop.

*Staggered sowing* Salad plants which mature and then are quickly past their best, such as many lettuces and summer radish, need to be sown frequently in small quantities so that they mature over an extended period rather than arriving at peak condition all at the same time. It is difficult to plan staggered sowing accurately. Sowing seeds every 1-2 weeks is not exact enough, as the speed of plant growth can be erratic, affected by the weather. Rather than sowing at 10 or 14 day intervals, you may find it more reliable to start off a new batch when the last sown seedlings appear or reach a certain size.

Experiment to find out what works best for you, keeping a note of dates sown, and when the same plants are harvested. This will give you some idea of how often and how much you need to sow to provide the quantities you require.

To some extent, a staggered crop can also be obtained by planting out the larger size seedlings from one sowing first, then planting out another lot from the same group when these have reached the larger size and so on. Always keep a few seedlings ready to plant in a vacant space when it arises.

*Seedling crops* Use a vacant space, even a small one, early in the summer or in the autumn, to grow a seedling crop. Protected, many seedlings can even be

**Successional sowing**
*Sow quick-growing crops, like lettuces, at frequent intervals to give you a steady supply of fresh produce.*

grown into the winter. Plants are cut and eaten when they are still small, tasty and very nutritious and it is possible to get up to three cuttings from one sowing. Many lettuce seeds can be used in this way – experiment with any leftover seeds you have. Corn salad, or lamb's lettuce, and radish are other suitable salad plants for a seedling crop. Utilize growing bags left empty after tomatoes or peppers are harvested in this way, but bear in mind the soil will have few nutrients left in it by then and extra feeding will probably be necessary.

**PROVIDING PROTECTION** A greenhouse or walk-in polythene tunnel will not only allow you to bring on plants early and to grow more exotic salad plants successfully in summer, but also to grow a supply of leafy salad plants almost around the year. Where space is limited, use cloches and frames to provide valuable protection from cold and wind for low-growing plants allowing them to be harvested earlier in the year and grown further into the winter. The introduction to Fruiting Vegetables, on page 32 gives more information on protecting plants. Cloches can also be used inside a greenhouse or walk-in tunnel to give extra winter protection.

**PESTS, DISEASES AND DISORDERS**
*Aphids* Greenfly may attack the plants. Remove by hand where possible or spray with insecticidal soap.
*Bolting* A check to growth, overcrowding or lack of water causes lettuces to flower, making them bitter and inedible. Transplant as soon as seedlings are large enough and keep well watered.
*Damping off* Seedlings collapse at ground level if affected by this disease. Always raise seeds in sterilized compost, do not sow too thickly and do not overwater.

## GLOBE BEETROOT

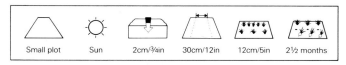

| | | | | | |
|---|---|---|---|---|---|
| Small plot | Sun | 2cm/¾in | 30cm/12in | 12cm/5in | 2½ months |

This type of beetroot has small, globular roots and is best for summer use and for pickling.

**GROWING** Light, sandy soils are best. Soil that is flinty or stony or which has been recently manured will produce mis-shapen roots. Deep digging should be done in the autumn, leaving the surface rough over winter. Prepare a fine tilth and work in a general purpose fertilizer just before sowing. Plants from sowings made too early may 'bolt', even if bolting-resistant varieties are used. Sow seed clusters from mid spring to early summer, soaking seed overnight to assist germination. Provide cloches to protect the earliest sowings and in colder districts. Keep weeds under control, but be careful not to damage the roots when hoeing. Water sparingly except in very dry summers, when beetroots tend to become woody.

**HARVESTING** Pick from early summer, lifting carefully to avoid damaging the roots, which will 'bleed' when pierced. Pick by hand if possible, or use a flat-tined fork and grasp the leaves like a handle. Twist off the tops carefully to keep the roots intact for cooking.

**POSSIBLE PROBLEMS** Keep aphids at bay on the young leaves. Plants sown too close together may attract carrot fly.

## LONG BEETROOT

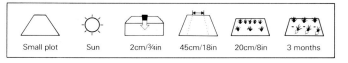

| | | | | | |
|---|---|---|---|---|---|
| Small plot | Sun | 2cm/¾in | 45cm/18in | 20cm/8in | 3 months |

Long varieties of beetroot can be stored over winter, making this an all-the-year-round vegetable. Beetroot make a delicious winter vegetable, served hot with creamy white sauce.

**GROWING** Soil requirements are as for globe beetroot, remembering that even heavy soils can be used, provided they have been lightened by the addition of peat or organic compost when digging in the autumn. Maincrop long beets should be sown in late spring, and the seedlings thinned 2-3 weeks after they emerge. Keep on top of weeds, always being careful not to damage the beets.

**HARVESTING** Long beetroot may either be left in the ground until required – in which case they should be strawed over to give protection against the severest frosts – or the roots can be lifted, cleaned and stored. Lift before late autumn as described for globe beets, discarding any that are damaged or diseased. If you cut the leaves off rather than twisting them, don't cut too close to the crown or 'bleeding' will occur.

**STORAGE** Place the trimmed beetroot on their sides in boxes of slightly damp sand. Keep the boxes in an airy frost-free place and inspect them at regular intervals.

**POSSIBLE PROBLEMS** Boron deficiency causes heart rot.

### ■ COOK'S TIP

*Young beetroot leaves can be used in salads raw or can be lightly cooked and eaten like spinach. Raw beetroot can be grated and used in salad in place of cooked beet. One of the most delicious soups, borsch, is made from beetroot cooked with other vegetables and stock. Tomato sauce, sugar and lemon juice are added towards the end of cooking. Finally it is topped with soured cream. Or try hot cooked beetroot coated in creamy white sauce.*

### ■ ORGANIC TIP

*While seedlings are young hoe around them to keep weed free. Later the covering of beet leaves should keep weeds at bay. Layers of newspaper can be used as a mulch as they will eradicate the light from any growing weeds.*

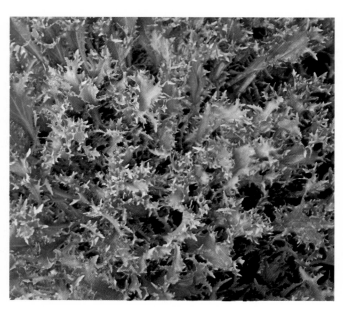

## SUGARLOAF CHICORY

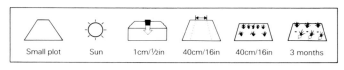

| Small plot | Sun | 1cm/½in | 40cm/16in | 40cm/16in | 3 months |

This variety of chicory, called *Pain de Sucre*, is the best if you want to use the leaves in salads, because they do not require blanching. It looks rather like a cos lettuce in shape.

**GROWING** A deep, fertile soil which has been well-manured for the previous crop is suitable. Sow seeds in the open from early to mid summer, and keep the rows well-hoed to eliminate weeds.

**HARVESTING** Sugarloaf chicory can be picked as soon as a heart has formed. Unlike lettuce, it can be left in the ground until it is needed without going to seed, a great advantage in dry seasons.

**POSSIBLE PROBLEMS** Watch for slugs and caterpillars.

## CURLED-LEAVED ENDIVE

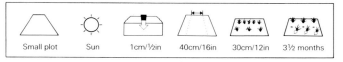

| Small plot | Sun | 1cm/½in | 40cm/16in | 30cm/12in | 3½ months |

Curled-leaved endive is the type most commonly eaten in salads. Its pale green, crisp leaves are deeply dissected and curled. As in the case of broad-leaved endive, for which see page 46, blanching is necessary to counteract its naturally bitter taste. Curled-leaved endive provides a summer and autumn crop.

**GROWING** As with most salad crops light, well-drained fertile soils are best, with a dressing of general, balanced fertilizer before sowing. Sow successively from early spring to late summer. Sow the seed in 1-cm/½-in deep drills spaced 40cm/16in apart. When the seedlings are 5-7.5cm/2-3in high, thin them out to 30cm/12in apart.

**BLANCHING** Endive plants are usually ready for blanching about 3 months after sowing and it may be done in one of two ways. The leaves can be gathered together when dry (damp plants may rot during blanching) and tied round with raffia string. This keeps the light away from all but the outer leaves. Alternatively, the plants can be completely covered with containers.

**HARVESTING** Blanching takes about 2 weeks in later summer. Only blanch the plants you require for immediate use, for they will soon rot once blanched.

**POSSIBLE PROBLEMS** Watch out for greenfly during the summer months, and avoid running to seed or bolting by correct watering during dry periods.

### ■ ORGANIC TIP

These chicories can be grown and harvested during autumn and winter when other salad materials are scarce. However, they will need protection in colder areas. Mix green-leaved chicories with the decorative red and variegated varieties which are expensive to buy and easy to grow. These start life green but their colour changes when the weather turns colder and, at the same time, they also form small, tight hearts.

### ■ ORGANIC TIP

Even dew can cause rot when blanching so dry leaves are very important. In summer, blanch plants in position using an upturned flower pot (cover any holes up first) or a bucket. You can also use a plate placed over each plant head.

# LAND CRESS

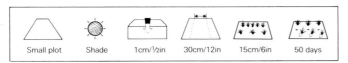

| Small plot | Shade | 1cm/½in | 30cm/12in | 15cm/6in | 50 days |

Otherwise known as American cress, land cress is a useful sub-stitute for watercress (which is difficult to grow in the kitchen garden as it needs an uncontaminated stream of gently running water). Similar in flavour, land cress is easy to grow in a shady, damp corner.

**GROWING** Prepare the soil by forking in plenty of organic material and rake to a fine tilth. Sow seed thinly from early spring to late summer at 3 week intervals. Thin the young plants when they are large enough to handle. Late summer sowings should be protected by cloches to give useful supplies of winter cress.

**HARVESTING** Sowings made in spring and summer will be ready for cutting in 8-10 weeks. Cut the young tender shoots as soon as they are ready. If left to stand they may flower and become tough and bitter.

**POSSIBLE PROBLEMS** Flea beetle can be a problem in the early stages.

# MUSTARD AND CRESS

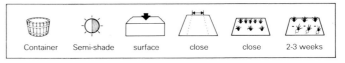

| Container | Semi-shade | surface | close | close | 2-3 weeks |

This combination of slightly peppery leaves is easy to grow, and is delicious in salads and sandwiches or as a garnish.

**GROWING** To grow mustard and cress indoors during the winter, fill a small box with bulb fibre or a moist peat/soil mix-ture and strew cress seeds on top. Press the seeds into the grow-ing medium with your fingers. Cover the box to exclude light. Mustard germinates faster than cress. After 4 days, strew mus-tard seeds over the cress, dampen slightly and cover again. When the seeds have germinated, bring the box into the light. During the spring and summer, mustard and cress can be grown in the open on light, moisture-retentive soils in the same way. Sow about every 2 weeks for a steady supply.

**HARVESTING** Snip off the fine stems and leaves when they are 4cm/1½in high.

**POSSIBLE PROBLEMS** Trouble-free.

■ ORGANIC TIP

*If you do not have a shady spot to grow land cress, position plants near to climbers like runner beans, or tall plants like sweet corn. These will provide the necessary shade and help to stop plants drying out. Water well on dry days.*

■ HEALTH TIP

*Mustard and cress are high in vitamins and minerals, so they are a specially valuable addition to winter salads. Children will enjoy growing this quickly harvested crop. Use damp blotting paper, cotton wool or a flannel and spread the pre-* *soaked seeds evenly over the base. Keep in the dark, rinsing daily. To do this, before the seeds have rooted, hold them in place with the back of a spoon. Bring out into the light to green up before harvesting.*

# RIDGE CUCUMBER

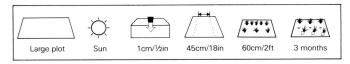

| | | | | | |
|---|---|---|---|---|---|
| Large plot | Sun | 1cm/½in | 45cm/18in | 60cm/2ft | 3 months |

If you do not have a heated greenhouse and live in a cooler climate, you can still grow cucumbers if you choose the small variety that can be eaten in salads or pickled.

**GROWING** Dig the land deeply and thoroughly in the autumn and leave it rough for over-winter weathering. Before planting, take out a trench 30cm/12in deep and 45cm/18in wide. Half-fill it with manure and replace the soil to form a ridge. Plants must not be set out until all danger of frost is past. You can raise plants in the greenhouse and set them out in early summer, or sow seeds directly into the ridges at the end of spring covering them with cloches or jam jars. Sow seeds in pairs, and if both germinate, discard the weaker plant. Stop the plants after the sixth leaf and restrict side shoots to the space available. On ridge cucumbers both male and female flowers are needed to ensure fertilization. Water well and after the fruits have begun to set give the plants a high-nitrogen liquid feed.

**HARVESTING** Pick cucumbers when 15-20cm/6-8in long for salads, 5cm/2in long for gherkins.

**POSSIBLE PROBLEMS** Cucumber mosaic virus causes mottled leaves and fruits and stunted plants. Keep aphids under control.

## ▦ GARDENER'S TIP

*For the best use of space train cucumbers up canes. Create a wigwam shape by trying the canes together at the top. This also keeps the cucumbers out of the reach of slugs. Use soft string, to avoid damage, and tie the plants in as they grow.*

# CUCUMBER

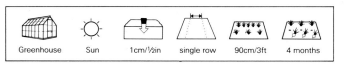

| | | | | | |
|---|---|---|---|---|---|
| Greenhouse | Sun | 1cm/½in | single row | 90cm/3ft | 4 months |

Greenhouse cucumbers need careful attention but as few as two plants can be very productive.

**GROWING** Three weeks before planting, prepare a special cucumber bed on the greenhouse floor, using a mixture of 2 parts well-rotted organic manure to 1 part peat or loam. Build the beds 60cm/2ft wide, 45cm/18in deep with a domed top. Cover with a 15cm/6in layer of peat or loam. Water liberally and keep the temperature constant at 21-25C/70-75F. In late winter/early spring sow seeds singly in 9-cm/3½-in pots at the above temperature. After germination, give the seedlings maximum light and reduce the temperature slightly. At the three-leaf stage, pot on to 14cm/5½-in pots. Water and spray very thoroughly to maintain essential humidity. After 4 weeks, work a general purpose fertilizer into the prepared beds and plant the cucumbers out with a little of the rootball showing (this helps water drain away). The plants need the support of wires or strings as they grow upwards and outwards. Stop the main stem when it reaches the roof and allow the cucumbers to develop on side branches, which should be stopped after 2 leaves. Grow all-female plants in order to avoid fertilization, which causes bitterness. Maintain high temperatures and humidity.

**HARVESTING** Pick cucumbers when young and succulent, at about 30cm/12in.

**POSSIBLE PROBLEMS** Glasshouse whitefly; root rot fungi; grey mould.

## ▦ COOK'S TIP

*For a refreshing salad, slice up the cucumber and arrange in a bowl. Pour over a dressing made from strained yogurt, oil and lemon juice plus crushed garlic, chopped mint and seasoning. Add more yogurt to turn this into a dip for eating outdoors* *with warmed pitta bread. Cucumber, onions, garlic and mushrooms sautéd, then simmered in chicken stock and garnished with soured cream and chives make a mouth-watering cold soup.*

# BUTTERHEAD LETTUCE

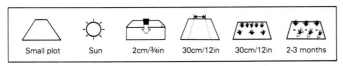

| | | | | | |
|---|---|---|---|---|---|
| Small plot | Sun | 2cm/¾in | 30cm/12in | 30cm/12in | 2-3 months |

Of all the varieties of lettuce available, this cabbage lettuce is the most popular. The name butterhead refers to the 'buttery' texture of the smooth, flattened leaves in named varieties such as Suzan and Fortune.

**GROWING** Butterhead lettuces can be raised in the open in the same way as crisphead types. The difficulty of watering lettuces under cloches makes the moisture-retentive quality of the soil even more important for over-wintering crops that can be picked in late spring. Sow seed of hardy varieties out in early autumn; alternatively, raise seedlings in trays and plant out in late autumn (in sheltered districts) or early spring (in more exposed areas). Apply fertilizer in the form of a top dressing just as growth recommences in the spring. Crops protected by unheated greenhouses, frames or cloches should be raised from transplanted seedlings. Sow in late summer and transplant a month later for mature plants in early winter; autumn plantings will be ready in early spring, while seeds sown in mid-winter and transplanted in late winter will be ready for cutting in mid to late spring.

**HARVESTING** Since lettuces contain a high percentage of water they wilt rapidly after cutting. Freshness will be improved by immersing the lettuce in ice-cold water for 15 minutes. Shake off the water and place the lettuce in the refrigerator until needed.

**POSSIBLE PROBLEMS** Aphids are the worst pest.

## ▮ ORGANIC TIP

*Slugs are often a major problem when lettuces are small. One of the most effective methods of reducing numbers is to go out in the late evening with a plastic bag and pick up any that are feeding. Drop them in paraffin to kill them quickly. You can also use a mulch of pine bark or surround plants with soot or lime. On young lettuces use plastic bottles with the base removed and slip one, right way up, over each plant to protect it.*

# COS LETTUCE

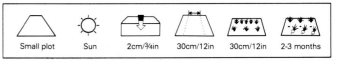

| | | | | | |
|---|---|---|---|---|---|
| Small plot | Sun | 2cm/¾in | 30cm/12in | 30cm/12in | 2-3 months |

The leaves of cos lettuce are long and crisp, with a sweeter flavour than cabbage types. Since the plants take longer to reach maturity, they take up space in the vegetable garden for an extended period. In smaller gardens, a dwarf variety like Little Gem may be recommended for this reason.

**GROWING** For summer crops raised in the open, apply a base dressing of a general-purpose fertilizer before sowing and/or transplanting. Thin seedlings when large enough to handle, reducing the distances for Little Gem to 25cm/10in between the rows and 15cm/6in between the plants. Keep weeds in check. For over-wintering, see Butterhead lettuce, and choose a suitably hardy variety.

**HARVESTING** Cos lettuces are less likely to bolt than cabbage lettuces, but in hot, dry weather inspect the plants regularly and pick them as soon as they mature.

**POSSIBLE PROBLEMS** As well as aphids and slugs, lettuces are susceptible to damping-off diseases and mildew.

## ▮ GARDENER'S TIP

*If some cos lettuces are grown close together they grow upright, produce good leaves more quickly and do not form hearts. Space 10cm/4in apart. Stumps of lettuces can also be left in the ground to regrow and provide a second crop.*

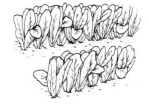

## CRISPHEAD LETTUCE

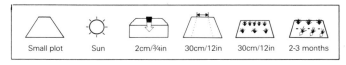

| | | | | | |
|---|---|---|---|---|---|
| Small plot | Sun | 2cm/¾in | 30cm/12in | 30cm/12in | 2-3 months |

The leaves of crisphead lettuce are large, curled and, as the name suggests, pleasantly crunchy. The old favourite, Webb's Wonderful, withstands heat and drought better than most.

**GROWING** Lettuces need light, moisture-retentive soil. For unprotected plants, sow seed in the open at fortnightly intervals from mid spring to late summer. Crisphead varieties of cabbage lettuce are not as well suited to over wintering as butterhead types. Thin out the seedlings as soon as they can be handled. Keep the beds free of weeds and water the plants well.

**HARVESTING** In warm weather, lettuces of all types run to seed ('bolt') quickly, so check regularly and pick mature plants as soon as they are ready. Pick in the cool morning if you can.

**POSSIBLE PROBLEMS** Aphids; slugs. Diseases include damping-off diseases and mildew if weather conditions are cold and damp.

## LOOSE LEAF LETTUCE

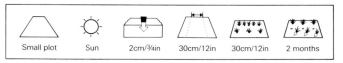

| | | | | | |
|---|---|---|---|---|---|
| Small plot | Sun | 2cm/¾in | 30cm/12in | 30cm/12in | 2 months |

Sometimes called chicken lettuce, these varieties are not harvested whole, nor do they form a heart like cabbage and cos lettuces, but individual leaves are picked as required. This cut-and-come again approach is useful as it allows space to be used for other crops. With the advent of frilly varieties like Lollo Rossa with red leaves, these lettuces are becoming very popular in gourmet salads. The long-established variety Salad Bowl is now also available with red leaves as well as the standard green.

**GROWING** Leaf lettuces should be grown as outdoor summer crops like crispheads, and need the same light, moisture retentive soil as other types.

**HARVESTING** Leaves are produced throughout the summer. Pick a few from each plant as needed. When all leaves have been used or died down, lift and discard the plant.

**POSSIBLE PROBLEMS** Aphids, which may carry virus diseases; slugs are a nuisance. Cold and wet weather encourages mildew and mould.

### ■ GARDENER'S TIP

*When growing hearting lettuces stagger the plants in adjacent rows for the best use of space. While these are young grow a seedling crop in the spaces, using up leftover seeds of loose leaf varieties and cutting off young leaves.*

### ■ COOK'S TIP

*Grow an alternating border of differently coloured and shaped loose-leaf lettuces to provide a decorative edging to a vegetable, herb or flower bed. Choose from red and green oak-leaved, the frill-edged red and green Lollo or red-leaved Marvel of Four*

*Seasons. Picking a few leaves from each plant will give you an attractive salad that can be enhanced by adding borage or nasturtium leaves and flowers. These ingredients are costly to buy but easy to grow.*

## CORN SALAD

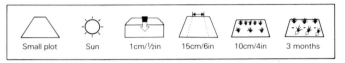

| | | | | | |
|---|---|---|---|---|---|
| Small plot | Sun | 1cm/½in | 15cm/6in | 10cm/4in | 3 months |

Also known as lamb's lettuce, this hardy annual has tender lettuce-like leaves ideal for a winter salad.

**GROWING**  Corn salad grows over winter on well-drained soil in a sheltered site, preferably following a well-manured summer vegetable. It can also be grown in summer on deep rich soil. For winter crops, sow at 14-day intervals from late summer to early autumn; for summer, sow from late spring to early summer. Thin the seedlings as soon as possible. Cover the early autumn sowing with cloches in mid-autumn to give leaves in early winter; from unprotected sowings, you can pick leaves in spring.

**HARVESTING**  In winter and early spring, gently pick a few leaves from each plant to make a good serving; in summer, lift the whole plant like lettuce.

**POSSIBLE PROBLEMS**  Relatively trouble-free.

## NASTURTIUM

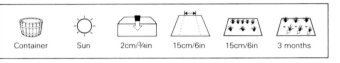

| | | | | | |
|---|---|---|---|---|---|
| Container | Sun | 2cm/¾in | 15cm/6in | 15cm/6in | 3 months |

This round-leaved trailing or climbing annual plant with brilliantly coloured flowers of red, yellow or orange makes a lively addition to salads. It has a strong peppery flavour similar to watercress, and is a valuable source of vitamin C and iron.

**GROWING**  Nasturtiums grow well in light sandy soil. Sow seed in early summer in open ground where they are to flower. They are successful in window boxes and other containers. If space is at a premium, grow the variety Tom Thumb which reaches only 30cm/12in and does not trail.

**HARVESTING**  The leaves and flowers should be eaten fresh and young, though the leaves can be dried successfully.

**POSSIBLE PROBLEMS**  The worst pest is blackfly: do not grow nasturtiums near broad beans. Aphids such as these carry virus diseases.

### ■ ORGANIC TIP

*Mix corn salad with stronger tasting chicory, or crisp cabbage for a winter salad and include citrus fruit, banana or apple. Crunchy roasted nuts or sesame seeds give extra flavour. Add yogurt to a vinaigrette dressing.*

### ■ COOK'S TIP

*Nasturtiums are specially valuable in the salad garden as flowers, leaves and seeds can all be eaten. Leaves and flowers have a peppery taste. The seeds can be pickled and used in the same way as capers. For a highly decorative effect in salads choose the variety Alaska which has flowers in traditional colours, but the green leaves are marbled and striped with cream. Alaska grows to 30cm/12in in height.*

# Radish

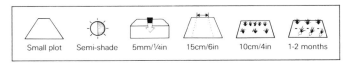

| | | | | | |
|---|---|---|---|---|---|
| Small plot | Semi-shade | 5mm/¼in | 15cm/6in | 10cm/4in | 1-2 months |

This popular vegetable can be grown for most of the year, adding colour, texture and taste to salads.

**GROWING** Rapid growth is essential to produce crisp, tender roots. Do not dig in fresh manure prior to sowing, but grow on rich soil which has sufficient organic matter to retain moisture. Always sow into a deep, fine bed. Because radishes are in the ground for a relatively short time, they are usually grown as a catch crop, between the rows of other vegetables that take longer to mature. Make the first sowing in mid-winter under frames or cloches, using varieties suitable for forcing such as Red Forcing. The first outdoor sowings of maincrop types like Cherry Belle can be made as soon as the ground is workable, in late winter/early spring, and thereafter fortnightly until late summer. Seed can be broadcast and lightly raked in or set at the recommended spacings. Water well, and give protected crops plenty of air on mild days.

**HARVESTING** Pick and eat as soon as they are ready. It takes up to 8 weeks for mid-winter sowings to mature but only 3-4 weeks for summer crops.

**POSSIBLE PROBLEMS** Damping off affects plants sown too thickly. Like brassicas, radishes are susceptible to club root, but if the soil is adequately limed this should not cause much damage as the plants are in the ground for such a short time.

# Winter Radish

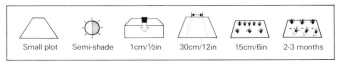

| | | | | | |
|---|---|---|---|---|---|
| Small plot | Semi-shade | 1cm/½in | 30cm/12in | 15cm/6in | 2-3 months |

Otherwise known as Chinese or Spanish radishes, depending on country of origin, winter radishes have solid roots, much larger than their summer cousins, which can be lifted and stored without becoming hollow. The skin can be red, white or black, the roots round or long. They can be peeled and grated to serve as a peppery garnish to roast meats or cooked like turnips.

**GROWING** Make sowings on fine, fertile soil in mid to late summer, thinning the plants when they are large enough to handle. Keep the seedbed moist and free of weeds.

**HARVESTING** Winter radishes will be ready to eat 2-3 months after sowing. Lift the plants and twist off the tops. Use fresh or store as described for long beetroot.

**POSSIBLE PROBLEMS** As for summer radishes.

■ GARDENER'S TIP

*Allow one or two of the early radish plants to go to seed and therefore supply you with a quantity of seeds for the next year for use as sprouted seed or as a seedling crop. As a catch crop sow with early carrots above potatoes or between rows of lettuce, beetroot or carrot. As radishes tend to bolt in hot weather sow mid-summer plants in a more shady position than earlier plants.*

■ COOK'S TIP

*Seed pods of radishes that have run to seed are excellent in salads. Pick when they are crisp and young; the bigger the radish the better the seed pod. In spring when a winter radish crop is ready for digging up, leave some plants to seed.*

# FRUITING VEGETABLES

Although in a hot summer aubergines, peppers and tomatoes will produce fruit outdoors, the harvest is likely to be small in comparison with protected plants, and in poor summers all but non-existent. The ideal way of growing fruiting vegetables is in a greenhouse or walk-in polythene tunnel.

**GREENHOUSE PROTECTION** The glass of a greenhouse not only allows plants plenty of light but also helps to trap heat so that night temperatures do not drop as sharply as they can outside. It also provides protection from wind. Windows and roof vents allow ventilation. Good ventilation is vital as this is an important way of controlling the temperature inside the greenhouse.

The disadvantage of a greenhouse is that if plants like tomatoes and cucumbers are grown directly in the soil over a number of years soil pests and diseases can become a serious problem and the soil has to be replaced or sterilized.

Heating the greenhouse just enough to keep it frost free allows you to grow a far wider choice of vegetables through the winter and a greenhouse allows you to raise healthy vegetables from seed. Started off in the house, seedlings can never be as strong as those raised in a greenhouse because even on a window sill they will only receive light from one direction.

**WALK-IN TUNNEL** The less expensive alternative to a greenhouse is a walk-in polythene tunnel. This has the advantage of being comparatively easy to move to another site to avoid pest and disease build-up in the soil. However, the polythene will need replacing about every three years and ventilation is much more difficult. In winter, condensation can be a major problem, bringing the danger of disease with it. Providing a door at each end of the tunnel and incorporating ventilation panels will help. Added ventilation can be provided in summer by cutting out small, low level vents along the sides. These can be taped over with spare polythene in winter. Alternatively, open mesh panels in doors and along the bottom of each side panel will provide extra ventilation. It is not feasible to heat a polythene tunnel.

**COLD FRAME AND CLOCHE PROTECTION** It is important that outdoor varieties of tomatoes are not planted outside until early summer or they can suffer a severe setback in a late cold spell. Put them into cold frames in late spring to harden off first. Both bush and tall varieties can be started off under cloches or in a cold frame with the protection removed when plants outgrow it. Also, towards the end of the season, plants can be covered by cloches to help any green fruit to ripen. Upright varieties of tomatoes can be carefully removed from the stakes and lain on the ground on a bed of straw.

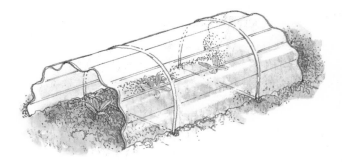

**Cloches**
*A corrugated PVC cloche, held in position with wire hoops, is long-lasting and serves many uses. It is light and easy to move.*

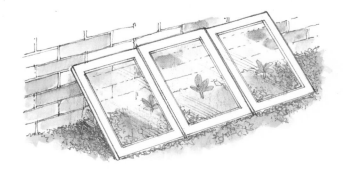

*An improvised cloche, made by leaning some spare window panes against a wall.*

**Training cordon tomatoes**
*Drive in a bamboo cane, before planting seedlings. They are ready when flowers on the first truss are opening.*

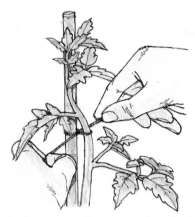

*As the tomato plant grows, loosely tie the main stem to the bamboo cane, using string.*

*Where a leaf stalk joins the main stem, side shoots will grow. Pinch these out, before they grow too large, sapping strength from the plant.*

**CULTIVATION** In the greenhouse plants can be grown in pots, in growing bags or in the ground, but avoid growing plants in the same greenhouse soil for more than three years. As peppers grow best if their roots are restricted, they do well in pots.

In hot weather it is important to damp down the greenhouse. This means spraying plants and the greenhouse floor at least once a day to keep the temperature down and provide a humid atmosphere. Spraying is also important when fruit is setting.

Mature plants will need feeding every time they are watered; see specific plants for recommended fertilizers or use organic fertilizers. Liquid seaweed can be used on tomatoes and peppers, liquid animal manure fertilizer on tomatoes, peppers or aubergines. See the Organic Tip on page 40 for making liquid manure.

**PESTS, DISEASES AND DISORDERS**

*Aphids* Greenfly and blackfly, both aphids, are usually obvious as they group on plant stems, especially at new growth tips. They suck the sap but are unable to use the sugar in the sap and so excrete it as sticky honeydew. Where there is a large amount of honeydew, sooty mould will grow and virus can develop. Remove the insects by hand or hose them off. Use an insecticidal soap to spray badly infected plants. The organic solution is to attract ladybirds, lacewings and hoverflies, who eat quantities of these pests (see page 15).

*Blotchy ripening in tomatoes* Shading fruit in hot weather and watering frequently should help to prevent this. Another year, try growing a different variety.

*Red spider mites* Mottled leaves and fine webbing are signs that you have an infestation of this tiny green or red mite. It is too small to actually see. A problem in greenhouses, red spider mites are a sign that the atmosphere is too dry. To avoid this pest, make sure you keep the atmosphere humid (see above). Spray small infestations with derris, following manufacturer's instructions. Alternatively, control by buying and introducing the predatory mite that feeds on red spider mites. Don't mix the two methods.

*Tomato blight* Black or brown spots appear on the leaves, tomatoes turn brown and rot. This is a problem that particularly occurs in warm, wet weather. Spray with Bordeaux mixture once a fortnight as soon as you discover the problem.

*Tomato leaf mould* This appears as yellow patches on the upper side of leaves, often with brown patches below. Spray with copper fungicide. Grow resistant varieties in the future.

*Virus* Yellowing and mottled leaves plus stunted plants is a sign of virus. Pull up and burn plants. This disease is carried by aphids.

*Whitefly* A common problem in greenhouses, these small white flies suck the plant's sap and can rise in clouds if you touch the plant.

Use a yellow grease-covered card to collect whitefly, as described on page 15. You can spray with derris. Do this three times at 5-day intervals, or alternatively use the parasitic wasp as a biological pest control. Don't use both methods as the derris will kill off the wasps.

Blotchy ripening

Tomato blight

# Aubergine

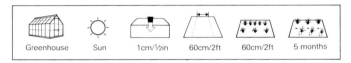

| Greenhouse | Sun | 1cm/½in | 60cm/2ft | 60cm/2ft | 5 months |

In cool districts aubergines can be raised only in a heated greenhouse, though if a sheltered, sunny site is available plants in pots can be moved outside in summer.

**GROWING** In late winter, or early spring for plants you plan to move outside, sow seeds thinly in trays of seed compost, cover lightly with compost and keep moist at a temperature of 21C/70F until germination occurs. When they are large enough to handle, prick the seedlings out into 9-cm/3½-in pots of proprietary compost. They can be planted out in late spring, either into the greenhouse bed or in 20-cm/8-in individual pots. A well-drained, moisture-retentive soil is necessary, and as with all greenhouse cultivation, it must be free of soil-borne diseases. Pinch out the leading shoot when the plant reaches 15cm/6in to encourage bushy growth. Aubergines like heat and humidity, so spray frequently with water and feed regularly with a nitrogenous fertilizer. Provide stakes for the plants to allow 3 or 4 shoots to develop on each.

**HARVESTING** The first fruits should be ready in mid summer. Cut them off with a sharp knife.

**POSSIBLE PROBLEMS** Aphids, glasshouse whitefly and red spider mite must be kept under strict control in the greenhouse. Control whitefly with the parasitic insect *Encarsia formosa*. Keep the atmosphere humid.

# White Aubergine

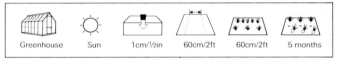

| Greenhouse | Sun | 1cm/½in | 60cm/2ft | 60cm/2ft | 5 months |

These fruiting vegetables are recently developed relatives of the familiar purple aubergine. They can be used in the same way and are particularly attractive pickled in vinegar in the Japanese style.

**GROWING** Sow seeds in late winter in trays of seed compost. Cover lightly with compost and keep moist at 21C/70F until germinated. When the seedlings are large enough to handle, prick them out into 9-cm/3½-in pots of proprietary compost. Maintain a constant temperature of 17C/65F. Set the plants into the greenhouse border or into 20-cm/8-in individual pots in late spring, using well drained, moisture retentive soil that is free of soil-borne diseases. Pinch out the leading shoot when the plants reach 15cm/6in. Keep the temperature steady, spray frequently to increase humidity and feed regularly with a nitrogenous fertilizer. Stake the plants so that 3 or 4 shoots develop in each: in good seasons it may be necessary to limit each plant to no more than 6 fruits. If you have a sun-trap patio, plants in pots can be moved outside in favourable weather.

**HARVESTING** The first fruits should be ready in midsummer. Cut them off with a sharp knife.

**POSSIBLE PROBLEMS** Keep greenhouse pests under control, spraying against aphids, whitefly and red spider mite.

## ▪ GARDENER'S TIP

*Grow plants on a sunny balcony or in front of a south facing wall, which will reflect warmth and give protection. Buy sturdy plants from a nursery and plant out in organic soil grow-bags in early summer.*

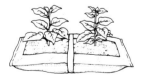

## ▪ COOK'S TIP

*Imam bayeldi is a famous Turkish dish made with aubergines. It is said that the sultan who first tasted it fainted from delight. Make it by frying 2 chopped onions and 2 garlic cloves; add a 400g/14oz can of tomatoes and cook until some but not all of the liquid is reduced. Fry slices of 2 large aubergines, add to the mixture and garnish with chopped parsley and toasted pine nuts. Eat while still warm, but not hot, with fresh crusty bread.*

# PEPPER

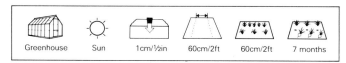

| Greenhouse | Sun | 1cm/½in | 60cm/2ft | 60cm/2ft | 7 months |

Peppers, the mature fruits of the capsicum plant are green, but if left on the plant will eventually turn red.

**GROWING** Peppers need very similar conditions to aubergines, and they make good companions in the greenhouse as well as the kitchen. Peppers are the less tender of the two, and can be grown outside in warm districts in good summers, in a sheltered site. All plants must be raised in a greenhouse. Sow seed thinly in trays of compost in late winter/early spring at 21C/70F. Pot the seedlings on into 9-cm/3½-in pots of proprietary compost when they are large enough to handle. Plant out in mid to late spring into the greenhouse bed or into 20-cm/8-in pots of soil into which plenty of well-rotted organic manure has been incorporated. Make sure the soil is warm when the plants are set out, and keep the temperature in the greenhouse at 18C/64F minimum. Keep the plants well watered and feed regularly with a high-nitrogen fertilizer. The developing plants need support, such as strings suspended from overhead wires, or canes if the plants are going outside. Pinch out the terminal flower in order to give continuous fruiting.

**HARVESTING** Begin picking green peppers in late summer, cutting them with a sharp knife. Pick regularly.

**POSSIBLE PROBLEMS** Watch out for aphids on young plants, red spider mite and whitefly in the greenhouse.

# CHILLI PEPPER

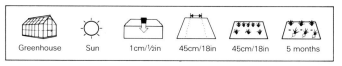

| Greenhouse | Sun | 1cm/½in | 45cm/18in | 45cm/18in | 5 months |

There are numerous varieties of capsicum, the smallest of which are chilli peppers. These are very hot to the taste, providing the characteristic flavour of strong Oriental curries and chilli con carne. Always wash your hands after preparing chillies for cooking, and take care not to touch your eyes or lips.

**GROWING** Chilli peppers need heat, humidity and light. Sow seeds in spring in seed trays of compost kept at a constant 21C/70F, and prick out when large enough into 9-cm/3½-in pots of proprietary compost. Grow on at 17C/65F. Pot on in late spring to 20-cm/8-in pots. Spray daily with water and feed regularly with nitrogenous fertilizer. Give a stake to each plant and pinch out when they reach 20cm/8in to encourage bushy growth.

**HARVESTING** Pick the chillies when they are plump and glossy and use immediately. They will keep for up to 2 weeks wrapped in baking parchment in a box in the refrigerator.

**POSSIBLE PROBLEMS** Keep all greenhouse pests under control.

## ▥ ORGANIC TIP

*To deter whitefly, surround pepper plants with French marigold plants. Grow outdoors against a sunny wall in home-made growing bags. Fill heavy duty plastic bags with garden compost and manure.*

## ▥ PRESERVING TIP

*Chilli peppers are best eaten fresh but they can also be dried to preserve them for use through the winter. Place the fruit on racks and put in the oven on a very low setting, leaving the door ajar. Chek regularly and remove when the fruits are crisp and dry.*

*Alternatively, place between sheets of absorbent kitchen roll and put in the microwave. Check every minute and turn the sandwich over. The chillies should be ready in 3-4 minutes.*

# GREENHOUSE TOMATO

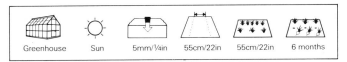

| | | | | | |
|---|---|---|---|---|---|
| Greenhouse | Sun | 5mm/¼in | 55cm/22in | 55cm/22in | 6 months |

A heated greenhouse gives a crop of early tomatoes. Choose a variety like Eurocross BB.

**GROWING** Bright light is essential. Sow in early winter to produce plants for setting out in late winter or in mid winter for an early spring planting. Sow seeds thinly in trays and cover lightly with compost. When 2 true leaves appear, pot the seedlings singly into 9-cm/3½-in pots using a proprietary potting compost. Plant out when the first flower on the first truss opens, earlier if they look pot-bound. The soil in the greenhouse border must be well-drained, moisture-retentive and completely free of soil-borne pests and diseases. Alternatively use 25-cm/10-in pots of a good proprietary compost. Water well after transplanting. Keep the temperature at a minimum of 17C/65F night and day. Support the growing plants with strings tied loosely around each stem and attached to an overhead horizontal wire. Remove the tiny side-shoots in the leaf axils. Feed the plants with a low-nitrogen, high potassium solution, gradually increasing the proportion of nitrogen. In mid summer wean the plants on to water only. Remove the growing point when the plants have 7-10 trusses. Spray regularly with water in hot weather.

**HARVESTING** Pick when the tomatoes are deep red.

**POSSIBLE PROBLEMS** The fungus cladosporum causes leaf mould: ventilate the greenhouse on hot days.

# TOMATO

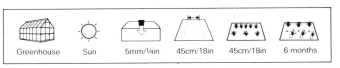

| | | | | | |
|---|---|---|---|---|---|
| Greenhouse | Sun | 5mm/¼in | 45cm/18in | 45cm/18in | 6 months |

Providing unheated protection is one of the most popular and successful methods of growing tomatoes.

**GROWING** Tomato plants raised from seed need the high temperatures and bright light described under greenhouse cultivation. Sow seed in mid/late winter. If you cannot raise plants in ideal conditions, it is better to buy sturdy plants from a nursery. Whether for an unheated greenhouse or outside under glass, prepare the soil by digging in generous quantities of well-rotted organic manure or compost the previous winter.
Harden off the young plants for 2-3 days before planting out in spring. Begin feeding with a medium-nitrogen feed and move on to a high-nitrogen solution when the plants are carrying fruit on the first 2 or 3 trusses. Water regularly. Support the plants as described for the heated greenhouse. Remove the side shoots from the leaf axils, and 'stop' the plants by pinching out the growing point when they have 7-10 trusses.

**HARVESTING** Pick the tomatoes with the calyx on, taking care not to damage the fruits. See outdoor tomato for ripening green tomatoes at the end of the season.

**POSSIBLE PROBLEMS**

To prevent the occurrence of soil-borne diseases, do not grow tomatoes on the same soil year after year.

**VARIETIES** Moneymaker, Tigerella (striped).

■ GARDENER'S TIP

*Use the plants themselves to hold the support strings in place at the base. Make a hole for a plant and fill with water. Take the tomato to be planted, loop the string end under the root ball, then firm the plant well in, anchoring the string.*

■ GARDENER'S TIP

*Tomatoes planted in an unheated greenhouse can be grown in the soil but, due to the fact that pests and diseases can build up in the soil over a number of years, it is best to grow the plants in large pots in garden compost on top of the soil. Some roots will find their way out of the pot into the soil but most will remain in the pot and this can be disposed of at the end of the season.*
*Alternatively stand pots in trays containing a layer of damp pebbles.*

## OUTDOOR TOMATO

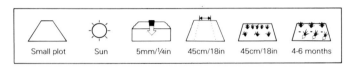

| Small plot | Sun | 5mm/¼in | 45cm/18in | 45cm/18in | 4-6 months |

Choose quick-maturing varieties like The Amateur for outdoor cultivation

**GROWING** To raise plants from seed, follow the instructions given under greenhouse cultivation, sowing up to early spring. If you cannot provide these ideal conditions, buy healthy plants from a nursery. Prepare the soil by digging in plenty of well-rotted organic manure or compost the previous winter. Set the plants out only after all risk of frost has passed and water well. Feed as for plants in an unheated greenhouse. Bush varieties do not need training, but long stemmed types should be staked. Water well every day. A useful protection technique is to plant 45cm/18in away from a wall and suspend a clear polythene sheet along the open side of the row. Remove weeds carefully or suppress them with a mulch of straw or grass cuttings. Bushy tomatoes grown outdoors do not need side-shooting, but as the fruits on the bottom truss begin to ripen, gradually remove the leaves below to allow light to enter and air to circulate.

**HARVESTING** Pick the ripe tomatoes with the calyx on. To ripen remaining green fruit, place in a single layer in a closed drawer with a ripening apple or pear.

**POSSIBLE PROBLEMS** Potato blight may strike in late summer if weather conditions are moist and warm.

**VARIETIES** The Amateur, French Cross.

## CONTAINER TOMATO

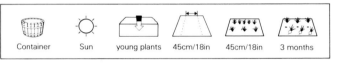

| Container | Sun | young plants | 45cm/18in | 45cm/18in | 3 months |

Miniature tomatoes can be grown very successfully in window boxes or large pots on balconies and patios as well as in growing bags.

**GROWING** If space is limited, you are unlikely to be able to raise tomatoes from seed in the ideal conditions described under greenhouse cultivation (although you may have a gardening friend who will do so for you). In early summer, buy healthy plants from the nursery and set them in 25-cm/10-in pots containing a proprietary compost such as John Innes no. 3. Choose a sunny spot out of the wind. Water the pots every day or twice a day in very warm weather, adding liquid tomato feed to the water. Stop the plants at 7 trusses. Bush tomatoes do not need training, but it is a good idea to tie the stems to supporting canes.

**HARVESTING** Inspect the plants daily and pick the tomatoes as they ripen, with the calyx on.

**POSSIBLE PROBLEMS** Magnesium deficiency shows itself as yellowing of the leaves, starting at the bottom of the plant. Spray regularly with a solution of Epsom salts at 9g per litre/1½oz per gallon. Very high temperatures can cause blotchy ripening: light shade may be necessary at the day's height.

**VARIETIES** Tiny Tim, Pixie Hybrid and Gardener's Delight.

### ◼ GARDENER'S TIP

*On all but bush tomatoes, remove the side shoots that appear in the angle between the leaf stems and main stem and remove lower leaves when they turn yellow. Use soft string to tie plants to canes to avoid damage.*

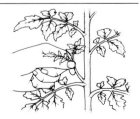

### ◼ COOK'S TIP

*The more tasteless, large-cropping tomatoes are cheap in the shops when home-grown tomatoes ripen. Instead choose to grow varieties with a wonderful flavour, like Gardener's Delight. If you are very short of space grow Pixie*

*F1, in a tub. It produces early tasty fruit. Cherry-sized Tiny Tim, expensive in the shops, do well in a window box or tub and look decorative, and taste good, whole in a salad.*

# LEAF VEGETABLES

Brassicas, which include broccoli, Brussels sprouts, cabbages, cauliflower, calabrese and kale, need a firm soil to help to give them anchorage, so do not dig the bed just before planting. They should always be moved to a new position each year to help to avoid the brassica disease, club root. In the rotation cycle on page 13, brassicas and leaf vegetables come under Plot C which follows peas and beans and salad vegetables. The plants in Group B will have been grown on very rich soil so fresh manuring may not be necessary and the peas and beans will have built up the supply of nitrogen in the soil from the bacteria in their root nodules.

**SPECIAL SOIL REQUIREMENTS** The soil pH is important and should be between 6.5 and 7.0 (see page 7). If your soil is too acid it is best to add lime in the autumn before growing brassicas. Do not lime and add manure or fertilizer at the same time as they do not mix. If you do not need to lime the plot, then it is a good idea to dig in well-rotted compost or manure in the autumn prior to planting as brassicas require a deep and fertile soil. Before planting, add a general fertilizer like dried blood, fish and bone meal. If plant growth is sluggish half way through the year, feed plants with a seaweed-based fertilizer, watered in, or top dress with a nitrogenous fertilizer.

**A CONTINUOUS SUPPLY** By planting a range of leaf vegetables, it is quite possible to have a fresh supply available throughout the year, both for salads and as cooked vegetables. Varieties of cabbage are available to harvest in spring, summer, autumn and winter. Spring greens, winter purslane and annual sprouting broccoli will provide greens in the spring, and in summer New Zealand spinach, spinach beet, summer purslane and spinach are available. Starting in the early autumn, both Swiss and ruby chard can be harvested, then Brussels sprouts, broad-leaved endive and winter cabbage will take you through most of the winter while perennial sprouting broccoli is available all year round.

*Planting* Details of when to plant each variety are given under the specific vegetable. Plant brassicas very

**Catch cropping**
*As broccoli and cauliflower are harvested, the ground they occupied is used for quick-growing crops.*

**Picking Brussels sprouts**
*As the plants grow, keep an eye on their progress and pick off any yellow leaves or loose-leaved sprouts from the bottom of the stem. This will create better air circulation.*

*When the sprouts are ready to harvest – they should be small and compact – pick them progressively from the base upwards a few sprouts at a time. There is an old saying that they taste better after a slight frost.*

firmly when they have three to four proper leaves and are about 5-8cm/2-3in high. The block method of planting is especially suited to cabbages. If you want large heads, space 45cm/18in apart. For smaller heads space only 35cm/14in apart. If cabbages are more widely spaced they can be intercropped, as described below. When plants are harvested, use the spaces left for catch crops or seedling crops of salad lettuce (see below).

Larger brassicas like cauliflower and Brussels sprouts may need staking and earthing up to protect them in stormy winters.

*Intercropping* Where plants are in the ground for a long time and grow slowly, like cabbages or Brussels sprouts, it is a good idea to make use of surrounding space while the plants are still small. This space can be used for fast-growing salad crops, or for raising seedlings for transplanting later. In the same way, where plants are spaced widely apart, it is possible to start off the next crop just prior to the one already in the ground being harvested.

*Catch cropping* When large plants are harvested, or a crop fails, the space can be used for a catch crop. Any plants which are normally successionally sown are suitable, such as beetroot, carrots, lettuces, spring onions or spinach.

*Watering* Leafy green plants need plenty of water while they are growing. In dry periods, water them thoroughly at least once a week or give one very heavy watering two to three weeks before you harvest. Seedlings and newly transplanted plants will need watering little and often, daily in dry weather until they have become established.

*Harvesting* Pick off any yellow leaves or loose-leaved Brussels sprouts from the bottom of the stem to create better air circulation. Pick the sprouts when they are small and compact, starting from the bottom of the stem.

Always remove roots and stems after harvesting brassicas to prevent club root.

**PESTS AND DISEASES** There are a number of diseases that can affect leaf vegetables but if you follow a crop rotation and the tips for growing healthy plants on page 15 these should be able to be kept to a minimum.

*Caterpillars* Appearing from early spring onwards they will eat holes in the leaves of most leaf vegetables. Remove them by hand and drop into paraffin. Look

Cabbage whitefly

Caterpillar

for eggs laid by moths and butterflies, on the plant, especially cabbages, and remove.

*Cabbage root fly* The larvae cause young plants to collapse. An adult female fly lays her eggs next to the stem in the soil and the larvae feed on the roots. Surround the stems of young plants with brassica collars at soil level so the fly cannot burrow down. These can be bought, or made from carpet underlay (see the Tip on page 42).

*Cabbage whitefly* Appearing from late spring to early autumn these tiny white flies can be found on the undersides of leaves of cabbages, Brussels sprouts and other brassicas. If the plant is touched a swarm will rise. Spray with insecticidal soap or derris. This fly can survive outside over winter so remove any old leaves and stems that it could feed on after harvesting.

*Club root* Young plants fail to develop and leaves yellow when this soil-borne fungus attacks the roots, making them swell and decay. There is no cure and the fungus can stay in the soil almost indefinitely. Pull up plants and burn them. Worst in acid soil and where there is poor drainage, so lime where necessary and improve drainage. By raising plants in pots in the greenhouse, then planting out later, you can produce crops after club root, except of cauliflower.

*Mealy cabbage aphid* A grey-green aphid that can appear in colonies on leaf undersides. Control as for cabbage whitefly above. Encourage ladybirds and hoverflies which are the predators of aphids, by growing a wide selection of plants.

*Mosaic virus* Also known as spinach blight, this virus causes yellowing of young leaves which then spreads to older leaves. There is no cure. Aphids spread the disease, so prevent it by controlling the aphids as soon as you discover them. Choose resistant varieties.

## ANNUAL BROCCOLI

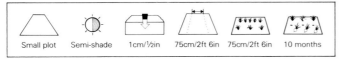

| Small plot | Semi-shade | 1cm/½in | 75cm/2ft 6in | 75cm/2ft 6in | 10 months |

Sprouting broccoli is similar to cauliflower, but produces a loose collection of flowerheads.

**GROWING** A well-drained, alkaline soil which has not recently grown a brassica crop is essential. It should be fertile, open and able to support a good root system. Broccoli plants thrive after well-manured crops such as early potatoes. Work in a top dressing of nitro-chalk in early spring. Sow seeds 2cm/³⁄₄in apart in an outdoor seedbed in mid spring, in drills 20-30cm/8-12in apart. In early summer, transplant the seedlings to the growing site, taking care not to damage the roots. Dip the roots in trichlorphon before planting to protect against cabbage root fly. Firm the plants in and water well. Mulch between the rows in summer to suppress weeds. Stake firmly against winter winds and earth up around the stems for extra support.

**HARVESTING** Sprouting may begin in mid winter, more likely late winter, and continues to late spring when the plants go to seed. Remove sprouting sideshoots when they are mature so that more will be produced further down. Snap off as close to the main stem as possible.

**POSSIBLE PROBLEMS** For club root, see Brussels Sprouts. Watch for aphids and whitefly.

**VARIETIES** Early Purple (or White) Sprouting; Late Purple (or White) Sprouting.

## PERENNIAL BROCCOLI

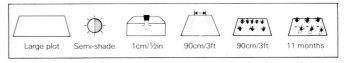

| Large plot | Semi-shade | 1cm/½in | 90cm/3ft | 90cm/3ft | 11 months |

This is a very useful winter-hardy vegetable, which matures in late spring and continues to be productive for several years. When the plants are exhausted, grub them up and do not use the plot for a brassica crop for at least 2 years.

**GROWING** Soil should be non-acid, fertile and well drained. Dig deep the winter before planting so that the soil texture will permit the formation of good strong roots. Raise plants by sowing seed in an outdoor seedbed in mid spring. Set the seeds 2cm/³⁄₄in apart in rows 20-30cm/8-12in apart. Choose only sturdy seedlings for transplanting in early summer to the permanent site, which should be given a worked-in top dressing of nitro-chalk in early spring. Dip the roots in trichlorphon to protect against cabbage root fly before firming the plants into place. Water well. To suppress weeds, put down a mulch in summer, and a layer of straw in winter. Stake firmly for support in winter winds.

**HARVESTING** In late spring perennial broccoli produces a large central head surrounded by about 6 smaller axillary heads. These must all be used to ensure continued productivity. Cut the central head first and remove all heads before the plant goes to seed.

**POSSIBLE PROBLEMS** See annual varieties.

**VARIETIES** Nine Star; Hen and Chickens.

---

■ ORGANIC TIP

*You can make an excellent liquid manure by suspending a sack of well-rotted animal manure in a water butt. Leave a couple of weeks before using and dilute it to the colour of weak tea before watering plants with it.*

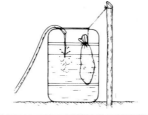

---

■ HEALTH TIP

*Broccoli is rich in vitamins A and B and has more vitamin C content even than oranges but it needs to be cooked in the right way to retain these important nutrients. Steam for only a few minutes or cook with a sprinkling of water in a microwave. After microwaving add yogurt to the cooking juices to create a sauce. Pour over the broccoli and sprinkle with toasted sesame seeds.*

# CALABRESE

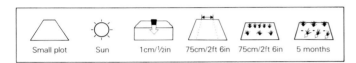

| Small plot | Sun | 1cm/½in | 75cm/2ft 6in | 75cm/2ft 6in | 5 months |

This delicious green relative of white and purple sprouting broccoli, hailing from Italy, is not winter hardy and must be harvested between late summer and mid autumn. It freezes beautifully.

**GROWING** To get the best results, calabrese must be grown rapidly. Soil must be non-acid, fertile and well drained but moisture retentive. Raise plants in an outdoor seedbed, sowing in mid spring. Place frames or cloches over the bed in advance to warm it up. Sow seeds 2cm/¾in apart in rows 20-30cm/8-12in apart and replace the frames/cloches. Water lightly. By early summer the plants are ready for transplanting, after a brief period of hardening off. Soak the seedbed before easing out the plants. Destroy any that are deformed or diseased. Dip the roots of sturdy specimens in trichlorphon and firm them in to the growing site. Dwarf types can be set closer together than the standards. Weed regularly. Constant supplies of water and nitrogenous fertilizer are needed if the necessary strong plant framework is to be produced.

**HARVESTING** Early-maturing varieties are ready for picking in late summer. Cut the terminal head first, using a sharp knife, to encourage formation of small axillary 'spears'.

**POSSIBLE PROBLEMS** See annual sprouting broccoli.

**SUITABLE VARIETIES** Mercedes (dwarf); Express Corona; Green Duke.

## ▪ FREEZER TIP

*Remove any outer leaves, trim the stalks and cut into sprigs, then wash well. Plunge into fast-boiling water for 3-5 minutes depending on stem thickness, then cool in ice-cold water for the same period. Pack head to tail in boxes.*

# BRUSSELS SPROUTS

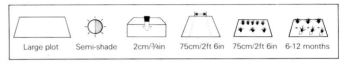

| Large plot | Semi-shade | 2cm/¾in | 75cm/2ft 6in | 75cm/2ft 6in | 6-12 months |

Brussels sprouts are hardy plants that stand over-winter, protected by the canopy of leaves.

**GROWING** Fertile soil is essential, worked deeply enough to sustain the deep root system necessary for a long growing season. Apply lime in the autumn/winter before planting. Raise plants outdoors in a seedbed in a sheltered part of the garden. Sow seed in early spring in drills spaced 25-30cm/10-12in apart. Transplant when the plants reach 15cm/6in, about 8 weeks later. Work a base dressing of a general purpose fertilizer into the soil of the growing site. Soak the seedbed before gently easing the young plants out with a fork. Discard any that are diseased, damaged or lack a growing point. Dip the roots into a bucket of trichlorphon to protect them against cabbage root fly. Firm them into place and give a good base watering. Weed well and water the base of the stems in dry seasons. Top-dress with a nitrogenous fertilizer in late summer. Tall varieties need staking.

**HARVESTING** Depending on variety, the first sprouts should be ready in early autumn. Pick from the bottom upwards, cutting with a sharp knife.

**POSSIBLE PROBLEMS** The most severe disease of all brassicas is the club root fungus. Do not grow on acid soils; rotate crops.

**VARIETIES** Peer Gynt; Roodnerf Early Button; Pegasus.

## ▪ ORGANIC TIP

*In winter birds are hungry too and may well take a liking to your Brussels sprouts. If you cover the leafy heads with a hood of wire or plastic netting, held aloft on long stakes, the birds will ignore the uncovered and easily-picked sprouts.*

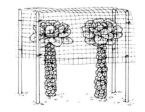

## SPRING CABBAGE

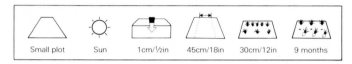

| | | | | | |
|---|---|---|---|---|---|
| Small plot | Sun | 1cm/½in | 45cm/18in | 30cm/12in | 9 months |

Very hardy varieties of cabbage stand over winter from summer sowings to mature at the beginning of the following year.

**GROWING**  Go for rich, deep soil which is moisture retentive but well drained. Incorporate plenty of well-rotted organic manure the autumn before planting. Do not grow on soil that grew brassicas the previous year. Sow seed in an outdoor seedbed in mid-late summer in shallow drills 20-30cm/8-12in apart. In early autumn, before transplanting, work a base dressing of a general purpose fertilizer into the growing site. Water the seedlings well before lifting, being careful not to damage the roots. Retain healthy specimens only and dip the roots in trichlorphon before planting to deter cabbage root fly. Firm the young plants in well and give them a good watering. They overwinter as small plants; so that they will grow rapidly in the new year, hoe in top dressings of nitrogenous fertilizer from late winter onwards.

**HARVESTING**  Spring cabbages are relatively small when mature. Pick as soon as they are ready and use fresh.

**POSSIBLE PROBLEMS**  Cabbage root fly, aphids, club root fungus – see summer/autumn cabbage.

**VARIETIES**  Harbinger (pointed, very early); Pixie (small, pointed); Durham Early (round).

### ■ GARDENER'S TIP

*Never let brassicas go short of water. Unless the weather is constantly wet, keep the soil deeply and evenly moist, especially for seedlings and new transplants.*

## EARLY SUMMER CABBAGE

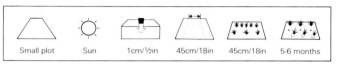

| | | | | | |
|---|---|---|---|---|---|
| Small plot | Sun | 1cm/½in | 45cm/18in | 45cm/18in | 5-6 months |

The first cabbages of the year can be harvested in late spring or early summer. Both round and pointed varieties are available.

**GROWING**  All cabbages prefer rich, deep soils which are moisture retentive but well drained. Incorporate plenty of well-rotted organic manure the autumn before planting. Do not grow on soil that grew brassicas the previous year. Sow seed in mid-late winter in cold or slightly heated greenhouses or frames (10C/50F), either in drills 20cm/8in apart directly into the soil or in seed trays. With the latter method the seedlings should be pricked out when large enough into other trays at 5 × 2.5cm/2 × 1in. Plant outside in mid spring, watering the seedlings well before lifting them carefully. Discard diseased or damaged specimens. Dip the roots of sturdy seedlings in trichlorphon to deter cabbage root fly. Firm in and water well. Continue to water the plants and give nitrogenous fertilizer regularly. Hoe weeds away.

**HARVESTING**  Early cabbages are best picked as soon as they are mature, and used fresh and crisp. Cut heads with a sharp knife.

**POSSIBLE PROBLEMS**  Cabbage root fly is prevalent in late spring. Spray with diazinon. Rotate crops to discourage club root disease.

**VARIETIES**  Golden Acre; May Express & Primo (round); Greyhound, Hispi (pointed).

### ■ ORGANIC TIP

*To outwit the cabbage root fly take a 15-cm/6-in square of foam-rubber carpet underlay, cut a slit from the centre of one side into the middle. Add a small cross slit at the centre and slip this around the plant base.*

## SUMMER/AUTUMN CABBAGE

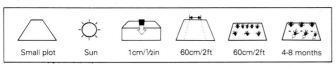

| Small plot | Sun | 1cm/½in | 60cm/2ft | 60cm/2ft | 4-8 months |

Cabbages sown outdoors in late spring are ready to pick from late summer to late autumn according to variety.

**GROWING** Cabbages prefer rich, deep soils which are moisture retentive but well drained. Incorporate plenty of well-rotted organic manure the autumn before planting. Do not grow on soil that grew brassicas the previous year. Sow seed in an outdoor seedbed during mid or late spring in drills 20-30cm/8-12in apart. Transplant to the growing site in early/mid summer, watering the seedlings well before lifting. Take care not to damage the roots. Retain healthy specimens only and dip the roots in trichlorphon before planting to deter cabbage root fly. Firm in well. Water generously and give top dressings of nitro-chalk to sustain growth. Hoe to control weeds until the leaves meet between the rows.

**HARVESTING** Most summer/autumn-maturing cabbages are best picked as soon as they are ready, but a few types stand well.

**POSSIBLE PROBLEMS** Spray against cabbage root fly in late spring. Spray young leaves against aphids. Rotate crops to discourage club root disease.

**VARIETIES** Autumn: Minicole (small, stands well); Holland Late Winter. Summer: Winnigstadt; Golden Acre.

## SAVOY AND WINTER-MATURING CABBAGE

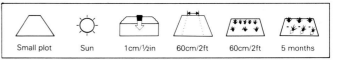

| Small plot | Sun | 1cm/½in | 60cm/2ft | 60cm/2ft | 5 months |

Savoy cabbage is distinguished from other winter-maturing cabbages, which are raised in the same way, by its beautiful crinkled leaves. All are frost-resistant, stand well and can be stored, unlike spring or summer/autumn types.

**GROWING** Soil should be rich and deep, moisture retentive but well drained. Incorporate plenty of well-rotted organic manure the autumn before planting. Do not grow on soil that grew brassicas the previous year. Sow seed in an outdoor seedbed during mid or late spring in drills 20-30cm/8-12in apart. Transplant to the growing site in early/mid summer, watering the seedlings well before lifting them. Take care not to damage the roots. Retain healthy specimens only and dip the roots in trichlorphon before planting to deter cabbage root fly. Firm in well. Water generously and give top dressings of nitro-chalk to sustain growth. Hoe to control weeds until the leaves meet between the rows.

**HARVESTING** Savoy cabbages mature from early autumn, while other winter cabbages stand throughout the winter. Cut the mature heads when required. To store white winter cabbages, cut in late autumn/early winter. Remove the outer leaves and stack the heads pyramid fashion in a cool, dry, frost-free shed.

### ▩ ORGANIC TIP

*Keep aphids at bay by encouraging hoverflies to inhabit your cabbage patch. Entice them with their favourite flat, open flowers like yarrow, fennel and French marigolds which will add colour to the area too. The larvae of hoverflies flourish on aphids,* *so are good friends to every organic gardener. Use a square of underlay to keep the cabbage root fly at bay (see early summer cabbage).*

### ▩ ORGANIC TIP

*To keep weeds at bay, plant seedlings through cross slits made in a sheet of biodegradable brown paper. Push down the paper edges into a narrow channel made in the soil, then cover the exposed sides with more soil.*

## RED CABBAGE

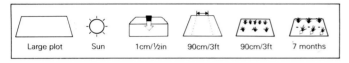

| Large plot | Sun | 1cm/½in | 90cm/3ft | 90cm/3ft | 7 months |
|---|---|---|---|---|---|

Red cabbages have large, firm spherical heads with deep purplish red leaves. Ready in late autumn, they stand well and have many uses in the kitchen, for pickling, grating in salads, or stewing with apple and onion to accompany roast meats.

**GROWING** Soil should be rich and deep, moisture retentive but well drained. Incorporate plenty of well-rotted organic manure the autumn before planting. Do not grow on soil that grew brassicas the previous year. Sow seed in an outdoor seedbed during mid or late spring in drills 20-30cm/8-12in apart. Transplant to the growing site in early/mid summer, watering the seedlings well before lifting them. Take care not to damage the roots. Retain healthy specimens only and dip the roots in trichlorphon before planting to deter cabbage root fly. Firm in well. Water generously and give top dressings of nitrochalk to sustain growth. Hoe to control weeds until the leaves meet between the rows.

**HARVESTING** Cut from late autumn onwards. To store, trim off the outer leaves and stack the heads pyramid fashion in a cool, airy, frost-free place.

**POSSIBLE PROBLEMS** See summer/autumn cabbage.

**VARIETIES** Ruby Ball; Red Drumhead.

## EARLY CAULIFLOWER

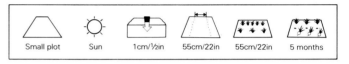

| Small plot | Sun | 1cm/½in | 55cm/22in | 55cm/22in | 5 months |
|---|---|---|---|---|---|

Tender early summer cauliflowers have the finest flavour.

**GROWING** An alkaline soil that has not recently grown another brassica is essential. It should be open, fertile and able to sustain rapid unchecked growth. If manured for a previous crop, moisture retention will be improved. Raise plants from seed sown in mid winter. Sow in seedtrays in the greenhouse at 13C/55F. When the seedlings are large enough to handle, prick them out into trays of potting compost, spacing them 5cm/2in apart. Before transplanting – in early or mid spring, depending on weather and location – dip the roots of the seedlings in trichlorphon to deter cabbage root fly and incorporate a general purpose fertilizer into the plot. If the soil is too cold, growth will be checked and a good head, or 'curd', will not form. Hoe to keep weeds down, and maintain growth with top dressings of nitrogen and regular waterings. Earth up the stems to prevent the plants shifting in the wind. To protect the developing curd from the sun and keep it white, break a leaf over it.

**HARVESTING** Cut cauliflowers as soon as they are ready throughout early summer, lifting them in the morning.

**POSSIBLE PROBLEMS** Watch out for aphids, whitefly, flea beetles and caterpillars as well as club root. Whiptail is a leaf distortion occurring on acid soils.

**VARIETIES** Snowball; Alpha.

■ DECORATIVE TIP

*Add colour to autumn flower borders by planting decorative and colourful cabbages in groups. Apart from red cabbages use ornamental cabbage, Brassica oleracea, with pink, green and white variegated foliage.*

■ ORGANIC TIP

*Cauliflowers will immediately react to a soil deficient in nutrients. Check that you have included lime to ensure that the soil is not too acid, then use a liquid seaweed fertilizer. This contains potash and all the trace elements necessary to quickly correct any deficiencies. However, extra feeding should only be used when deficiencies are noticed. In an organic garden the well-fed soil should be able to supply all the nutrients that vegetables will need.*

## SUMMER/AUTUMN CAULIFLOWER

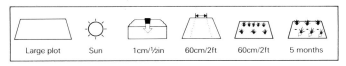

| Large plot | Sun | 1cm/½in | 60cm/2ft | 60cm/2ft | 5 months |

Summer- and autumn-maturing cauliflowers are the easiest to grow. While they are not frost-hardy, the flavour is more delicate than that of winter types.

**GROWING**  Give cauliflowers a non-acid, open fertile soil, manured for a previous crop. Work in a base dressing of general purpose fertilizer before planting. Raise plants from seed sown in early spring in an outdoor seedbed that has not recently grown a brassica crop. Sow throughout spring in shallow drills 20-30cm/8-12in apart. Move the young plants to the growing site 8-10 weeks later, first dipping the roots in trichlorphon to deter cabbage root fly. Firm in well. Growth must be unchecked – give a top dressing of a nitrogenous fertilizer and water regularly. Keep weeds down and earth up the stems to keep the plants steady. If the variety you are growing has upright leaves, bend one over the maturing head to prevent it yellowing.

**HARVESTING**  Cut cauliflowers as soon as they are mature, in the cool of the morning. Depending on variety the crop will be ready from late summer to late autumn.

**POSSIBLE PROBLEMS**  See early cauliflower. Frost may damage late autumn crops.

**VARIETIES**  All The Year Round; Wallaby.

## WINTER CAULIFLOWER

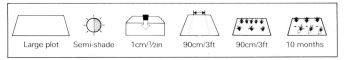

| Large plot | Semi-shade | 1cm/½in | 90cm/3ft | 90cm/3ft | 10 months |

Winter-maturing cauliflower varieties, though relatively hardy, do better in mild coastal areas where frost damage is minimal. The leaves tend to be wrapped protectively around the white 'curd'.

**GROWING**  Go for a non-acid, open, fertile soil that has been manured for a previous crop. Good drainage is important: a strong root system must develop to anchor the plants during windy winter months. Winter cauliflower plants are produced by sowing seed in an outdoor seedbed in mid/late spring as described for late summer/autumn crops. Thin the seedlings if necessary to 2cm/¾in to encourage short sturdy plants. Transplant to the growing site in mid summer, dipping the roots in trichlorphon to deter cabbage root fly. Keep weeds down during the winter and earth up the plants to keep them steady. When growth begins again in late winter apply a top-dressing of nitro-chalk, hoed in around the base of the plants.

**HARVESTING**  Depending on variety, winter cauliflower are ready for picking from late winter to late spring. Cut at the base of the stem with a sharp knife.

**POSSIBLE PROBLEMS**  See early cauliflower. Soil-borne fungi may cause damping off of seedlings.

**VARIETIES**  Early White; Angers (south and west districts); Asmer Pinnacle (northern districts).

■ GARDENER'S TIP

*Try growing mini-cauliflowers, which taste good and look very decorative. Choose a variety like Gorant or Predominant which will produce miniature curds, and space at 10cm/4in intervals in rows 22.5cm/9in apart. Then grow as for summer cauliflowers,* *above. All will be ready about the same time but some can be frozen for use later. Raw cauliflower is delicious in a salad with nuts and raisins.*

■ GARDENER'S TIP

*Before transplanting a seedling, check that it has developed the tiny central bud from which the curd will come. If the seedling lacks this bud no head will form later on, so it is best to discard it at this point.*

## CHICORY

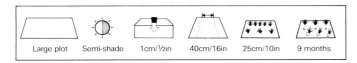

| | | | | | |
|---|---|---|---|---|---|
| Large plot | Semi-shade | 1cm/½in | 40cm/16in | 25cm/10in | 9 months |

The blanched chicon, or heart, which is forced from the roots of chicory plants is used in salads and braised as a vegetable.

**GROWING** Good chicons can only be produced from nicely shaped, healthy roots, which require soil, that has been enriched for a previous crop, such as leeks. Recently manured soil will make the roots forked and misshapen. Sow in mid-late spring. Thin the seedlings when they reach the third leaf stage.

**LIFTING** When the most of the leaves have died down, in late autumn at the latest, carefully lift the long roots, discarding any that are damaged or forked, and trim the leaves to 2.5cm/1in of the crown. Store the roots on their sides on boxes in a cool frost-free place. Cover with sand or peat to prevent drying out.

**FORCING AND BLANCHING** Force a few roots at a time. Stand them upright about 6.5cm/2½in apart in deep boxes or pots in sand or light soil with 2.5cm/1in showing. Water lightly and then cover the containers completely to exclude all light.

**HARVESTING** Pick the chicons when 10-15cm/4-6in long. Discard the used roots and start again with a fresh batch from store.

**POSSIBLE PROBLEMS** Inspect for slugs when blanching.

## BROAD-LEAVED ENDIVE

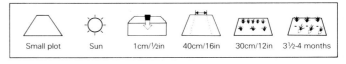

| | | | | | |
|---|---|---|---|---|---|
| Small plot | Sun | 1cm/½in | 40cm/16in | 30cm/12in | 3½-4 months |

A half-hardy annual and close relative of chicory, endive is blanched before picking to counteract its naturally bitter taste. Cook or eat raw in salads.

**GROWING** A well-drained, fertile soil is best, with a dressing of general, balanced fertilizer before sowing. Sow the seed into its final position from mid summer to early autumn for late autumn and winter picking. Transplanting the seedlings can damage the tap root and check growth. Sow the seed in 1-cm/½-in deep drills spaced 40cm/16in apart. When the seedlings are 5-7.5cm/2-3in high, thin them out to 30cm/12in apart in the rows.

**BLANCHING** Endive plants are usually ready for blanching about 3 months after sowing and it may be done in one of two ways. The leaves can be gathered together when dry (damp plants may rot during blanching) and tied round with raffia or string. This keeps the light away from all but the outer leaves. Alternatively, the plants can be completely covered with containers.

**HARVESTING** Blanching takes up to 3 weeks in the winter. Don't treat too many plants at a time because endive will not keep very long after blanching.

**POSSIBLE PROBLEMS** Watch out for greenfly during the summer months. Broad-leaved endive will need the protection of cloches in winter.

### ▪ PRESERVING TIP

*Once the chicons have been harvested they will need to be used fairly quickly or they will deteriorate, becoming green and bitter on exposure to light. Keep them chilled in the refrigerator and out of the light and wrap in foil.*

### ▪ COOK'S TIP

*Endive goes well with other salad greens. Alternatively, toss with orange segments and watercress sprigs in a vinaigrette to which toasted almonds have been added. For a tasty hot bacon dressing to toss endive and dandelion leaves in, melt butter in* *a saucepan and add slices of bacon chopped up small, cook until the bacon starts to go crisp, then pour over the salad. Heat a little wine vinegar in the pan and pour this over the top. Serve at once.*

# KALE

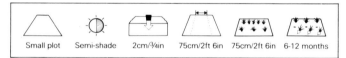

| Small plot | Semi-shade | 2cm/¾in | 75cm/2ft 6in | 75cm/2ft 6in | 6-12 months |
|---|---|---|---|---|---|

Kales are hardy winter greens that will stand very severe weather indeed. The type grown in vegetable gardens is curly kale – plain-leaved kale has a very strong flavour and is usually fed to livestock. Dwarf curly kales are useful for small gardens.

**GROWING** Kales do best if they follow well-manured crops such as early potatoes or peas. The soil should be non-acid and well drained. Raise plants in an outdoor seedbed, sowing seed thinly in mid/late spring, in drills 30cm/12in apart. Transplant the seedlings to the growing site in mid summer, setting dwarf varieties at the shorter distances of 45cm/18in each way. Fertilizer levels should be kept low to start with but increased by giving top dressings of nitrogenous fertilizer in mid winter.

**HARVESTING** Pick the young leaves off the plants from mid winter onwards. Regular picking will encourage sideshoots to develop which will produce more tender shoots in early and mid spring.

**POSSIBLE PROBLEMS** The usual brassica pests and diseases will need to be dealt with. See Brussels sprouts.

**VARIETIES** Dwarf Green Curled; Ragged Jack; Pentland Brig.

# KOHLRABI

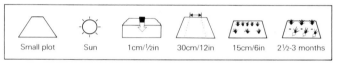

| Small plot | Sun | 1cm/½in | 30cm/12in | 15cm/6in | 2½-3 months |
|---|---|---|---|---|---|

This member of the cabbage family is grown for its swollen stem which is treated by cooks as a root – in fact its popular name is turnip-rooted cabbage. Gardeners like it because it can be grown quickly between rows of peas or carrots as a catch crop.

**GROWING** To sustain rapid growth, well-drained soil is important. Apply lime in late winter. Sow seed thinly from mid spring to mid summer, thinning the seedlings as soon as they are large enough to handle. Sow the white-skinned variety at the beginning, switching to the purple one for later sowings (both have creamy flesh). The plants withstand heat and drought but regular light watering assists development. Hoe carefully to control weeds, taking care not to damage the stems.

**HARVESTING** Do not let the globes exceed 7.5cm/3in in diameter before picking or the flavour will be coarse. Use immediately, as kohlrabi do not store well.

**POSSIBLE PROBLEMS** Relatively trouble-free.

**VARIETIES** Early White Vienna; Early Purple Vienna.

## ORGANIC TIP

*Club root cannot be cured and the fungus lives in and affects the soil for up to ten years. So it is important to grow plants that are as healthy as possible. Make sure the soil is not acid, is properly drained and rich in humus and dig up brassica stumps after harvesting. Some organic gardeners believe that a chunk of rhubarb or a moth-ball popped into the hole before planting a seedling helps mask the brassica smell from the fungus.*

## COOK'S TIP

*Kohlrabi has a sweet, nutty flavour. To cook, scrub the bulb-shaped stems, then steam or boil for 15-25 minutes, depending on size. Peel just before serving and coat with a creamy sauce. Kohlrabi can also be sliced and stir-fried.*

## RUBY CHARD (SEAKALE BEET)

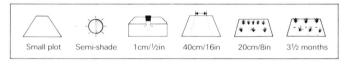

| Small plot | Semi-shade | 1cm/½in | 40cm/16in | 20cm/8in | 3½ months |

A showpiece in the vegetable garden, ruby chard's ornamental red stems can be eaten as a separate vegetable from the leaves, as in the case of Swiss chard. The leaves have a milder flavour than those of true spinach.

**GROWING** As is true of the other leaf beets – spinach beet and Swiss chard – any well-drained fertile garden soil is suitable for growing ruby chard. It should be given plenty of organic manure to encourage succulent leaf growth. The best results are obtained from spring-sown crops. Sow the seed thinly in 1-cm/½-in deep drills during mid spring. Leave 40cm/16in between rows and thin the seedlings to 20cm/8in apart when they are large enough.

**HARVESTING** A little ruby chard can be pulled in winter, but mainly in late summer and early autumn. Take only the young outer leaves while they are tender and pull them off complete with the base, being extra careful not to pull up the plant.

**POSSIBLE PROBLEMS** Weed control is particularly necessary during the early stages of this crop and extra watering in dry weather will help to prevent bolting.

## SWISS CHARD (SEAKALE BEET)

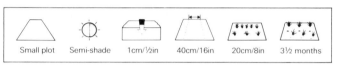

| Small plot | Semi-shade | 1cm/½in | 40cm/16in | 20cm/8in | 3½ months |

This distinctive-looking vegetable is grown for its wide white stalks as well as its leaves: the leaves are substituted for spinach and have a milder flavour than those of true spinach. The leaf stalks may be substituted for seakale itself. It is easier to grow than true spinach.

**GROWING** Any well-drained fertile garden soil is suitable. Swiss chard should be given plenty of organic manure to encourage succulent leaf growth. Sow the seed thinly in 1-cm/½-in deep drills during mid spring. Leave 40cm/16in between rows and thin the seedlings to 20cm/8in apart when they are large enough. Swiss chard can be sown in mid/late summer for an over-wintering crop, but the best results are obtained from spring-grown crops.

**HARVESTING** A little Swiss chard can be pulled in winter, but mainly in late summer and early autumn. Take only the young outer leaves while they are tender and pull them off complete with the base, being extra careful not to pull up the plant.

**POSSIBLE PROBLEMS** Weed control is particularly necessary during the early stages of this crop and extra watering in dry weather will help to prevent bolting. Feed with comfrey liquid if plants are not growing well.

### ■ DECORATIVE TIP

*The red stems of ruby chard and the large spear-shaped leaves make it decorative enough to grow amongst flowering plants or as a border edging plant. The stems of rainbow chard can be red, yellow, orange, purple or white.*

### ■ ORGANIC TIP

*Grow comfrey as a plant food. The leaves of comfrey contain as much nitrogen and phosphorus as manure, plus far more potassium. Use a sunny position for a comfrey patch and cut down leaves to dig directly into the soil or use them as a mulch.*

*Make a concentrated feed by stuffing the freshly cut leaves into a plastic container with a hole in the bottom. The liquid that seeps out should be diluted with water 1:20 before use.*

## SPINACH BEET

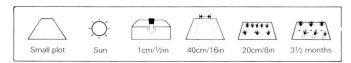

| Small plot | Sun | 1cm/½in | 40cm/16in | 20cm/8in | 3½ months |

Spinach beet belongs to the same family as garden beetroots. It is sometimes called perpetual spinach and is grown for the leaves and stalks, which are eaten whole for the spinach-like flavour. Its leaves have a milder flavour than those of true spinach.

**GROWING** Any well-drained, fertile garden soil is suitable. Spinach beet should be given plenty of organic manure to encourage succulent leaf growth. Spinach beet can either be sown in spring – for harvesting in the summer or autumn – or in late summer for harvesting in winter and early spring. The best results are obtained from spring-sown crops. Sow the seed thinly in 1-cm/½-in deep drills in mid spring. Leave 40cm/16in between rows and thin the seedlings to 20cm/8in apart when they are large enough.

**HARVESTING** Cut the entire leaves when young and tender. Regular harvesting encourages growth.

**POSSIBLE PROBLEMS** Weed control is particularly necessary during the early stages of this crop and regular watering is very useful in hot, dry summers. Aphids are a continual problem, especially on summer crops. Downy mildew produces the typical yellow blotches on the top of the leaves, accompanied by white fungal patches below. Protect winter spinach beet by lagging the plants with straw or bracken.

## NEW ZEALAND SPINACH

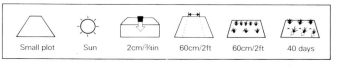

| Small plot | Sun | 2cm/¾in | 60cm/2ft | 60cm/2ft | 40 days |

New Zealand spinach is a useful vegetable for dry soils, and can be cropped regularly over a long period. It is a half-hardy sprawling plant.

**GROWING** New Zealand spinach must either be sown indoors in mid spring, hardened off and planted out in late spring after risk of frost has passed, or sown directly outdoors in early summer – or a little earlier under cloches. To assist germination, soak the seed in water overnight before sowing. Grow in stations 60cm/2ft apart. Sow 3 seeds per station, about 2cm/¾in deep, and pull out the two weakest seedlings as they grow. New Zealand spinach does best in hot summers, so choose a site in full sun with a light, well-drained soil.

**HARVESTING** New Zealand spinach should crop from early summer to early autumn, and must be picked regularly – otherwise it becomes tough, and knobbly seedheads are formed. Pick carefully, by nipping off the leaves without tearing. The plants are quite robust and up to half the leaves may be picked at a time.

**POSSIBLE PROBLEMS** Pick off any flowers to keep leaves growing. Hungry spinach of any kind will be bitter and possibly earthy flavoured. Give extra base dressing and liquid feed well throughout the summer.

### ▪ ORGANIC TIP

*Mulch plants well, spreading around them garden compost, animal manure, seaweed, dried bracken, old straw, dried lawn mowings, or leaf mould. This will help to conserve moisture and keep the soil temperature stable.*

### ▪ FREEZER TIP

*Spinach and its substitutes, like New Zealand spinach, freeze well. Use young leaves and wash carefully to make sure no grit is left, then blanch, a little at a time, for two minutes, shaking the basket to separate the leaves. Cool fast by running very cold* *water over the leaves for a further two minutes. Then press leaves to remove as much moisture as possible and freeze leaves whole in bags or chop up.*

## SPINACH

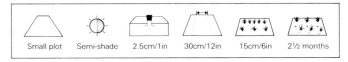

| Small plot | Semi-shade | 2.5cm/1in | 30cm/12in | 15cm/6in | 2½ months |

Spinach is very sensitive to day length, which is why it is apt to 'bolt' in the long days of summer. Steadier growth in autumn, winter and early spring allows several pickings.

**GROWING** A moist, rich, deeply dug soil is essential. For a summer supply, frequent small sowings are advisable, as in general only one cut can be made before spinach runs to seed. In warm parts of the country, the first sowing can be made under cloches in late winter, followed by outdoor sowings in early spring. Sow the seed thinly in 2.5cm/1-in deep drills spaced 30cm/12in apart. Water the bottom of the drill before sowing in dry weather. Thin the seedlings to 15cm/6in apart to allow reasonably sized plants to develop and to prevent excessive moisture loss and therefore bolting. Make further sowings at 2-3 week intervals until mid summer.

Winter spinach, which can be cropped between mid autumn and late spring, is sown in late summer and early autumn. In this case, however, growth rate and the danger of bolting will be less so the seedlings can be thinned, if necessary, to 7.5-15cm/3-6in apart. The plants will benefit from cloche protection from mid autumn.

**HARVESTING** Leaves can be eaten very small or allowed to grow larger. Pick them off the plant as required.

**POSSIBLE PROBLEMS** Copper spray will combat downy mildew. Pick off any flowers to keep leaves growing.

## SPRING GREENS

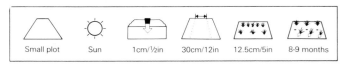

| Small plot | Sun | 1cm/½in | 30cm/12in | 12.5cm/5in | 8-9 months |

Spring greens are actually spring cabbages, cut before a heart forms, or the thinnings of a spring cabbage crop.

**GROWING** Spring greens are best sown in mid to late summer in their final positions with the shallow 1-cm/½-in drills spaced 30cm/12in apart. Once the seedlings have one or two true leaves, thin them to 7.5-12.5cm/3-5in apart in the rows. All members of the cabbage family prefer rich, deep soils which are moisture-retentive – but well drained – and have been given plenty of well-rotted organic manure. Spring greens over-winter as relatively small plants and must be encouraged to grow rapidly in the spring by hoeing in nitrogenous top dressings.

**HARVESTING** Harvest the first pickings of spring cabbages carefully so that the plants left have a 30cm/12in space between them. These can be left to heart up.

**POSSIBLE PROBLEMS** The soil will tend to become compacted during the winter, and this should be broken up when the fertilizer top dressing is hoed in during the spring. The fungus disease, club root, which causes the roots to become thick and swollen, is soil-borne, and most likely to occur in wet, acid soils which have grown continuous crops of brassicas without adequate rotational breaks. Mealy aphid can be treated with environmentally-sound soap sprays, with their combined insecticidal and wetting properties.

### ■ COOK'S TIP

*Spinach has a distinctive taste and is delicious cooked or raw. Use young leaves in salads. Make a delicious appetizer with raw spinach leaves. Add to these hot streaky bacon bits, fried in butter until crisp, plus fried croutons. Toss the mixture in the hot butter from the frying pan and add a little warmed wine vinegar. Spinach makes a tasty soup too. Add to it chicken stock, puréed tomatoes, a few carrots and potatoes plus freshly chopped dill leaves.*

### ■ COOK'S TIP

*Spring greens freeze well: wash, then blanch for two minutes in boiling, salted water, cool in icy cold water and press out any excess moisture before packing. Cook in a minimum of water for 5-10 minutes.*

## SUMMER PURSLANE

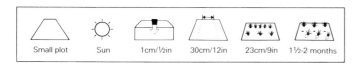

| Small plot | Sun | 1cm/½in | 30cm/12in | 23cm/9in | 1½-2 months |

Summer purslane is not a commonly grown leaf vegetable. It is worth trying if only because it grows very quickly. A low-growing plant, it can be cooked or eaten raw in salads.

**GROWING** Sandy soil suits summer purslane best, and a warm and sheltered position. Mixing the fine seed beforehand with moist sand will make sowing easier. Sow the seed broadcast from late spring until late summer. The plant usually grows well under the protection of glass or plastic cloches, but during wet, cold summers it often fails in the open.

**HARVESTING** Summer purslane is ready for picking in about 6 weeks – it may be ready in as little as 4 weeks, if the weather is warm or if it is grown under cloches. A length of stalk is usually picked with the leaves.

**POSSIBLE PROBLEMS** Over-close planting and over-watering can result in the fungus disease smoulder.

## WINTER PURSLANE

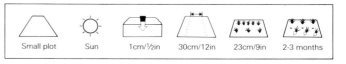

| Small plot | Sun | 1cm/½in | 30cm/12in | 23cm/9in | 2-3 months |

Late-sown crops of winter purslane survive mild winters and form a useful ingredient in the vegetable garden in early spring. Winter purslane is a low-growing, succulent salad plant.

**GROWING** Sow the seed from early spring to late summer in its final position. Most ordinary soils will be suitable and the plants tolerate light shade. Thin the seedlings to 10-13cm/4-5in apart each way.

**HARVESTING** The young leaves are ready for picking from 30 days.

**POSSIBLE PROBLEMS** Over-close planting and over-watering can result in the fungus disease smoulder. Protect winter purslane from frost by covering with cloches.

---

### ■ COOK'S TIP

*When picking purslane leave a short length of stalk and a couple of leaves to encourage regrowth. Purslane has a crunchy texture and a rather bland taste that makes this salad plant best mixed with stronger tasting salad ingredients like rocket, sorrel,* *endive or chicory. The golden form adds an attractive yellow-green colour to a salad. Purslane can also be boiled briefly and eaten as a hot vegetable. It used to be pickled for winter use.*

### ■ ORGANIC TIP

*To reduce the slug and snail population encourage their predators: a pile of leaves in a dry and undisturbed corner could bring a hedgehog, an open-fronted nest box shaded and hidden by climbers may draw a pair of thrushes.*

# STALK AND SHOOT VEGETABLES

If you are following the crop rotation plan on page 13, stalk and shoot vegetables come into Plot B. Most need a well-drained soil that has been thoroughly dug to incorporate plenty of manure, but look under specific vegetables for more detail.

**BLANCHING**  Blanching is done by excluding the light from stalks, shoots or leaves. This makes them more decorative, less bitter and crisp. Forced in the warm darkness new shoots of rhubarb can produce early supplies. Blanching can be done at any time of the year but colder weather produces the best results.

Plants can be blanched either while they are still in the ground or they can be lifted and transplanted for blanching in a dark position under cover in a frame, the greenhouse, garden shed or indoors where they will be protected from winter frosts.

*Blanching in the ground*  There are a number of methods for doing this, suited to different plants.

*Tying up plants*  The leaves are bunched up and then tied together with raffia or string either once about two-thirds up the plant or when necessary at two points. As light still reaches the outer leaves, they remain green but the inner leaves will be pale and crisp in 10-15 days. This method is used on endive.

*Covering plants*  Light is totally excluded in this method where the plant is covered by a bucket, an inverted plant pot with the holes covered, black polythene-covered cloches or straw held in place with wire hoops or wire netting. Tie up the leaves to keep them off the ground.

Endive will take about 10 days; rhubarb protected and forced by this method in late winter will take about 5-6 weeks and seakale forced in mid winter takes longer, about 3 months.

*Self blanching*  In this method, used for some varieties of celery, the plants are placed in squares, 30cm/12in apart, or 15cm/6in for larger quantities of smaller sticks. Because the plants exclude light from each other, they blanch without any additional work.

*Covering stalks*  Cardoon stems are blanched by tying collars made of light-proof material, such as black polythene, around each stem. This method can also be used on Florence fennel and on celery instead of, or in conjunction with, earthing up where the collar is mainly used to stop the soil getting between the stalks.

*Earthing up*  Here the plant stems are gradually covered with earth, increasing the height of the ridge in stages as the plants grow to keep out the light. This method is used on celery, asparagus, chard, leeks and Florence fennel.

If you leave a few salsify and scorzonera plants in the ground these can be completely covered in earth to provide blanched leaves for winter salads.

*Lifted plants*  In winter plants can be lifted to be stored, then forced as required. Seakale can be blanched in this way. Blanching may be done in the dark in any frost-proof place; the greenhouse, a garden shed, a frame or in the house itself. A large flower pot, or a deep box filled with soil can be used to force and blanch the plants but the container needs to be covered with another of identical size and shape so that the light is completely excluded.

The plants are dug up in autumn, carefully to avoid damage, and the roots are stored until required for blanching. Those plants which are forced in warmth in the dark are not considered to have as much flavour as those which are blanched at low temperatures. Really early rhubarb can be produced by simulating forcing shed conditions used by commercial growers. Roots

**Trench-grown celery**
*Dig a trench about 30cm/12in deep and 38cm/15in wide. Loosen the bottom to another spade's depth, add manure.*

*Tread down, return topsoil and firm to 10cm/4in of top. Ridge remaining soil and plant celery when it is 10cm/4in high. Tie polythene round plants when 30cm/12in high.*

*Earthing up is done in three stages, at three-weekly intervals. After the last earthing up only the leaves of the celery plants should be visible.*

are lifted in the autumn and left on the soil surface until they have been frosted several times to break their dormancy. They are then taken into heated sheds where they are planted either in the soil or in boxes. After a thorough watering the crowns are then forced into growth – in absolute darkness – at temperatures around 13-18C/55-65F. Regular watering is necessary and the forced rhubarb is ready for pulling, at the higher temperature, in about 4 weeks. Home forcing should follow the same pattern but using smaller containers for the crowns. If tubs, pots or boxes are used then it should be possible to provide complete darkness by inverting a similar sized container over the top. After forcing in this way the crowns will be exhausted and should be thrown away.

*Tips for successful blanching* Make sure that plants are very dry before blanching. If damp they are likely to rot. In bad weather cover with cloches for a few days before excluding the light.

Remove any dead or rotting leaves before you blanch vegetables.

Handle plants with great care as damage to leaves or roots can lead to disease.

Once blanched a plant will quickly deteriorate so blanch only small quantities at a time for immediate use.

## PESTS, DISEASES AND DISORDERS

*Asparagus beetle* This small orange beetle and its grubs may severely damage leaves, stripping the foliage, and encircle the stem, killing the plant. As soon as you see any sign of attack, dust with derris or use insecticidal soap.

*Carrot fly* Celery can be damaged by the larvae of the tunnelling carrot fly. To keep the carrot fly away from plants, surround the bed with a carrot fly barrier (see Tip on page 66). The insect has to fly up to go over the barrier and so misses the crop.

*Celery fly* The maggots appear in spring and leave brown blotches on leaves which then shrivel. They can kill the plant. Remove damaged leaves immediately and burn them.

*Club root* This disease of brassicas where roots distort and plants fail to develop can also affect seakale on acid soils. See page 39 for more information.

*Damping off* This is a fungus disease causing stems to blacken and decay on seedlings and plants to collapse. It should be prevented by sowing seed more thinly and watering less. Use sterilized compost.

*Frit fly* The growing points of sweetcorn will be stunted if larvae of the frit fly burrow in. Spray young plants with BHC.

*Frost* Asparagus shoots may be damaged by late frosts. In this likelihood, protect the tips with straw.

*Leaf spot* Dark, irregular spotting on celery leaves spreads and the leaves fall off. Remove and burn any affected leaves. Spray the plant with a copper fungicide.

*Slugs* Celery and young artichokes are attractive to slugs. Put a layer of soot or lime around the stems and weed regularly.

*Violet root rot* This fungus causes asparagus plants to wilt and die and the roots to turn purple and mouldy. This is rare but there is no cure. Make a bed in another part of the garden and do not use this area for asparagus again for at least three years.

# GLOBE ARTICHOKE

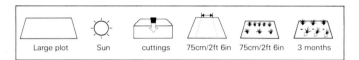

| Large plot | Sun | cuttings | 75cm/2ft 6in | 75cm/2ft 6in | 3 months |

# ASPARAGUS

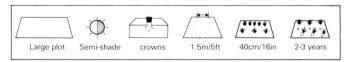

| Large plot | Semi-shade | crowns | 1.5m/5ft | 40cm/16in | 2-3 years |

Although this vegetable needs a considerable amount of space, it is rewarding to grow. It is a handsome ornamental plant which produces edible flowerheads. The artichoke is an almost hardy perennial which will be productive for about 5 years.

**GROWING** Like all perennials, globe artichokes must be grown on well-prepared, manured and weed-free land. They prefer sheltered districts and light, well-drained soils. The best plants are raised from offsets detached from the parent plant in early spring or mid autumn. Early spring offsets are set into their permanent positions immediately; put autumn offsets into 9-cm/3½-in pots and keep in a cold frame until the following spring, when they can be planted out. Replace one quarter of the artichoke bed annually with offsets. Protect plants over winter with straw. Remove this covering in the spring, apply a top dressing of fertilizer and keep well-watered in dry seasons. Weed regularly or suppress weeds with a mulch.

**HARVESTING** Heads will be ready for cutting from midsummer onwards. Cut the terminal (king) head first: these are the largest, but the smaller lateral heads are very tender. To encourage continual cropping, harvest the heads as soon as they are mature.

**POSSIBLE PROBLEMS** None likely.

Start with 1-year-old crowns from a reputable supplier.

**GROWING** The ideal soil is a light, easily worked and well-drained loam. Dig deeply in the autumn before planting and work in well-rotted organic manure or compost. Remove all traces of perennial weeds. In late winter, rake in a general purpose fertilizer. In early spring/late spring, prepare double trenches 30cm/12in wide and 20cm/8in deep, 60cm/2ft apart. Replace a mound of soil 7.5cm/3in deep in the trench. Place the crowns on top, spreading out the roots. Quickly cover the roots with 5-7.5cm/2-3in of fine soil. Hoe the soil between the trenches regularly, each time drawing a little soil over the plants until the trench is filled. Continue earthing up as the shoots appear to make steep-sided beds.

**HARVESTING** Do not cut any spears in the first or second year. In the third year, cut for a 6-week period beginning in mid spring. Hold the tip of the spear and cut below the surface with a sharp knife, taking great care not to damage the crowns. At the end of the cutting period, leave the foliage to build up next year's crowns.
Cut down the foliage of mature plants when it changes colour and before the berries begin to drop.

**POSSIBLE PROBLEMS** Adult asparagus beetles and their larvae feed on shoots and foliage. Violet root rot fungus produces purple threads on the roots.

## ■ ORGANIC TIP

*Save water and time by watering large, single plants efficiently. Sink a porous clay flower pot into the soil close to the plant and pour in water. It will seep down to the roots and a minimum will be lost by running away or evaporation.*

## ■ ORGANIC TIP

*Preparing the ground before planting is essential, since asparagus will crop for 40 years. When cutting back the foliage, cut as low as possible as the pupae of the asparagus fly overwinter in the stems. Slugs can be a problem with young* *asparagus. Distract them by growing a highly favoured crop nearby such as Chinese cabbage, hostas or sunflowers. Better still attract hedgehogs, thrushes, frogs and toads to do the work for you.*

## CARDOON

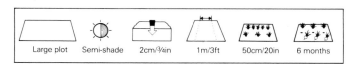

| Large plot | Semi-shade | 2cm/¾in | 1m/3ft | 50cm/20in | 6 months |

Cardoons are related to globe artichokes, but are cultivated for the leaf-stalks and ribs, although the thistle-like flowerhead is also edible. The stalks must be blanched in the same way as celery but the flavour is relatively bitter. Wear thick gloves when handling the prickly stems.

**GROWING** A fertile, free-draining but moisture-retentive soil is required. Prepare trenches 30cm/12in deep and 45cm/18in wide with well-rotted organic manure or compost dug into the bottom. Leave the soil from the trenches in ridges alongside. In mid spring, sow seeds at each station in the trench and later thin out all but the strongest seedlings. Alternatively, raise plants under glass at 15C/60F and harden off before planting out in late spring. Water lightly during the summer and keep weeds under control. Remove flowerheads and use as globe artichokes. On a dry day in early autumn, cut out any dead or yellow leaves before earthing up the plants. Tie up the tops and wrap the paper around the stems. Replace the soil from the ridges around the plants.

**HARVESTING** Blanching will be complete in four weeks. Remove the soil and use the stems – in salads, soups, and stews – as required, making sure all are harvested before the onset of severe winter frosts.

**POSSIBLE PROBLEMS** Relatively trouble-free

## TRENCH CELERY

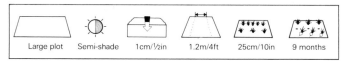

| Large plot | Semi-shade | 1cm/½in | 1.2m/4ft | 25cm/10in | 9 months |

Trench celery is winter-hardy and soil drawn up around the developing sticks blanches them.

**GROWING** Celery likes fertile, free-draining yet moisture retentive soil that is slightly acid. In early spring, dig trenches 30cm/12in deep and 40cm/16in wide, 90cm/3ft apart. Pile the soil you have removed in flat-topped ridges between the trenches. Fork over the trench bottom and work in well-rotted organic manure or compost. Earliest crops can be raised from seed in early spring. Sow thinly in trays, do not cover with compost and keep moist at 18C/65F to germinate. Prick out the seedlings after about 5 weeks into other seed trays, spacing them 9cm/3in apart each way. Do not let the temperature drop below 15C/60F. In late spring, transfer the plants to a cold frame for a few days to harden off before planting them in the trench. They are ready for planting when 10-12cm/4-5in tall. Plant firmly but carefully and water in well. Keep weeds down. When the plants reach 30-40cm/12-16in, begin to place earth from the ridges around the stems to the half-way point. Put a loose tie round the top to prevent soil getting into the heart. Repeat twice more at 3-weekly intervals, on dry days, making the soil slope away from the leaves.

**HARVESTING** Dig up bunches from mid autumn onwards.

**POSSIBLE PROBLEMS** As for Self-blanching Celery.

## ▨ COOK'S TIP

*Remove the tough outer stalks, cut the remaining stems into 5-10cm/2-4in lengths, after discarding the leaves. Boil in water, to which a little lemon juice has been added, until tender, about 20-30 minutes.*

## ▨ COOK'S TIP

*Serve celery chopped up with apple and walnut with a creamy dressing by adding equal parts of cream cheese and Greek yogurt to vinaigrette. Celery is also good stir-fried. Chop small 1 onion, 1 clove garlic and 1cm/½ in ginger and fry quickly, stirring all the time. Add chopped up lengths of 450g/1lb celery, lower the heat and cook for 2-3 minutes. Add a little sherry, and soy sauce, sprinkle with sesame seeds, cook for a further minute and serve.*

## SELF-BLANCHING CELERY

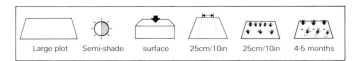

| | | | | | |
|---|---|---|---|---|---|
| Large plot | Semi-shade | surface | 25cm/10in | 25cm/10in | 4-5 months |

All celery must be blanched for a good flavour. In contrast to trench celery, self-blanching types are grown on the flat. They are not frost hardy: their season of maturity stretches from mid summer until onset of frosts. Blanching is actually achieved by planting them close together in blocks and thus excluding the light.

**GROWING** Self-blanching celery needs the same soil type as trench varieties, and should also have well-rotted organic material dug in. Raise plants in the same way as for trench celery, but plant them out in a block, not in rows. Regular watering and a top dressing of nitro-chalk in mid summer are vital to encourage rapid growth.

**HARVESTING** Self-blanching celery will be available from mid summer. Lift the whole plant, and make sure harvesting is complete before the frosts begin.

**POSSIBLE PROBLEMS** Use seed treated against leaf spot fungus. Watch out for carrot and celery fly larvae. Seedlings can be affected by damping-off. Yellowing of the leaves and cracks in stems are caused by boron deficiency.

**VARIETIES** Golden Self-Blanching, Galaxy.

## RHUBARB

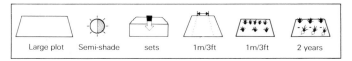

| | | | | | |
|---|---|---|---|---|---|
| Large plot | Semi-shade | sets | 1m/3ft | 1m/3ft | 2 years |

Rhubarb is a perennial plant which can be forced to produce stems in late winter. The leaves are poisonous.

**GROWING** Because rhubarb occupies the ground for 5-10 years, the soil must be well prepared by incorporating plenty of organic compost or manure and digging deeply. Light soil is best. Start with healthy 'sets', obtained by dividing a mature crown in autumn, or buy in sets from a nursery. Remove all the roots and make sure each set has at least one bud. Plant with the crown just below the soil surface. Water lightly and do not let the new plant dry out. Clear away weeds and cut off flowering stems. Do not pull stalks for use in the first year. Remove them after they die down in winter, tidy the crowns and dig compost around the plants.

**HARVESTING** The first crop can be picked in the second season. Remove only half the stalks, twisting them off near the crown. Take more stalks in subsequent years.

**FORCING** Use an early variety. Cover the crowns with boxes or terracotta forcing pots if possible in early winter. Pack round with straw or fresh manure for warmth. After eight weeks, check that the growth has started. Pick stalks when 20-30cm/8-12in long. Let the plants crop naturally the following year.

**POSSIBLE PROBLEMS** Destroy any crowns affected by crown rot.

### ■ ORGANIC TIP

*Feed with a seaweed-based fertilizer. Tuck straw around and between the plants to increase blanching. Also try growing leaf celery, a close relation of wild celery. It is hardy, usually continues to grow throughout the year and self seeds.*

### ■ GARDENER'S TIP

*Force rhubarb indoors to harvest in mid winter. Dig up clumps and leave exposed for 1-2 weeks. Place roots in a box, cover with a thin layer of soil and water, then another box and black polythene. Keep warm and moist for 4-5 weeks.*

## SEAKALE

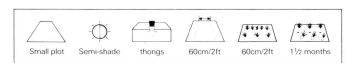

| | | | | | |
|---|---|---|---|---|---|
| Small plot | Semi-shade | thongs | 60cm/2ft | 60cm/2ft | 1½ months |

The edible parts of this excellent spring vegetable are the shoots, which are blanched to eliminate bitterness.

**GROWING** A well-drained sandy loam is best. Seakale does not like acid soils. Shoots are forced from good healthy crowns. Cut the roots to 15-cm/6-in lengths (thongs) the size of your little finger. Trim the end which was nearest the crown horizontally, making an angled cut at the other end. Bundle the thongs together and heel them in under a cold frame over winter. In spring, remove all the buds except the strongest. Plant the thongs in early spring, angled ends downwards, so the tops are 1cm/½in below the soil's surface. In the growing season, control weeds, water regularly and remove flowering stems in order to build up the crown. Do not force the crowns in the first winter after planting.

**FORCING** Place pots or boxes over the crowns late in the second winter. To increase the temperature inside, fermenting organic manure can be packed outside.

**HARVESTING** Cut off the blanched, tender stems with a sharp knife. When all the shoots have been cut, clean up the crowns, apply a mulch and top-dress with fertilizer. Good crowns can be forced for at least 5 consecutive seasons, and from these new root cuttings can be taken.

**POSSIBLE PROBLEMS** Club root can occur on acid soils.

■ COOK'S TIP

*Blanched seakale has a delicate, nutty flavour. It is best steamed for about 20-25 minutes. Don't overcook. Serve with a knob of melted butter or with a coating of bechamel sauce. Alternatively, use cheese sauce, top with nuts and breadcrumbs and put in a moderate oven for about half-an-hour until the topping becomes brown and crusty. A good flavour is produced, too, if the shoots are simmered in chicken stock. They can also be added raw, to salads.*

## SWEET CORN

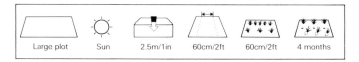

| | | | | | |
|---|---|---|---|---|---|
| Large plot | Sun | 2.5m/1in | 60cm/2ft | 60cm/2ft | 4 months |

Plant this half-hardy annual in square blocks rather than long rows to assist wind-pollination

**GROWING** Sow seeds in mid spring in seed trays at 10-13C/50-55F. Keep moist and when the seedlings are large enough to handle transfer them to 9-cm/3½-in pots. The plants need full light and good ventilation on warm days. Harden off before planting out in late spring. In warm districts, seeds can be sown in the open from late spring. Set 3 seeds at each station. in a well-drained and fertile soil on a sunny, sheltered site and retain the strongest seedling only. Incorporate plenty of well-rotted organic manure or compost the winter before sowing to assist fast vegetable growth, which is important to produce 2 cobs per plant (you may get only 1). Provide continual supplies of water and nitrogenous fertilizer during the growing season. Hoe the weeds out until the plants are tall enough – 60cm/2ft – to shade out further weed growth, being careful not to damage the stems. 'Tassels' and 'silks', the male and female parts of the plant, appear from mid-summer.

**HARVESTING** Pick about 4 weeks after the silk begins to wither. The ideal time is when a milky white fluid shoots out from the grains if pressed with your thumbnail.

**POSSIBLE PROBLEMS** Birds damage young plants. Fruit fly larvae tunnel into the stems.

■ HEALTH TIP

*Because the sugar starts to turn to starch as soon as a cob is picked, home-grown corns that are cooked immediately after picking are more nutritious and taste far better than those you buy in a shop.*

# SQUASHES

Squashes do not need to be rotated to another plot yearly so they can be grown on a permanent site, Plot D on the crop rotation plan, page 13. They do, however, need well-drained soil and a sunny site. They also need a soil rich in organic matter.

**PREPARING THE SOIL**  As roots do not reach down far into the soil each plant can be treated individually by providing it with its own supply of organic matter. Dig out a 30-cm/12-in cube where each plant is to be grown. Half fill the holes with well-rotted manure or garden compost then replace the soil on top and mix the two together to form a mound. Alternatively, if a row of plants is being grown you can dig a trench if you prefer.

When plants begin to fruit they will need feeding once a week with seaweed fertilizer or comfrey liquid (see page 48).

**SEED GERMINATION**  Squash seed germination can be erratic. The best way to germinate the seeds is to place them on moist kitchen paper in a plastic container with a lid. Keep the container, covered, in a warm spot, such as the airing cupboard, and the seeds should start to germinate within 2-3 days. As squashes also dislike root disturbance, it is best to grow the seedlings individually in 7.5-cm/3-in pots or soil blocks. Sow in mid spring to plant out in early summer. Early courgettes to be grown under cloches may be sown in early spring and transplanted to the garden in late spring.

Alternatively, seeds can be sown outdoors, three to a mound, in late spring. Thin to leave one plant to each mound. A minimum of three plants of any squash variety is needed so that, in the early stages, there will be enough male and female flowers out at the same time for pollination to take place.

**BUSH OR TRAILING**  There is a choice between growing bush or trailing varieties of most squashes. For small gardens, where space is at a premium, bush varieties are an obvious choice although trailing varieties can be grown up canes in a wigwam shape. In this case, pinch out the growing shoot when each plant reaches the top of its cane and support fruit other than courgettes in net bags.

Trailing varieties grown along the ground should have each branch stopped at 60cm/24in.

**FROST TENDER**  Any squash planted out too early will suffer a severe setback that can be terminal if there is a late frost or even a cold spell, so don't be tempted to plant out before late spring or early summer, unless you are growing plants under cloches. It is also important to harden plants off gradually so that they adjust to the outdoor temperature before being planted out. A garden frame is ideal for this but a cloche can also be used. Place plants in the frame or under the cloche and during warm daytime hours gradually increase the

**Growing squashes**
*Dig out a 30-cm/12-in cube where each plant is to be grown. Half fill the holes with well-rotted manure, replace the soil and mix with the compost.*

*When seven leaves have formed on each young plant, pinch out the growing tip. This encourages the side shoots – which will bear fruit – to develop. Select a support system of wire or canes.*

*Any side shoots which do not have flowers when their seventh leaf forms should have their tips pinched out. Water around the plants in dry weather and feed regularly with a liquid fertilizer.*

time they are left uncovered. Protect at night until finally they are left uncovered altogether. They are then ready for transplanting.

**EARLY COURGETTES** By protecting courgette plants with cloches or a polythene tunnel you can bring forward the planting and fruiting dates by about a month. Prepare the soil as described on page 58, opposite, and place the cloches over the mounds about 4 weeks before planting out. If you dig out a trench instead of separate blocks of soil, you can cover the resulting soil and manure ridge with black plastic or biodegradable paper, then plant through this and finally replace the polythene tunnel. The plastic or paper will act as a mulch, conserving moisture and controlling weeds and will help to maintain soil temperature through the night.

**MULCHING AND WATERING** The fruit of squash plants contain a high proportion of water and plants need to be kept moist. Mulching the plants will help to conserve the moisture. It will also help to keep the fruit clean. It is also a good idea to place a piece of glass, a small square of timber or plywood or a brick under larger squash fruit to keep them away from slugs and help against fungal attack.

Large plants, like squashes, can be watered by sinking a clay plant pot into the soil close to the stem and filling this with water. The water will gradually sink through the soil providing a constant supply with a minimum of evaporation.

**GARDEN COLD FRAME** Really a miniature greenhouse, a cold frame is very useful for raising young plants and for hardening off seedlings prior to planting out. In winter a frame can be used for overwintering seedlings, for growing lettuce or for forcing chicory. In spring it can protect the first crops of many plants including lettuce, carrot and radish. Tomato and pepper plants can be grown safely here until the weather is right for planting them out. A frame's use will be governed by its height. A low 23-cm/9-in frame can be used for seedlings and for salad plants like lettuces, but one of 45cm/18in high allows you to use it for a much wider range of plants.

Traditionally, garden frames are a permanent fixture, constructed of timber or bricks with glass, removable lights (top lid). These materials provide good insulation and the lights can be covered with an old piece of carpet for top protection in winter when forcing and blanching chicory.

Modern frames are lighter, with an aluminium frame and glass sides as well as glazed lights. They are also portable.

Like greenhouses, frames provide a restricted environment in which diseases can build up and pests multiply. Always clean the frame thoroughly at the end of the season.

**PESTS AND DISEASES**

*Aphids* Aphids are especially unpopular as the carriers of cucumber mosaic virus so need to be dealt with as soon as you see them. Remove small numbers by hand. Spray plants with insecticidal soap (direct on to the pests as this acts on impact) which is harmless to humans, animals, bees and other beneficial insects. Alternatively, spray with derris.

Greenfly                    Cucumber mosaic virus

*Cucumber mosaic virus* This can affect all types of squashes. Leaves become mottled and yellow and the virus stunts growth. There is no cure. Pull up and burn an affected plant to stop it spreading. Take steps to remove aphids as soon as you see them as they carry the disease.

*Foot rot* Badly drained soil suffocates the roots and young plants rot at the stem. Keep the soil open and well-cultivated and observe recommended crop rotation patterns.

*Leaf distortion* A virus disease affecting marrows (and strawberries) causes the leaves to become crinkled and undersized. Burn diseased plants.

*Slugs* Slugs can be a problem when growing any squashes. Surround plants with a lime or soot circle which slugs hate going through or use a bark mulch which will also deter them. Attract the predators of slugs: toads and frogs, slow worms, birds and hedgehogs (see page 15).

# COURGETTE

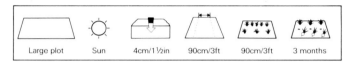

| Large plot | Sun | 4cm/1½in | 90cm/3ft | 90cm/3ft | 3 months |

Courgettes are marrows specially bred to be ready to pick and use at 15-20cm/6-8in long As well as the more common green types, yellow varieties are available as a colourful summer vegetable.

**GROWING** Fertile, well-drained soil is essential. Prepare ridges as for marrows or, alternatively, dig out planting holes 30cm/12in deep and 30cm/12in square and half fill with well-rotted organic manure before replacing the soil to make mounds. Like marrows, seeds need help germinating. Place on sheets of soaked kitchen paper and keep at 18C/65F until the roots appear. Plant immediately in pots if sowing in mid spring or directly into the growing site in late spring. The earlier sowings should be kept moist at 15-18C/60-65F and hardened off briefly before planting out in late spring. Feed and water liberally while growing. In cold weather pollination may need to be done by hand with a camel-hair brush or by removing the male flowers and inserting them into the open female blossoms. Leave the flowers in place.

**HARVESTING** As soon as they are large enough to use, pick regularly to encourage the formation of further fruits. Unlike marrows, courgettes cannot be restored.

**POSSIBLE PROBLEMS** Aphids attacking young shoots carry virus diseases. Spray with a suitable insecticide.

**VARIETIES** Zucchini; Green Bush; Eldorado (yellow)

## ▪ ORGANIC TIP

*For extra colour, mix varieties. Fruits can range from dark to light green, grey and yellow. Some are attractively striped. The flowers look effective in a saucer as a table decoration and can also be stuffed and cooked as a starter.*

# CUSTARD MARROW

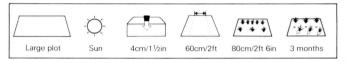

| Large plot | Sun | 4cm/1½in | 60cm/2ft | 80cm/2ft 6in | 3 months |

These members of the marrow and pumpkin tribe are very attractive fruiting vegetables which can be cooked like pumpkins.

**GROWING** Like long marrows, these plants need fertile, well-drained soil. Prepare a trench or planting holes as for courgettes, half filling with well-rotted organic compost before replacing the soil. Start the seeds into growth in mid spring by placing them on sheets of soaked kitchen paper kept moist at 18C/65F until the roots appear. Plant immediately, either into 9-cm/3½-in pots kept at 15-18C/60-65F until planting out in late spring or directly into the growing site, again in late spring. Feed and water generously during the growing period. Assist pollination if necessary, either using a camel-hair brush or by inserting the male flowers into the open female flowers (the females have a swelling behind the blossom).

**HARVESTING** Pick the circular fruits as soon as they reach 15cm/6in in diameter in order to encourage further fruiting. Not suitable for storage.

**POSSIBLE PROBLEMS** Slugs: lay down bait; aphids: spray with suitable insecticide. If virus diseases strike, destroy affected plants.

**VARIETIES** Custard Pie; Custard Yellow.

## ▪ ORGANIC TIP

*Make sleeves from plastic bottle sides to protect young plants from slugs; later surround them with lime or soot, both of which slugs hate crawling over. Use hoverfly larvae to control aphids (see summer and autumn cabbages) or, on a bad*

*infestation, spray with insecticidal soap directly on to the insect. Aphids also carry the cucumber mosaic virus and it pays to keep them at bay as there is no cure for this.*

# Marrow

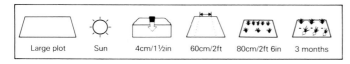

| Large plot | Sun | 4cm/1½in | 60cm/2ft | 80cm/2ft 6in | 3 months |

These half-hardy members of the cucumber family may be trailing or bushy in habit.

**GROWING** Marrows need fertile, well-drained soil. Prepare the growing site in late spring in a sheltered position, having dug the land deeply in the previous autumn. Dig out trenches 30cm/12in deep and 45cm/18in wide. Half fill with well-rotted manure and replace the soil to form a ridge. For early plantings, raise plants from seed sown in mid spring. To assist germination, place the seeds on sheets of soaked kitchen paper and keep at 18C/65F until the roots appear. Immediately transfer to individual 9-cm/3½-in pots of potting compost and keep moist at 15-18C/60-65F until planting out in late spring. Germinated seed may be sown directly into the ridges in late spring. Water very generously while growing and conserve moisture with a mulch of organic manure, peat or grass cuttings. Give regular feeds of liquid fertilizer.

**HARVESTING** Pick marrows as soon as they reach 30cm/12in for a tender texture. Those ripening in early autumn can be stored in an airy, frost-free place for winter use.

**POSSIBLE PROBLEMS** Spray with derris against aphids, which carry virus diseases. Watch for slugs.

**VARIETIES** Tender & True; White Bush (white).

# Round Marrow

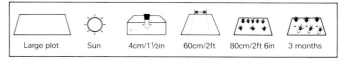

| Large plot | Sun | 4cm/1½in | 60cm/2ft | 80cm/2ft 6in | 3 months |

Very like melons in appearance, round marrows are good cooked with a savoury stuffing.

**GROWING** Prepare the site in the autumn for a spring sowing. Dig out trenches or planting holes 30cm/12in deep and half fill with well-rotted manure. Replace the soil to make a ridge or mound. In mid spring, prepare the seeds for sowing by placing them on sheets of kitchen paper soaked in water. Keep at 18C/65F until roots appear, then plant in individual 9-cm/3½-in pots. Keep moist at 15-18C/60-65F and transfer to the growing site in late spring. Water liberally, apply a moisture-retaining mulch and feed regularly with a liquid fertilizer. It may be necessary to hand-pollinate with a camel-hair brush if the weather is cold. Bush plants do not require staking.

**HARVESTING** Pick the marrows when they are about 30cm/12in in diameter. Late ripening specimens can be stored for winter use.

**POSSIBLE PROBLEMS** Aphids; slugs.

**VARIETY** Twickers.

## ■ COOK'S TIP

*A whole marrow may be cooked remarkably easily in the microwave oven, provided it fits! Allow about 10 minutes for a stuffed 2kg/4½lb marrow, cooking it in a roasting bag on Full power.*

## ■ GARDENER'S TIP

*If you have only a small garden, you may well feel that you do not have the space to grow marrows. You can grow trailing varieties up tripods of canes but the fruit needs to be carefully supported. Alternatively, towards the end of the season, allow courgettes on a few plants to remain and grow large to provide you with a supply of marrows.*

## SPAGHETTI MARROW

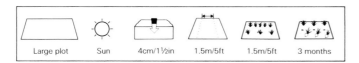

| | | | | | |
|---|---|---|---|---|---|
| Large plot | Sun | 4cm/1½in | 1.5m/5ft | 1.5m/5ft | 3 months |

Sometimes called vegetable spaghetti, these curious fruiting vegetables look like elongated melons. They are boiled whole, and when split in two reveal tender flesh in spaghetti-like strands, eaten simply with butter and seasoning.

**GROWING** Prepare planting holes as for courgettes but at the greater distances recommended. Raise plants from pre-germinated seed (see marrows). Sow seed in mid spring in individual pots of potting compost at 15-18C/60-65F and harden the seedlings off briefly before planting out in late spring, firming the plants in well. Alternatively, sow seed directly into the growing site, again in late spring. Feed and water well to encourage rapid growth. Because of its trailing habit, this plant needs training, on fences or tripods of 2-m/7-ft poles, if it is not to wander all over the garden. Support systems also help to keep the fruits out of slugs' way.

**HARVESTING** Pick spaghetti marrows at 20cm/8in long; do not leave them until the skin is so hard your fingernail cannot penetrate it. The plant will continue producing fruits for several weeks if they are harvested regularly.

**POSSIBLE PROBLEMS** Aphids carry serious virus diseases. Spray with a suitable insecticide.

## MELON

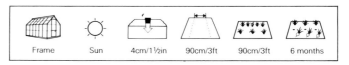

| | | | | | |
|---|---|---|---|---|---|
| Frame | Sun | 4cm/1½in | 90cm/3ft | 90cm/3ft | 6 months |

Some melon varieties must be greenhouse grown, but for others the protection of a frame is enough.

**GROWING** Sow seed in mid spring for planting in late spring/early summer. Strew seeds on a wad of wet kitchen paper. Keep moist at 18C/65F. Some of the seeds will root within 2 days. Plant them 4cm/1½in deep in individual 9-cm/3½-in pots of compost. Keep the temperature steady until the first true leaf appears, then gradually reduce it to 15C/60F. Harden off for 2-3 days before planting out, 1 plant per frame. To prepare the frame, see Tip below. Set the plants into the mounded beds with the rootball 4cm/1½in above the surface. Water in well. Spray regularly. Ventilate only on very hot days. Stop the plants after 3-4 leaves, again after another 4-5. Train 3-4 laterals into the corners, peg them down and stop them when they reach the edges. Open the frame on hot days to admit pollinating insects. After flowering, withhold water. Water the bed again when the fruits are egg-sized, keeping the atmosphere dry. Give liquid fertilizer every 10 days.

**HARVESTING** Fruits are ripe when they yield to gentle pressure and smell sweet. Cut off with a short stem.

**POSSIBLE PROBLEMS** Red spider mite; root rot fungi.

■ GARDENER'S TIP

*Place ground-level developing fruit on sheets of glass or plywood. This helps to keep slugs away and discourages fungal attack.*

■ GARDENER'S TIP

*To prepare the frame, in late spring take out a 30-cm/ 12-in cube at the back and fill with well-rotted manure. Replace the soil to make a mound. Water the bed and cover the frame to create warmth and humidity.*

## PUMPKIN

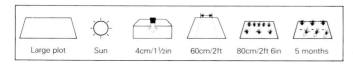

| | | | | | |
|---|---|---|---|---|---|
| Large plot | Sun | 4cm/1½in | 60cm/2ft | 80cm/2ft 6in | 5 months |

Although large pumpkins are impressive exhibition pieces and useful at hallowe'en, for cooking purposes smaller specimens are better. In fact it is difficult to grow giant pumpkins in the British climate. Full sun is essential. Both bush and trailing types are available.

**GROWING** In fertile, well-drained soil, prepare planting holes as for courgettes but at the greater distances recommended. To raise plants under glass, sow pre-germinated seed (see marrows) in mid spring and keep the seedlings moist at 10-13C/50-55F until planting out in early summer. Alternatively, sow directly into the growing site in late spring, covering the seeds with jars or cloches until they have sprouted two true leaves. Feed and water generously. Stop trailing types at 45cm/18in to encourage the flower-bearing sideshoots. For bigger pumpkins, leave only 1 or 2 fruits per plant.

**HARVESTING** Pumpkins are usually eaten as they mature in summer, but types that bear larger fruits should be left until autumn. Store in a cool, frost-free place.

**POSSIBLE PROBLEMS** Grey mould on the leaves: treat with benomyl. Use a systemic fungicide if powdery mildew appears on the leaves. See also courgettes.

## SUMMER SQUASH

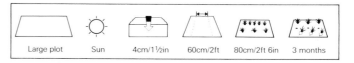

| | | | | | |
|---|---|---|---|---|---|
| Large plot | Sun | 4cm/1½in | 60cm/2ft | 80cm/2ft 6in | 3 months |

Summer squashes are popular vegetables in North America. Related to pumpkins and marrows, they cannot be stored but – like courgettes – should be used soon after picking.

**GROWING** Full sun and fertile soil is important. Prepare the site in autumn by digging out planting holes 30cm/12in deep, half-filling them with well-rotted manure and replacing the soil to form mounds. In late spring, prepare the seeds by placing them on sheets of soaked kitchen paper kept at 18C/65F until roots appear. Plant the seeds immediately after germination, one to each site, and cover with an upturned jar until the first true leaves appear. Feed and water generously. Stop trailing varieties at 45cm/18in to encourage the production of flower-bearing side shoots. Bush types are more compact and better for small gardens.

**HARVESTING** Pick squashes when they are young and tender for the best flavour. Harvest regularly to encourage the formation of more fruits.

**POSSIBLE PROBLEMS** Slugs; aphids.

**VARIETIES** Baby Crookneck.

### ■ COOK'S TIP

*To make the traditional pumpkin pie in a 18-20-cm/7-8-in flan tin, you will need 1kg/2lb fresh pumpkin. Cut the flesh into cubes and steam in a bowl over simmering water for 15-20 minutes, then purée. When cool, add to this 3 eggs, 75g/3oz caster sugar, ½ tsp ground cinnamon, ½ tsp ground ginger and a pinch of nutmeg. Mix well, then beat in 150ml/¼ pint single cream. Place in a pastry case and bake for about 55 minutes in a moderately hot oven (190C, 375F, gas 5).*

### ■ GARDENER'S TIP

*When the weather is cold early in the season, push a pollen-releasing male flower into an open female flower to pollinate.*

# ROOT VEGETABLES AND TUBERS

Following the crop rotation plan on page 13, roots are grown in Plot A. Because there is a danger of roots forking in freshly manured ground, in this plan they are grown on ground which was manured two years previously. However, if you use well-rotted manure or compost this should not occur.

**PREPARING THE SOIL**  Land that has been deep dug, to the depth of two spades rather than one, is ideal for growing root crops as this improves the drainage and allows the roots to go downwards. For double digging see page 10. This greater depth of cultivated ground also allows you to grow plants much closer together which is a great advantage in a small plot. Plan beds to a width that allows you to work on them comfortably from both sides without moving on to the soil. This is important on all cultivated soil but specially so on deep dug beds. Somewhere between 1m/3ft and 1.25m/4ft depending on what is comfortable for you, is about the right size.

**FLUID SOWING**  This is a method used by commercial growers to evenly sow small pre-germinated seeds and can be used on parsnips as well as many other vegetables.

First sow the seed on moist kitchen or tissue paper.

When the majority have produced a first root or shoot, wash them carefully in a sieve to remove the paper. Mix up a wallpaper paste – make sure you choose one that does not contain fungicide – and gently stir the seeds into it until they are evenly distributed throughout.

Pour into a polythene bag and tie up. When the seed drill is prepared cut off a corner of the bag and, like icing a cake, squeeze the mixture along the drill then cover in the usual way. Water regularly (very important or the wallpaper paste could harden) and tend the crop as usual.

**TRANSPLANTING**  Most root crops cannot be transplanted as there is too much danger of damage to the single tap root causing distorted growth and double roots. They can however be planted individually in peat pots, then planted out pot and all. The roots produced by thinning can provide the wonderful tiny root vegetables that are so prized by nouvelle cuisine chefs.

**INTERCROPPING**  Root vegetables, many of which are in the ground for some time, are ideal subjects for intercropping with fast growing crops like lettuces. Early carrots can be planted in spaces between slow-growing crops too, like cabbages.

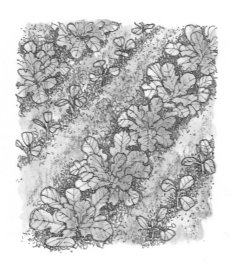

**Intercropping**
Left *While long-term crops are still young, use the ground in between for quick-growing crops.*

**Earthing up potatoes**
Right *Use a draw hoe to pull the earth between the rows up and around the top growth. If the tops are short, the soil can be drawn right over to cover the foliage, protecting it from frost.*

When intercropping, remember to choose plants to grow together which require the same conditions. Don't try to crush too many plants into the space. It is important to give both slow and quick growing plants plenty of space, light and moisture and enough room for you to cultivate and harvest them. Because the ground is being so heavily used it will need to be kept fertile with regular manuring and feeding.

*Tips on keeping winter supplies* Many roots such as parsnips, salsify, swedes and Jerusalem artichokes can be left in the ground to be lifted when required.

When harvesting roots and tubers, lift them carefully to avoid damage.

Pick only perfect vegetables for storage, eating any that are less than perfect first.

Potatoes should be lifted, cleaned of soil and left outdoors to dry for a few hours before sorting then storing in paper or hessian bags.

Most root crops are best lifted in late autumn. Store in layers in boxes in moist vermiculite or sand (see below). Small quantities can be stored in plastic bags.

Cool temperatures are best for storing vegetables: just above freezing is ideal.

Check stored supplies regularly and remove any roots or tubers that are starting to rot.

## PESTS, DISEASES AND DISORDERS

*Carrot fly larvae* Both carrots and parsnips can be damaged by the carrot fly maggots which tunnel through the roots. Signs of attack are young seedlings that die or foliage of older plants that reddens. Avoid thinning as the smell attracts the fly. Surround beds with a plastic mesh barrier, described in Tip on page 66 to keep the fly away from plants.

*Celery fly larvae* The maggots leave brown blotches on the leaves of parsnips and celeriac which can then

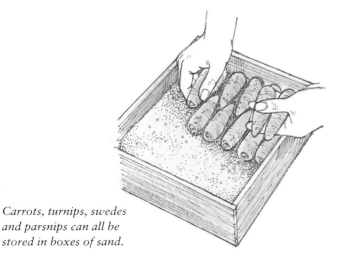

*Carrots, turnips, swedes and parsnips can all be stored in boxes of sand.*

wither and the plant may die. Remove affected leaves as soon as you see them and burn.

*Flea beetle* These jumping beetles make small holes in the leaves of turnips. As they act like fleas, leaping into the air when approached, they can be caught by running a small piece of wood over the crop which has been coated on the lower side with thick grease.

*Forked roots* Forked roots are caused by carrots or parsnips being grown on soil where fresh manure or compost has been used. Grow on ground manured for a previous crop or store manure and compost for a year, until it is well rotted.

Carrot fly      Parsnip canker

*Parsnip canker* Reddish, orange brown or black cankers spread into the root and cause it to rot. In future dress the soil with lime and use good methods of cultivation plus resistant varieties.

*Potato blight* This is a fungus that causes black spotting on leaves and withered stems. Ultimately the tubers rot. Spray with Bordeaux mixture.

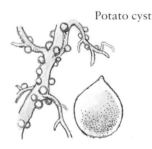
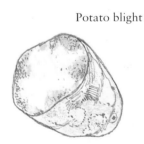

Potato cyst      Potato blight

*Potato cyst eelworm*
A minute pest that attacks potatoes between mid and late summer causing smaller tubers and plants to die. Rotate the crop to avoid this problem and grow resistant varieties.

*Powdery mildew* This powdery grey fungus thrives when days are hot and nights cool. It coats leaves and can eventually get into the plant and kill it if nothing is done about it. Spray with a copper fungicide.

*Split roots* Split roots can occur if plants suffer a very dry period followed by a very wet one. Do not allow the soil to get too dry before watering.

## FORCING CARROT

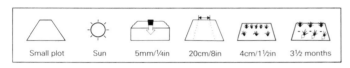

| | | | | | |
|---|---|---|---|---|---|
| Small plot | Sun | 5mm/¼in | 20cm/8in | 4cm/1½in | 3½ months |

The carrot varieties suitable for forcing or early cultivation are the stump-rooted types.

**GROWING** All carrot crops like a light, open-textured soil, and this is essential for early plantings. The soil must also be fertile and moisture retentive if good-sized roots are to develop. Dig over the plot in the autumn and leave it rough over winter for a tilth to form, but do not dig in organic manure, which will cause forking of the roots. Rake over the soil in mid winter to give a fine tilth, incorporating a general purpose fertilizer. Sow seed in shallow drills and lightly rake it in. Water evenly and regularly and cover with cloches or frames. Ventilate on warm, sunny days. Remove the cloches/frames in mid spring. Thinning the seedlings is unnecessary.

**HARVESTING** Pull the tender carrots for use as soon as they reach the required size. This crop will continue until late spring.

**POSSIBLE PROBLEMS** Early sowings escape the worst problems, but aphids may attack the leaves. Spray with a suitable insecticide.

**VARIETIES** Amsterdam Forcing; Nantes.

## EARLY OUTDOOR CARROT

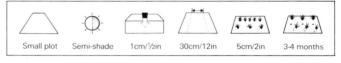

| | | | | | |
|---|---|---|---|---|---|
| Small plot | Semi-shade | 1cm/½in | 30cm/12in | 5cm/2in | 3-4 months |

If sown successively at fortnightly intervals, early outdoor sowings will produce carrots continuously throughout the summer. Like forced crops, stump-rooted types should be used.

**GROWING** The soil for early carrots should be light, open-textured and fertile with enough moisture to allow roots to develop to a good size. Prepare the plot by digging deeply in the previous autumn and leaving it rough to allow a tilth to develop. Apply a general purpose fertilizer, raking the soil to a fine tilth, as soon as the ground is workable, in early spring or a little later. Warm up the soil by covering it with cloches or polythene tunnels before the first sowing. Sow thinly in shallow drills. Water evenly and regularly and thin the seedlings as soon as they are large enough to handle. It is not usually necessary to water after this point. A further thinning may be necessary to produce really large roots. Thin in the evening, scattering soil over the holes from which carrots have been removed, to deter carrot fly. Keep weeds down, hoeing with care.

**HARVESTING** Lift the roots as soon as they have reached the required size and use immediately.

**POSSIBLE PROBLEMS** Carrot fly and aphids, which carry a virus which causes the leaves to be stunted and yellowed and the roots underdeveloped.

---

### ■ FREEZER TIP

Small, young carrots are ideal for freezing whole. Scrub under running water then blanch by plunging into boiling water for 3 minutes then into ice-cold water. Pack in bags. They will keep well until the next year's crop. Steam the carrots or cook quickly in the microwave in a minimum of water and serve with butter, a squeeze of lemon juice and a pinch of sugar. Sprinkle with chopped fresh herbs, like parsley, marjoram, dill, chives or mint.

### ■ ORGANIC TIP

Carrot flies are fairly easily foiled. As they fly low, simply erect a barrier around a carrot crop and they will move up to pass over it and miss your carrots too. Use plastic or fine mesh and put in place as soon as carrots have been thinned.

## MAINCROP CARROT

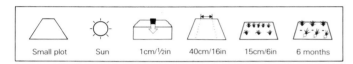

| | | | | | |
|---|---|---|---|---|---|
| Small plot | Sun | 1cm/½in | 40cm/16in | 15cm/6in | 6 months |

For maincrop carrots to be used in late summer both stump-rooted and long tapering varieties are available. Those picked in the autumn for winter storage must be long-rooted types.

**GROWING** While maincrop carrots prefer the light, open-textured soil essential for early crops, it is possible to grow them on heavier soils using stump-rooted types. If the soil needs manuring, this should be done for the previous crop. Dig the plot deeply in the autumn, leaving it rough over winter for a natural tilth to develop. Around mid spring, rake to a fine tilth, evenly incorporating a general purpose fertilizer. The first sowings can be made at this point, but seedlings will be vulnerable to carrot fly and it is better to wait until late spring or early summer if possible. Water regularly. Thin the seedlings when they are large enough to handle and withhold water unless conditions are very dry.

**HARVESTING** Maincrop carrots can either be left in the ground and dug up as needed – in which case they will need protection with straw during severe weather – or they can be lifted in mid autumn and stored. Place undamaged carrots only in boxes of sand in an airy frost-free place. They should keep until mid spring.

**POSSIBLE PROBLEMS** Carrot fly larvae feed on the roots and can kill young seedlings or damage older plants.

## CELERIAC

| | | | | | |
|---|---|---|---|---|---|
| Small plot | Semi-shade | surface | 40cm/16in | 40cm/16in | 4-6 months |

This close relative of celery is not a true root crop since the edible part is the swollen stem base. The flavour is very like celery and the 'roots' can be cooked variously.

**GROWING** Deep, fertile, well-drained soil is essential. Dig in plenty of organic manure during the winter and incorporate a nitrogenous fertilizer when preparing the plot for planting. Raise plants in a heated greenhouse, sowing the seed thinly on the surface of compost in seed trays in early spring. Do not cover the seed with compost. Keep a steady temperature of 16C/61F and never let the trays dry out. After about a month, prick the seedlings out into small individual pots and grow on for another 4-5 weeks. Harden the plants off before setting them out in late spring/early summer. Water in well and continue to water generously through the season. If growth slows down give a light dressing of nitro-chalk and water it in. Keep weeds down.

**HARVESTING** Celeriac is ready for lifting from early autumn, but the roots will be bigger if left until late autumn. They can be left in the ground until required, covered with a protective layer of straw in severe weather.

**POSSIBLE PROBLEMS** Celeriac suffers from the same pests and diseases as celery. In poor growing seasons the flesh may be streaked brown.

**VARIETIES** Globus; Alabaster; Tellus.

### ▪ PRESERVING TIP

*If you are short of space, use a plastic dustbin to store carrots in a garden shed. If they are left in the ground during a wet winter they may split. Twist off leaves and store in layers in sand, positioned so that they do not touch each other.*

### ▪ COOK'S TIP

*A classic French salad is made with raw grated celeriac coated with a mustard mayonnaise. Celeriac is also delicious cooked and served in a white sauce. Alternatively, layer celeriac and mushrooms in white sauce, cover with cheese and breadcrumbs and* *put in the oven to give a crusty topping. Yogurt or soured cream are also good partners for cooked or raw celeriac.*

## HAMBURG PARSLEY

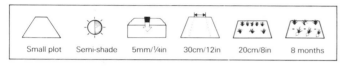

| Small plot | Semi-shade | 5mm/¼in | 30cm/12in | 20cm/8in | 8 months |
|---|---|---|---|---|---|

This hardy biennial, also known as turnip-rooted parsley, is grown for its roots, which taste rather like celeriac.

**GROWING** Sow seeds in early spring in well-drained soil manured for a previous crop. Thin the seedlings when they are large enough to handle. Keep weeds under control and water the plants regularly throughout the growing season.

**HARVESTING** Hamburg parsley needs a long growing season to develop the large roots which have the best flavour. Delay lifting the roots until late autumn or even late autumn. They can be left in the ground all winter, but are better lifted and stored, as beetroot, for winter use.

**POSSIBLE PROBLEMS** Root fly or fungus diseases can be problems.

## JERUSALEM ARTICHOKE

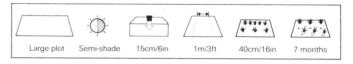

| Large plot | Semi-shade | 15cm/6in | 1m/3ft | 40cm/16in | 7 months |
|---|---|---|---|---|---|

This hardy perennial is a relative of the sunflower rather than the globe artichoke. It has underground tubers which are whitish in colour and club-like with knobbly protrusions. The delicate flavour is best appreciated if Jerusalem artichokes are served alone or as a creamy soup. The plants reach 2.5m/8ft and make excellent screens.

**GROWING** Jerusalem artichokes can be grown in even the poorest soils – in fact very fertile soils encourage too much foliage at the expense of the tubers. Save some tubers from a previous crop and plant them in early spring. The plants will need little attentiion but in exposed positions support the tall leafy stems with posts and wires.

**HARVESTING** The foliage dies down in the autumn. Pick some tubers in mid autumn if you wish, but the flavour improves if they are left in the ground to be lifted during the winter as needed. Make sure you lift all of them or they will come up again the following year.

**POSSIBLE PROBLEMS** A trouble-free crop.

### ■ GARDENER'S TIP

*Early sowing is necessary because of the long growing season but if the soil temperature is too low seeds may fail to germinate. Warm up the soil for a couple of weeks before sowing using cloches and keep them in place for a few weeks after sowing.*

### ■ ORGANIC TIP

*These tall plants, when supported, can provide a useful windbreak to other delicate plants in the garden.*

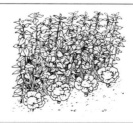

## PARSNIP

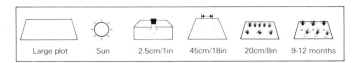

| Large plot | Sun | 2.5cm/1in | 45cm/18in | 20cm/8in | 9-12 months |

Because parsnips occupy the ground for such a long time – often a whole year – they are best in large gardens that can spare the space.

**GROWING** Parsnips need deep, rich, open-textured soils, free of stones and manured for a previous crop. Freshly manured soil produces misshapen roots. Work in a base dressing of a well-balanced fertilizer before sowing. Sow as early as possible to get the maximum length of growing season; late winter/early spring is ideal. As germination is erratic, sow seed liberally in the drills and thin seedlings later. Alternatively, sow 4-5 seeds at each station and discard all but the strongest seedling after emergence.

**HARVESTING** The leaves will go yellow and begin to die down from late autumn, and the roots can then be lifted as required. Tradition has it that the flavour is at its best when parsnips have been frosted. It is certainly better to leave them in the ground until you want them as they quickly go soft if stored. Regrowth begins in early spring so they must all be used by then.

**POSSIBLE PROBLEMS** Canker is a fungus which rots the roots and ruins the crop. Always grow resistant varieties.

**VARIETIES** Avonresister; White Gem.

## LONG PARSNIP

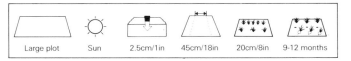

| Large plot | Sun | 2.5cm/1in | 45cm/18in | 20cm/8in | 9-12 months |

Because the sweet creamy flesh is high in sugar and starch, parsnips have always been valued as a winter vegetable.

**GROWING** Parsnips need deep, rich, open-textured soils, free of stones and manured for a previous crop. Freshly manured soil produces misshapen roots. Work in a base dressing of a well-balanced fertilizer before sowing. Sow as early as possible to get the maximum length of growing season; late winter/early spring is ideal. Sow 4-5 seeds at each station and discard all but the strongest seedling after emergence. Hoe regularly to keep weeds down.

**HARVESTING** The leaves will go yellow and begin to die down from late autumn, and the roots can then be lifted as required.

**POSSIBLE PROBLEMS** Aphids may infest young leaves. Spray with a suitable insecticide. Carrot fly larvae tunnel into the roots in summer. Spray with diazinon.

**VARIETIES** Lancer; Tender and True.

### ORGANIC TIP

*Parsnips need a constant supply of water or roots can crack, so always water in dry periods. Use sub-surface irrigation; placed about 1m/3ft 3in apart the pipes are not difficult to install. Water leaks out through the pipes' surface and spreads out evenly in the ground. This method uses a tenth of the water a hose does to obtain the same result.*

### GARDENER'S TIP

*Forked roots in carrots and parsnips are caused by over-manuring. To avoid, use land which has been manured for a previous crop; do not add more.*

## FIRST EARLY POTATO

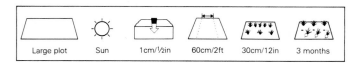

| Large plot | Sun | 1cm/½in | 60cm/2ft | 30cm/12in | 3 months |
|---|---|---|---|---|---|

For the first plantings, choose varieties like Arran Pilot.

**GROWING** Soil should be freely drained yet moisture retentive and preferably slightly acid. Double-dig the ground in the autumn, incorporating plenty of organic manure or well-rotted compost into the lower spit. Leave the top surface rough over winter to allow a natural tilth to develop. Before planting, evenly work in a general purpose fertilizer. Only use 'seed' potatoes that are certified virus-free. Order first earlies for mid winter so that they can be sprouted before planting. Growth begins from 'eyes', most of which appear at the rose end. Place the tubers close together, rose end upwards, in slatted-bottom trays. Leave in a light, frost-free but unheated place for shoots to develop. In mid or late spring, make 15-cm/6-in deep trenches with a hoe and plant the tubers, without damaging the shoots. Rake the soil back to cover and leave the surface slightly mounded over each row. Ridge up the plants as described for second earlies. Water when the tubers are 1cm/¹/₂in in diameter. Avoid watering late in the season.

**HARVESTING** Lift in early summer when the foliage is still green. Yield increases rapidly through mid until late summer.

**POSSIBLE PROBLEMS** Frost is a danger to young foliage. Aphids cause distortion of the foliage and may spread viruses from other plants.

## SECOND EARLY POTATO

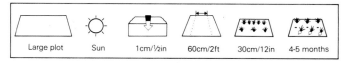

| Large plot | Sun | 1cm/½in | 60cm/2ft | 30cm/12in | 4-5 months |
|---|---|---|---|---|---|

To ensure a succession of new potatoes in late summer, and if space permits, plant varieties such as Craig's Royal or Pentland Dell.

**GROWING** The soil conditions for all types of potatoes are the same as for first earlies. Give them a site which provides maximum protection against frost. If spring frosts kill off young foliage there will be a 2-3 week setback to the crop. Second early varieties do not need to be sprouted before planting. Prepare a trench as for first earlies and set the tubers out in mid or late spring.

**RIDGING** When the potato shoots are 15cm/6in tall, loosen the soil between the rows with a fork and then draw it up around the plants with a hoe so that the sloping ridges meet near the top of the plants. Repeat at 3 week intervals until the foliage is touching.

**HARVESTING** Second earlies can be lifted in late summer and early autumn as needed. Neither first nor second earlies are suitable for storage, so do not lift the potatoes until you need them. Carefully dig up the potatoes using a flat-tined fork.

**POSSIBLE PROBLEMS** Keep aphids under control. Potato cyst eelworm is a pest living in the soil which attacks the roots, causing cysts to form. Long crop rotation is essential to eradicate it.

### ■ GARDENER'S TIP

*To avoid ridging up, lay a film of black polythene over the ground, make slits in the earth at the sides and push the polythene edges in this, holding in place with the soil as well. Make slits in the film and plant through these.*

### ■ ORGANIC TIP

*Attract the predators of aphids, like ladybirds and hoverflies, by growing French marigolds as a companion plant to potatoes. These will also add a wonderful splash of colour. Aphids can be removed with a strong spray and insecticidal soap. If you grow* *your own potatoes organically you have the added confidence that no persistent chemicals, including fungicides, have been used in their production.*

# MAINCROP POTATO

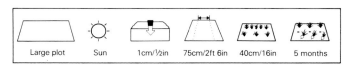

| | | | | | |
|---|---|---|---|---|---|
| Large plot | Sun | 1cm/½in | 75cm/2ft 6in | 40cm/16in | 5 months |

Maincrop potatoes like Desirée are the last to be harvested but can be stored through the winter.

**GROWING**  Prepare the soil and make trenches as for early varieties. Maincrop varieties do not need to be sprouted before planting. Set the tubers out during mid spring. If frost threatens emerging shoots, scatter straw over them for protection. Ridge up the developing plants as described for second earlies.

**HARVESTING**  Maincrop potatoes, harvested in early or mid autumn, will be easier to dig if the haulm (foliage) is removed about 3 weeks before. This also reduces the risk of disease spreading from the foliage to the tubers.

**STORAGE**  Potatoes should be allowed to dry before storing. In warm, dry weather this can be done by leaving them in the open for 2-3 hours. Discard any damaged or diseased specimens. It is useful to grade the potatoes by size before placing them in boxes, trays or sacks. Keep in a dark, frost-free place. Dark is essential to prevent the tubers developing green areas containing poisonous substances which make them inedible. Inspect the tubers monthly. Remove rotting specimens and rub off developing 'sprouts'.

**POSSIBLE PROBLEMS**  Potato blight affects foliage and tubers. Spray with fungicide from mid summer onwards whenever wet, humid conditions last for more than 2 days.

# CONTAINER POTATO

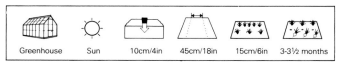

| | | | | | |
|---|---|---|---|---|---|
| Greenhouse | Sun | 10cm/4in | 45cm/18in | 15cm/6in | 3-3½ months |

If your garden is small, but you have a heated greenhouse, you can still grow some of your own delicious new potatoes. Choose a very early variety like Ulster Chieftain.

**GROWING**  Sprout the tubers in mid winter as described for first earlies. In mid to late winter, plant the sprouted tubers 2 to a 25-30-cm/10-12-in pot containing a fairly rich potting compost. Water the pots well. Keep them at a temperature of 6-7C/43-45F at first and then at 10-13C/50-55F. Water regularly using a weak liquid fertilizer.

**HARVESTING**  About 12 weeks after planting the tubers should be large enough to lift. Take the plants from the pot to remove the potatoes.

**POSSIBLE PROBLEMS**  Usually trouble free.

---

■ GARDENER'S TIP

*Most of the food value in a potato lies just beneath the skin and is lost when the potato is peeled. The skin itself also provides some important fibre, so cook potatoes in their skins whenever possible.*

---

■ GARDENER'S TIP

*Use a home-made automatic watering system to provide a constant supply of water to pot-grown plants. Fill a bucket with water and place on a higher level than the plants. Cut soft water-retentive material into 2-cm/¾-in wide strips to make wicks and* *place one end of each in the bucket and the other end on the soil in the pot. The water is taken up by the wicks and seeps along them into the soil in each pot keeping it damp.*

## SALSIFY

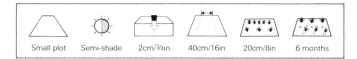

| Small plot | Semi-shade | 2cm/¾in | 40cm/16in | 20cm/8in | 6 months |

The common name of this long white root, vegetable oyster, gives a clue to its unusual flavour.

**GROWING** Deeply cultivated, moisture-retentive soils which have not been recently manured or limed are best. Sow seed thinly in mid spring, thinning the seedlings when they are large enough to handle. Keep weeds down, but do not damage the developing roots with the hoe – like beetroot, they 'bleed'. Keep plants well watered.

**HARVESTING** The best-flavoured roots are 5cm/2in wide at the crown and 25cm/10in long. Leave them in the ground and lift from mid autumn as required or store the whole crop in boxes of sand in an airy, frost-free place. The roots will keep until early spring. If roots are left in the ground until spring they will send up new shoots (chards) which can be cooked like asparagus.

**POSSIBLE PROBLEMS** None likely.

## SCORZONERA

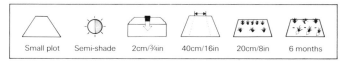

| Small plot | Semi-shade | 2cm/¾in | 40cm/16in | 20cm/8in | 6 months |

The delicate flavour of these black-skinned, white-fleshed roots is rather like Jerusalem artichoke, and is best simply boiled and served well seasoned with butter.

**GROWING** Fertile, well-drained soil is necessary, cultivated deeply to allow unchecked root growth. The roots will be mis-shapen if grown on recently manured soil. Sow seed in mid spring and thin the seedlings as soon as they are large enough to handle. Keep weeds under control and water well. A mulch of straw or grass cuttings will help to prevent the roots drying out.

**HARVESTING** Lift from mid autumn for immediate use or leave in the ground until required. Alternatively, lift the entire crop and store in boxes of sand in a frost-free place.

**POSSIBLE PROBLEMS** None likely.

■ COOK'S TIP

*This root has a taste similar to turnip. Cook gently for about 15 minutes until just tender then serve with a white sauce or a little butter. Otherwise salsify can be cooked in any way you might cook parsnips. The roots discolour quickly when preparing, so scrub them and place in water to which lemon juice has been added.*

■ ORGANIC TIP

*Mulches can be made from a wide range of decaying materials. Do not use fresh, but allow to rot down for two to three months first and use fairly coarse. Other mulches are a 5cm/2in layer of pine needles or softwood bark.*

# SWEDE

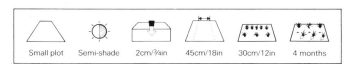

| Small plot | Semi-shade | 2cm/¾in | 45cm/18in | 30cm/12in | 4 months |
|---|---|---|---|---|---|

This hardy relative of the turnip is much larger and sweeter than its cousin. The skin may be white, purple or yellow but the flesh is usually yellow, sometimes white. Swedes store very successfully and are particularly popular in the north.

**GROWING** Any fertile, non-acid soil is suitable, manured for a previous crop as freshly manured ground will give forked roots. Work a little well-balanced fertilizer into the seed bed before sowing. Sow seed in drills in late spring/early summer in more exposed areas, and thin out when the seedlings are large enough to handle. Water well throughout the season.

**HARVESTING** Swedes are hardy enough to be left in the ground and lifted as required from early autumn through the winter. They store well in clamps, which is useful if the ground is likely to be frozen.

**POSSIBLE PROBLEMS** Flea beetle damage may occur on young seedlings. Spray with diazinon. Boron deficiency causes the flesh to discolour and harden. Water lightly with a solution of borax at 15g per 4.5 litres/¹/₂oz per 1 gallon.

**SUITABLE VARIETIES** Marian; Chignecto; Purple Top.

# TURNIP

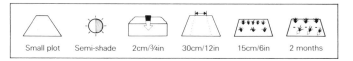

| Small plot | Semi-shade | 2cm/¾in | 30cm/12in | 15cm/6in | 2 months |
|---|---|---|---|---|---|

Turnips are best in spring and summer, young white globes flushed green and violet, but good varieties are also available for traditional winter use.

**GROWING** Fertile, well-drained yet moisture-retentive soil is best. Summer turnips must be grown rapidly, and can be treated as catch crops. Earliest sowings can be made outdoors in late winter. Sow 3 or 4 seeds to a station, soak the seedbed thoroughly and cover with frames or cloches. For summer crops, sow seed in drills in early spring. Winter turnips are grown from sowings made from mid summer to late summer and thinned so that the plants are spaced 40cm/16in apart each way.

**HARVESTING** Lift very early turnips when they are the size of a golf ball. Let summer turnips reach a maximum of 7.5cm/3in in diameter before lifting: this should be in late spring. Pick as soon as they are ready to be sure of a nice crisp texture. Winter varieties are ready in mid autumn for immediate use. They can also be stored: twist off the tops and place in boxes of sand in a cool, frost-free place. Roots which are left in the ground over winter will regrow in the spring, and the new tops can be used like spring greens.

**POSSIBLE PROBLEMS** Turnips share the problems of the cabbage family. Young seedlings may be attacked by flea beetle: dust the leaves with derris.

■ GARDENER'S TIP

*Lift roots around mid winter, trim, pack in boxes in soil and put in part-darkness, such as the garden shed. The roots will sprout and the taste of the young, semi-blanched growth which results is delicious.*

■ GARDENER'S TIP

*Floating cloches made of woven polypropylene will float up with the crop as it grows beneath. Spread loosely over the ground and secure with bricks around the edge or hold in slits in the ground about 5cm/2in deep.*

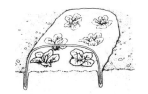

# BULB VEGETABLES

If you are following the crop rotation plan on page 13, bulb vegetables are grown on Plot B. It is important to rotate onion crops to protect plants from soil-borne problems like white rot and stem eelworm. The soil pH should be above 6.5, so add lime if necessary. Bulbs require a sunny, sheltered position and a well-drained rich, fertile soil that has been previously dug and to which plenty of bulky organic matter, manure or compost has been added. As bulb plants have small leaves these are unable to smother weeds, so it is important to hoe around plants regularly to check weed growth.

**BLANCHING LEEKS**  Plant stems can be blanched in one of two ways. In the first, the seedlings are placed in individual holes that are filled with water only. Gradually the holes fill up with soil and stems are blanched. They can be further blanched by drawing up

soil around the plants in late summer. Alternatively, seedlings can be positioned in a row down the centre of a trench. Soil is then gradually added to the trench as plants grow. In this way longer white stems are obtained. Tie paper collars around the stems to keep them clean.

**HARVESTING AND STORAGE**  Onions are sown in autumn, winter and spring. Japanese onions, sown in autumn, provide the first harvest in mid summer. Onions store well, with the exception of Welsh onions which can be harvested fresh through winter in milder areas.

Spring onions are grown close together to keep the bulbs small and when sown in late winter under glass they are ready to lift in early summer. Sown in early summer, spring onions can be also harvested in the autumn.

Mild-tasting leeks, which can tolerate severe winter weather, are available to pull fresh when required from early autumn if sown in mid winter. Maincrop leeks sown in late winter are available for harvesting from late autumn to spring.

**PROTECTION FROM COLD**  Early sown leeks and onions, like many other plants, need the protection of cloches if they are to survive the cold. Cloches are invaluable for extending the season when you can grow plants outdoors, both early and later in the year and for protecting tender vegetables.

A cloche should be at least twice as high and one and a half times as wide as the nearly fully grown crop to be covered. In fact it is wise to buy the largest size you can, one that covers your bed width is ideal. Larger cloches ensure that there is plenty of air circulation underneath and therefore less risk of pest or disease outbreaks. Some cloches have vents incorporated in the design to provide ventilation; on others a side or end can be raised or removed. Some designs include extra side pieces which can be added when plants grow tall.

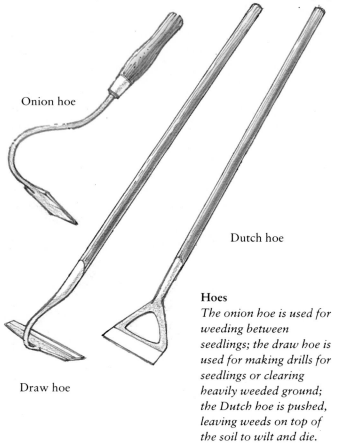

Onion hoe

Dutch hoe

Draw hoe

**Hoes**
*The onion hoe is used for weeding between seedlings; the draw hoe is used for making drills for seedlings or clearing heavily weeded ground; the Dutch hoe is pushed, leaving weeds on top of the soil to wilt and die.*

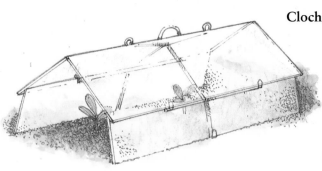
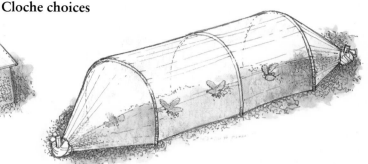

### Cloche choices

○ **Glass cloches** provide the best protection from cold, but are heavier than plastic cloches to move around, expensive and not advisable where there are children.

○ **Rigid plastic** is lightweight, so make sure plastic cloches can be anchored to the ground.

○ **Corrugated plastic** diffuses the light which is excellent for use in summer or for winter protection of mature plants but not so satisfactory for use on seedlings.

○ **Transparent plastic bottles** make excellent cloches for small individual plants. Add a few small holes for ventilation.

○ **Polythene film** stretched over wire hoops is cheaper. Polythene tunnels are easy to move from crop to crop and the sides can be raised for ventilation. Since they are very light you will need to incorporate a secure method of holding the sheeting down. The film will deteriorate, usually lasting for two to three years at the most.

○ **Floating cloches** are sheets of perforated plastic or woven polypropylene which you weight down at the edges. As the crop beneath grows the cloche floats up with it. Water and air can penetrate the material and the polypropylene type will protect the plants from a few degrees of frost. This is the cheapest form of cloche to buy.

*Tips on using cloches*

*Protection from draught* Cloches need to include end pieces as a through draught can cause considerable damage to young or tender crops. You can make your own ends from panes of glass or rigid plastic.

*Heating the soil* Position a cloche or tunnel over the soil to be used a month before you intend to sow or plant there to warm it up.

*Watering* Don't forget that the cloche will keep rain off the plants inside so you will need to water regularly. If you place a length of seep hose inside then you will only need to fit the end of the hose to water.

*Pollination* Covered plants cannot be pollinated by insects so open or remove the cover during the daytime when the plants are flowering.

*Ventilation* As temperatures rise quickly under the protection, ventilation is important; where vents are not included in the design raise a side or remove one end only. Remove covers completely during the day in hot spells.

## PESTS, DISEASES AND DISORDERS

*Downy mildew* In wet weather mildew may streak leaves with purple. Spray with zineb and rotate crops.

*Onion eelworm* Minute worms which get inside bulbs and cause distortion. Remove and burn plants. Move bed to another part of the garden and do not use this area for onions or potatoes for four to five years.

*Onion fly* Maggots, the larvae of the onion fly, can be a problem throughout the summer when they feed on the roots. First signs are yellowing leaves. Plants may die. The onion fly is attracted by the scent of the onions, specially strong when seedlings are thinned. If you grow onions from sets this avoids thinning. Hoe regularly around plants to expose grubs to birds.

*Rot on stored onions* A mouldy white growth can appear close to the neck of stored onions, which then become soft and rot. Others may become slimy due to fungal attack. Bending the tops of onions over to promote ripening can encourage the growth of mould later. Inspect stored onions regularly and remove any that are affected as soon as you find them. Only store ripe bulbs and store in nets or on strings to ensure air circulation.

*White or neck rot* This white fungus rots onions, leeks, shallots and garlic. Diseased plants turn yellow and die. Treat affected plants with Bordeaux mixture. Do not grow onions on the affected bed for at least three years as beds can be contaminated for up to eight years.

## FLORENCE FENNEL

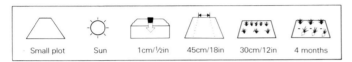

| | | | | | |
|---|---|---|---|---|---|
| Small plot | Sun | 1cm/½in | 45cm/18in | 30cm/12in | 4 months |

The bulbs for which this plant is chiefly cultivated are actually the swollen leaf bases. Florence fennel has a mild, sweet, aniseed flavour and has a range of culinary uses. The bulb can be sliced and used raw in salads or cooked in soups and stews, while the leaves make a useful flavouring.

**GROWING** Any reasonably fertile soil will do, but the best results are obtained on light, sandy soils. Because the leaf bases are blanched by earthing them up, an easily worked, stone-free soil is essential. Incorporate a base dressing of general fertilizer before sowing the seed thinly in mid spring. Thin the seedlings as soon as possible. Water well in dry weather and keep weeds under control. As soon as the bases start to swell, earth them up with soil to exclude the light. Alternatively, wrap them in paper collars secured with rubber bands.

**HARVESTING** Lift the plants as required during the late summer and autumn, once the bulbs have swollen. Cut the plants just below the swollen bases.

**POSSIBLE PROBLEMS** Florence fennel is a trouble-free crop.

## EARLY LEEK

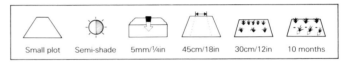

| | | | | | |
|---|---|---|---|---|---|
| Small plot | Semi-shade | 5mm/¼in | 45cm/18in | 30cm/12in | 10 months |

It is possible to bring the availability of leeks forward by raising plants of selected varieties under glass. This method is always used for growing leeks for exhibition purposes. Milder in flavour than onions, leeks are straight stems blanched at the base with green tops.

**GROWING** In mid winter sow seed thinly in trays in the greenhouse with the temperature at 10C/50F. When the seedlings are large enough to handle, prick them out into individual containers. They are slow-growing at first, but will be ready for planting out in late spring after a brief period of hardening off. Like maincrop leeks, early varieties can be grown on the flat or in trenches, as long as the soil is rich and deep and has been thoroughly cultivated in the previous autumn. Trench cultivation is necessary for exhibition leeks, which are fed regularly with a weak solution of nitrate of soda and superphosphate to increase size, staked to ensure straight stems and provided with cardboard collars packed with wood shavings to protect the foliage.

**HARVESTING** Early leeks are ready for lifting in early autumn but can be left in the ground until late autumn.

**POSSIBLE PROBLEMS** Relatively trouble-free.

**VARIETIES** Lyon Prizetaker; Early Market.

---

### ■ GARDENER'S TIP

*This plant does not like being transplanted so if you want to start seeds off indoors or in a greenhouse use soil blocks, peat pots or cardboard rolls from toilet paper, kitchen roll or freezer bags cut into short lengths as containers. These decompose in the soil and all avoid disturbing the roots. This type of fennel can be frozen satisfactorily to provide a winter supply. Scrub young stalks and blanch for 3 minutes. Pack in boxes in blanching water, cool and freeze.*

### ■ GARDENER'S TIP

*An ingenious method of keeping leeks clean as they grow is to place a cardboard roll from toilet paper over each plant.*

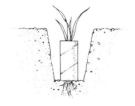

## MAINCROP LEEK

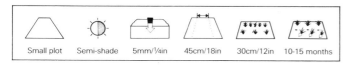

| | | | | | |
|---|---|---|---|---|---|
| Small plot | Semi-shade | 5mm/¼in | 45cm/18in | 30cm/12in | 10-15 months |

This hardy vegetable is particularly useful in the mid to late winter period, as it may well be available when the last of stored onion bulbs have been used.

**GROWING** Raise plants in a seedbed on light, well-drained soil. Sow in late late winter/early early spring in shallow drills 20-30cm/8-12in apart. Cover with cloches. When they are large enough to handle, thin the seedlings to 1-2cm/about ³⁄₄in apart. Hand-weed regularly or the emerging plants may be swamped. Water occasionally. Transplant to the growing site in early summer, watering the plants well before moving them. Here a rich, deep soil is best, well-cultivated in the previous autumn. Incorporate a base dressing of a well-balanced general fertilizer before planting. Make holes 15-25cm/6-10in deep with a dibber. Drop 1 plant in each and fill with water. During the season the holes gradually fill up and further blanching can be done by drawing up soil around the plants in early autumn. Hoe regularly to remove weeds.

**HARVESTING** Leeks are hardy enough to be left in the ground and lifted as needed from late autumn to mid spring, though late varieties will not be ready until mid winter. Do not leave them any later or they will start to regrow.

**POSSIBLE PROBLEMS** Relatively trouble-free.

**VARIETIES** Late autumn-mid winter: Musselburgh; mid winter-mid spring: Royal Favourite.

### ▓ COOK'S TIP

*To clean home-grown leeks, cut off the green top leaves, and the root, plus coarse outer skin. Then slit down the length to the centre, open out and wash under cold running water.*

## MAINCROP TRENCH LEEK

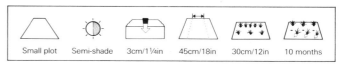

| | | | | | |
|---|---|---|---|---|---|
| Small plot | Semi-shade | 3cm/1¼in | 45cm/18in | 30cm/12in | 10 months |

Growing leeks in trenches produces a greater length of blanched stem and bigger specimens generally.

**GROWING** Raise plants from seed in exactly the same way as for cultivation on the flat. Before transplanting the seedlings, prepare the trenches well on rich-textured fertile soil. Make the trenches 30cm/12in deep and wide and heap the soil from the trenches in the pathways. Dig well-rotted manure or compost into the bottom. In early summer, set the leeks in a single row down the middle of the trench. Water in well. If birds pull out some of the seedlings, replant them immediately.

**BLANCHING** At monthly intervals, put soil from the pathways around the plants until the trenches are eventually filled in. To keep the plants clean and soil-free, wrap them in collars of corrugated cardboard before blanching begins. Weeding is important, but less of a problem as the regular movement of soil tends to discourage weed development.

**POSSIBLE PROBLEMS** Relatively trouble-free.

**VARIETIES** Late autumn-mid winter: Musselburgh; mid winter-mid spring: Royal Favourite.

### ▓ GARDENER'S TIP

*An alternative way of growing leeks is to place individual plants in 15-cm/6-in holes made with a dibber. Place holes at 15cm/6in intervals and in rows 30cm/12in apart. Drop a plant into each hole and fill with water but no earth. The water washes soil around and over the roots. When the seedlings have become established spread mulch around the plants. Harvest the plants as they are required.*

## ONION

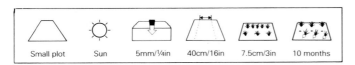

| | | | | | |
|---|---|---|---|---|---|
| Small plot | Sun | 5mm/¼in | 40cm/16in | 7.5cm/3in | 10 months |

Raise onions under glass for outdoor planting in spring.

**GROWING** Sow seed at the turn of the year (on Boxing Day, traditionally) in seed trays kept at 10C/50F. When the seedlings are large enough to handle prick them out into individual containers. Gradually harden them off from early spring before planting outside in mid spring. Fertile non-acid soil is essential. Dig in well-rotted manure or compost in the autumn and leave the ground rough to develop a natural tilth. Before planting, rake in a fertilizer with nitrogen and potassium in the ratio 1:2, as too much nitrogen encourages soft growth. Plant carefully: make a hole for each plant with a trowel or better still a dibber, deep enough for the roots to go their full depth but with the bottom of the bulblet not more than 1cm/½in below the surface. Firm each plant in well. Do not damage the leaves. Weed regularly with a short-handled onion hoe: don't damage the bulbs or cover them with earth. Water only in hot dry conditions. When the leaves wilt in late summer, fold them over neatly.

**HARVESTING** When the leaves are brittle, and on a warm sunny day, lift the bulbs. Lay them in the sun to dry, turning them frequently. When they are fully ripe, about 4 weeks later, store in wire-bottomed trays in a cool, frost-free place until the following spring.

**POSSIBLE PROBLEMS** Onion fly larvae tunnel into the bulbs: spray with diazinon.

## SPRING-SOWN ONION

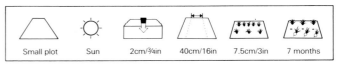

| | | | | | |
|---|---|---|---|---|---|
| Small plot | Sun | 2cm/¾in | 40cm/16in | 7.5cm/3in | 7 months |

Spring-sown onions are best in areas where cold, wet winters may damage an over-wintered crop.

**GROWING** A rich-textured, fertile soil is ideal. Onions do not tolerate acid soils, so it may be advisable to add lime. Prepare the ground in the autumn, digging in well-rotted manure or compost and leaving it rough over winter for a tilth to develop. In late winter, incorporate a fertilizer with nitrogen and potassium in the ratio 1:2, and rake the soil to a fine tilth. Firm the plot by treading up and down. Sow fairly thinly in the rows. While thinnings can be used for salads, the less disturbance to the plants the better. Watering is only necessary in dry seasons, but weeding must be carried out regularly. The bulbs begin to ripen in late summer, when the leaves fall over: if they don't, bend them over gently so that the ripening sun can get to the bulbs.

**HARVESTING** By the time the leaves are shrivelling the bulbs are ripe enough to lift. Choose a warm sunny day and pick the bulbs by hand or ease them out with a fork. Let them dry in the sun if possible, otherwise spread them out in the greenhouse. When the leaves are brittle, store the onions in wire-bottomed trays or make them into ropes. It is essential that they are in an airy, frost-free, dry place.

**POSSIBLE PROBLEMS** Many of the diseases afflicting onions can be avoided by observing crop rotations.

### ■ COOK'S TIP

*To avoid crying when peeling onions, leave the root end of the onion in place until you have finished peeling and chopping each individual vegetable, then remove it. Alternatively, remove any necessary layers of skin under water.*

### ■ PRESERVING TIP

*Onions can also be stored hanging up: place them, one above the other, in an old stocking, making a knot between each one to keep them apart. Cut off the required number from the bottom as you need them.*

# ONION SETS

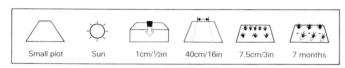

| | | | | | |
|---|---|---|---|---|---|
| Small plot | Sun | 1cm/½in | 40cm/16in | 7.5cm/3in | 7 months |

Onion sets are bulbs which have been partially grown in the previous season, then lifted and dried, and finally kept in temperature-controlled stores so that the small bulb continues to grow when it is replanted (rather than running to seed). Growing onions from sets means that less suitable soils can be used.

**GROWING** Prepare the soil as for onions grown from seed, digging and manuring in the previous autumn, and raking it to a fine tilth in early to mid spring. Firm the soil before inserting the bulbs so that only the necks protrude above the surface. If birds, worms or frost dislodge the bulbs, replant them immediately. Keep weeds down, while avoiding damage to the bulbs, and water only if prolonged dry conditions threaten to slow down growth. In late summer, when the leaves begin to topple, bend them over to speed up ripening.

**HARVESTING** In early autumn, when the leaves have shrivelled, the onions are ready for lifting. Pick on a warm sunny day and let the bulbs dry completely in the sun. A net supported on 4 low posts makes a good 'hammock' for drying the onions with warm air all round. Thick-necked onions must be used as soon as possible, but undamaged specimens can be stored in an airy, frost-free place until the following spring.

**POSSIBLE PROBLEMS** Rotate crops to avoid a build-up of diseases such as white rot and downy mildew.

# JAPANESE ONION

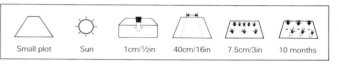

| | | | | | |
|---|---|---|---|---|---|
| Small plot | Sun | 1cm/½in | 40cm/16in | 7.5cm/3in | 10 months |

Japanese onions have been developed to mature from an autumn sowing, giving a midsummer crop before spring-sown onions are ready to use. Sowing onions in the autumn has a long tradition, but the crop was often spoiled by plants flowering in the spring warmth rather than producing a bulb. These can be relied upon to mature correctly, and can only be sown in the autumn.

**GROWING** A rich-textured, fertile, non-acid soil is essential. Incorporate well-rotted manure or compost in the previous winter and leave rough to allow a natural tilth to develop. Add fertilizer with nitrogen and potassium in the ratio 1:2 before planting and rake to a fine tilth. Firm the soil and sow seed in late summer. It is useful, but not essential, to protect the plot with cloches from mid autumn until frosts have passed. Not all the seeds will germinate, and some seedlings will not make it through the winter. Growth begins again in spring. Keep weeds down during the growing period.

**HARVESTING** The leaves begin to flag in early summer. Bend them over and let the bulbs ripen for 4-5 weeks before lifting. Pick on a warm sunny day and let the bulbs dry completely in the sun before use or before storing in a dry, airy place.

**POSSIBLE PROBLEMS** Rotate crops to avoid a build-up of soil-borne diseases. Grey mould sometimes appears after frost damage. Use a systemic fungicide.

## ▪ ORGANIC TIP

*Growing onions from sets helps to keep the onion fly away. Onion scent attracts the female fly and this is specially strong when seedlings are thinned. Before planting, trim off old stems to deprive birds of a grip to pull on.*

## ▪ COOK'S TIP

*The simple Italian way to cook tomatoes with onions is to blanch and peel 397-g/14-oz tomatoes and sprinkle with salt, pepper and a pinch of sugar, then slice 2 large onions; arrange with 100g/4oz breadcrumbs, in alternate layers in an ovenproof dish, finishing with a layer of breadcrumbs and grated cheese. Bake in a moderate oven for 30 minutes. Lightly fried onions are also delicious with pine nuts, raisins and white wine added.*

## PICKLING ONION

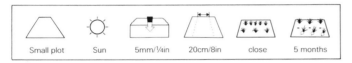

| | | | | | |
|---|---|---|---|---|---|
| Small plot | Sun | 5mm/¼in | 20cm/8in | close | 5 months |

Little yellow silverskin onions for pickling are very quick to mature and easy to grow. The flavour is milder than that of bulb onions.

**GROWING** While pickling onions prefer the fertile, rich-textured soil important for bulb onions, they can be grown on poorer soils as long as they are not acid. Rake the bed to a fine tilth in spring and tread it flat. Sow seed in mid spring in shallow drills, sowing very closely to make sure that the individual bulbs remain small. Water lightly but regularly to speed growth. Remove weeds by hand. The crop does not need thinning. In mid summer the leaves turn yellow and topple over – bend them over to speed up the ripening process.

**HARVESTING** Pick at the end of late summer. Fork up the onions and, if conditions are favourable, leave them on the ground for about a week to dry, turning them over from time to time.

**POSSIBLE PROBLEMS** See spring-sown onions. Onion fly is the most likely pest: spray with diazinon.

**VARIETIES** Paris Silverskin; Aviv.

## SHALLOT

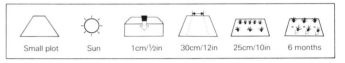

| | | | | | |
|---|---|---|---|---|---|
| Small plot | Sun | 1cm/½in | 30cm/12in | 25cm/10in | 6 months |

Shallots are small bulbs of the onion family about 2.5-5cm/1-2in in diameter, milder in flavour than large onions and commonly used for pickling or for flavouring casseroles and soups. They grow in clumps of 6-12.

**GROWING** Shallots are raised from the best bulbs saved from the previous year's crop and are planted like onion sets. They like the same soil as other onions: rich-textured, fertile and non-acid, manured in the autumn before planting. Rake the plot to a fine tilth and firm the soil before setting out the little bulbs. Plant as early in late winter as possible, firming them in well. Any bulbs dislodged by birds, worms or frost should be replanted immediately. Keep weeds down, taking care not to damage the bulbs. As they begin to dry off in early/mid summer, gently remove the soil from around the clumps.

**HARVESTING** The leaves will turn yellow and wither when growth has finished. Lift the shallots with care and spread them out individually in the sun to dry for a few days, or under protection if the weather is wet. Use immediately if required for pickling or store in an airy, frost-free place for future use. Select the best bulbs for planting next season.

**POSSIBLE PROBLEMS** There is a danger of soil-borne diseases building up if onions are grown on the same plot year after year, so rotate the crop.

### ■ COOK'S TIP

*To pickle onions place them, unpeeled, in brine for a day. Drain and peel the onions, put in jars and cover with spiced vinegar. Seal. To make brine, dissolve 450g/1lb coarse salt in boiling water, allow to cool, strain and make up to 4.5 litres/8 pints. To make spiced vinegar add to 1 litre/1³/₄ pints white cider vinegar, 5-cm/2-in piece cinnamon, 1 tsp cloves, 2 tsp allspice, 1 tsp black peppercorns, 1 tsp mustard seed, 2-3 bay leaves, cover and bring to boil.*

### ■ PRESERVING TIP

*To dry shallots, lay them on chicken wire nailed to four short posts stuck in the ground to create a hammock. To store, hang up in string or mesh plastic bags, the sort that you get oranges in from the supermarket.*

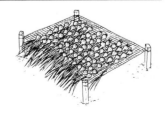

# SPRING ONION

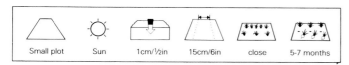

| Small plot | Sun | 1cm/½in | 15cm/6in | close | 5-7 months |
|---|---|---|---|---|---|

Otherwise known as salad onions, these small white bulbs with slender green stems are mild enough to be eaten raw but with enough pungency to enliven salads (the larger the bulb, the stronger the flavour).

**GROWING** Spring onions are grown close together to restrict the development of the bulb. The ideal soil is rich-textured, fertile and non-acid, and manured for a previous crop. Rake the plot to a fine tilth before sowing and tread it firm. For an early spring crop, sow seed of a hardy variety fairly thickly and protect with cloches. For lifting in early summer, sow in late winter under glass or early spring in the open. Seed sown in early summer will give onions for lifting in the autumn. All crops should be kept weed-free – hand weeding is best to avoid damaging the developing bulbs. No thinning is required.

**HARVESTING** Pull the onions as soon as they are big enough to use, with the leaves still green and tender. Unlike bulb onions, salad onions cannot be stored and should be used very fresh.

**POSSIBLE PROBLEMS** Rotate crops to avoid a build-up of soil-borne diseases. Onion fly larvae may be a problem on lighter soils: spray with diazinon.

**VARIETIES** For overwintering: White Lisbon Winter Hardy; spring and summer plantings: White Lisbon.

## ■ GARDENER'S TIP

*You can have spring onions almost around the year if you make successive sowings every three weeks from late winter until early summer. Plants should be ready to eat in about eight weeks. Sow seeds in 8-cm/3-in bands, 1-2cm/½-¾in apart with 23cm/9in between bands. In all but the coldest areas you can also sow hardier varieties in late summer to harvest the next spring.*

# WELSH ONION

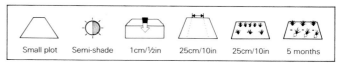

| Small plot | Semi-shade | 1cm/½in | 25cm/10in | 25cm/10in | 5 months |
|---|---|---|---|---|---|

Also known as the ever-ready onion, the so-called Welsh onion is in fact the most popular onion in Japanese and Chinese cooking. It is a perfectly hardy perennial and can be grown easily even in cooler zones. Plants grow in clumps in the same way as shallots or chives, reaching a height of 30cm/12in, but do not form large bulbs. Use the onions, stems and all, as a substitute for spring onions or for flavouring winter stews and soups.

**GROWING** Any fertile, well-drained soil will do in any handy part of the garden, perhaps as an edging to the vegetable or herb garden. The most satisfactory results are obtained by setting out new young plants rather than raising from seed. Set the bulblets out in mid spring, weed regularly and water lightly. The bulblets will multiply into thick clumps during the summer. Lift and divide the clumps every 3 years, replanting on new ground.

**HARVESTING** By early autumn you should be able to detach a few onions from each clump, continuing to pick throughout the winter. Use immediately – Welsh onions do not store. Always leave some onions in each clump to multiply the following year.

**POSSIBLE PROBLEMS** Trouble-free.

## ■ COOK'S TIP

*Both the leaves and bulbs of Welsh onions can be used in salads. They can be used in place of leeks. Chop, then steam them until just tender. Use hot, coated in a sauce, or allow to cool, then toss them in vinaigrette.*

# HERBS

The value of herbs for food and medicine has probably been recognized almost as long as man has been around. Cultivating these wild plants became popular in Britain with the arrival of the Romans and in medieval England they were mainly grown in monastery gardens. Mixed with flowers and vegetables they became an important component of the cottage garden.

With their capacity to add delicious natural flavours to food and a renewed interest in curing illness with natural herbal remedies, herbs have come back into their own in the last decades. Many people have discovered the delights of including herbs in the garden. They are easy to grow, have a wide range of leaf shapes that are decorative in flower arrangements, and often have their own richly scented and colourful flowers. Add to this the benefit of some herbs in keeping away a range of plant pests and their attraction for pollinating insects, essential in the fruit and vegetable garden, and you will see that a garden without herbs is sadly lacking.

**CREATING A HERB GARDEN** Even if you have only a balcony or backyard, or no outdoor space at all, it is still possible to grow a range of herbs in pots. A small area of, preferably sunny, free space will give you the chance to plan a decoratively-shaped herb garden. Alternatively, the plants can be intermingled with flowers, or grown in a bed on their own close to the kitchen.

**DESIGNING A DECORATIVE HERB GARDEN** First, design the garden on paper. In a square plot you could copy the old cartwheel shape, using treated timber fence posts in place of spokes and a bird bath or sun dial as the centre point. Or use the same shape but divide off the sections with 'spokes' of shingle, grass or brick paths. Paths can also be used to divide up a rectangle and form beds of triangles, diamonds and hexagon shapes to break up the space. On a long, narrow plot use an old wooden ladder, or timber laid in a ladder shape, to act as a decorative plant divider.

Leave some of the paving slabs out when designing a patio and plant low-growing evergreen herbs in the spaces, such as thyme and winter savory. Group a number of decorative pots together and grow tall herbs, such as lovage, angelica and fennel, in the larger pots at the back. Place smaller plants in the front. A line of lavender, rue or rosemary plants can form a low dividing hedge between patio and grass.

*Among the flowers* Herbs mingle well with flowers and fruit, encouraging pollinating insects with their wonderful scents. Group different varieties of one herb together. Thyme, sage and mint all come in a range of leaf colours and patterns. Create a border for a herbaceous bed with parsley, thyme, chives, marjoram or salad burnet. Tall herbs like angelica, lovage, fennel, southernwood and evening primrose will add decorative leaf shapes towards the back of a bed and shelter smaller, more delicate flowers.

*Kitchen herb bed* If the area outside your kitchen door is sunny then this is an ideal spot for a culinary herb bed and some pots. It also means that you don't have to make a damp dash for a fistful of parsley in wet weather. A bed about 1 by 3 metres/3.3 by 10ft is ideal. If it is wider, you will need stepping stones to help you care for and harvest plants at the back without treading on the soil.

*Limited space herb garden* Hanging baskets can be used for herbs that will trail decoratively, like marjoram, thyme, nasturtiums, tarragon and chamomile. Boxes will take the more upright varieties, or plant a number of window boxes, each containing plants for specific uses, one of culinary herbs, one of herbs for making herbal teas, one for those herbs used in beauty preparations.

A box on a bedroom or living room window sill could be used for strongly scented herbs so that on sunny days herbal fragrances fill the room.

Rampant herbs like lemon balm and mint are more easily controlled if you grow them in a container, so plant them in pots, even if you intend growing them in a window box, then sink them into the soil with the

*Herbs grow well in pots and hanging baskets. A good thick moss is required for lining the baskets to prevent loss of moisture.*

rims about 2cm/³/₄in above soil level. Delicate herbs like basil and lemon verbena are best grown in pots so that they can be brought indoors in the autumn for protection from frost.

*Indoor herb garden* Herbs grown or brought indoors will be available for picking later into the winter than those grown outdoors. However, plants raised indoors cannot be expected to grow to the same extent as outdoor plants. Therefore, more plants are needed to provide a comparable harvest.

Indoor-grown herbs need ventilation, but not draughts, humidity, a moderate temperature of about 15C/60F, good light, and sunshine. The kitchen, unfortunately, is not the ideal spot to grow herbs as temperatures tend to fluctuate too much and unless the ventilation is good, the plants' leaf pores can become clogged with grease and dust. Consider growing them in hanging baskets, pots, or a window box in a sunny window. If you are short of space just grow the herbs

necessary for a bouquet garni in a decorative pot: parsley, thyme and bay.

*Choosing the herbs to grow* The herbs you decide to grow will depend on your own requirements. Some herbs provide a wide range of uses and are found in all categories. Given below are some of the most widely used herbs under each of four main headings.

*For culinary purposes* Start off with a limited number of the herbs you use most, then gradually extend the range, experimenting with species new to you. The ten most popular culinary herbs are: parsley, thyme, bay, rosemary, chives, tarragon, mint, sage, marjoram and fennel.

*Medicinal herb garden* Most herbs are in one way or another good for health. Ten starter herbs to treat some minor ailments are: peppermint for indigestion and as a pick-me-up, chamomile for indigestion, fennel for flatulence, lemon balm for insomnia and to relax, bergamot for insomnia, hyssop for coughs and colds, and parsley to stimulate digestion and as a diuretic herb – it gives gentle stimulation to the kidneys. Rosemary helps to stimulate circulation and when steeped in oil is a help for rheumatism, if gently rubbed into the affected part; sage is an expectorant while thyme stimulates appetite and aids digestion.

*Cosmetic herb garden* Many herbs can be included in shampoos, conditioners, moisturizers, cleansers and for bathtime relaxation. Some aid a healthy skin, others hair, eyes, hands, feet or nails. Elder cleanses, softens and whitens skin and is helpful for freckles and wrinkles. It also makes a soothing eyebath. Chamomile, *Matricaria chamomilla*, is good for skin, hair and eyes. Lavender can be used for skin and feet, rosemary for hair and skin, dill for eyes and nails, sage for skin and fennel for cleansing.

*For scent* Close to a window plant lemon thyme, lemon verbena, lemon geranium, pineapple mint and sweet marjoram. To attract butterflies and bees include borage, hyssop and thyme.

**GROWING HERBS** Most herbs are a delight to grow. They take little from the soil, while giving off scent, taste and colour. Most also have an in-built rejection of pests and disease.

In fact even if you are totally committed to fertilizers and pesticides, this is an area of the garden where it is important to use organic principles, a start to becoming a committed organic gardener perhaps. As many herbs are used uncooked, and taste to some extent is lost through washing, it has to be better to refrain from including chemicals in their cultivation.

*Choosing a position* Choose a sunny corner if possible as most herbs thrive in the sun. Those suitable for more shady areas are angelica, fennel, mint, tansy, sorrel and bergamot. Some protection from wind, such as walls or fences, is valuable.

*Drainage* A well-drained site is important for almost all herbs so that air can circulate around the plant roots. Soggy soil is airless and cold. The aim is to have a soil that does not dry out too quickly but has good drainage. If you are unsure if your drainage is adequate you can do a simple test. Dig a hole twice the depth of your spade blade and leave it open for a few days. If water collects in the hole over this time it shows that the drainage is poor. The surest way to improve poor drainage is to install pipes laid on gravel and leading to a soakaway point. In practice this is expensive and troublesome for the amateur gardener. An easier, but still laborious, alternative is to dig narrow trenches and partly fill them with large stones before replacing the soil. In most domestic gardens it is enough to dig the ground over to twice the spade's depth and incorporate as much bulky organic matter as you can get.

*Soil and nutrients* Most herbs grow best in a slightly alkaline soil. The soil should be well dug before planting and organic matter, animal manure, green manure, or garden compost included. For more information see pages 7-8. A healthy organic garden includes a good worm population to aerate the soil, improve drainage and convert materials into plant food. See page 7 for attracting and increasing worm population. When making your own compost, include any herb refuse as this is specially valuable to the compost heap. Add organic matter in autumn and mulch with a thin layer of compost in spring. This should be all the feeding necessary.

**INCREASING HERBS** Annual herbs can be sown in warm weather on the spot where they will grow or started indoors to give earlier crops (see page 14 for sowing). Recycle seeds for use in the next season but buy new every two to three years.

Perennials can be increased by layering: mint, marjoram, lemon balm, southernwood and sage are all suitable for this method of propagation, which is described and illustrated in the Gardener's Tip for sage on page 96. During the growing season stem cuttings can be taken from healthy plants (as described and illustrated step by step opposite). In autumn or early spring when plants are dormant many can be dug up and divided (see below).

**HARVESTING** Small quantities of most herbs can be cut for use fresh throughout the growing season. However, if you wish to preserve them then the best time to pick is when the volatile oil content is greatest. The time of day and the time in the plant's cycle are the two points to consider. Most herbs should be cut in the morning when the dew has dried naturally but before the sun is fully on the plant. In bright sun the volatile oils, which carry flavour and value, diminish.

If it is the leaves you require, the ideal time to pick is between the formation of flower buds and the opening of the flowers, when the oil content is highest. If you wish to harvest flowers these should be picked when fully open, and in prime condition. Seeds are gathered when the flowerheads begin to turn brown. To check if seeds are ripe, tap a head lightly; the seeds will fall when ready. Cut the heads, including a length of stem, and hang upside down in a dry airy shed. You can either encase the head in a paper bag so that the seeds fall into it or place a basket lined with paper or a cotton cloth below to catch the seeds. Place seeds in airtight containers in the dark to retain the full flavour.

**Lifting and dividing chives**
*Lift mature or over-crowded clumps out of the ground, using a garden fork.*

*Divide the chives into smaller clumps by prising the roots apart with your hands or a small fork.*

*Plant out the new divisions, without delay, in the desired position. Make sure that the chives are well watered.*

**Taking cuttings of shrubby herbs**
*Take a cutting of a semi-ripened shoot in summer. Neaten off the end by making a sharp diagonal cut with a knife.*

*Carefully strip the leaves off the lower end of the cutting to leave sufficient stem bare to insert into the compost. Do this gently with your hands.*

*Wet the bottom end of the cutting with water and dip it in a pot of hormone rooting powder, which will encourage roots to grow.*

*Fill trays or pots with seed compost or a half-sand, half-peat mixture. Using a matchstick, make holes in the compost and insert the cuttings.*

*Firm in the cuttings carefully with your fingertips, then gently water them; it is best to use a fine rose on a watering can to do this.*

*Cover the cuttings with a clear polythene bag, keeping the polythene off the leaves. Place on a warm windowsill but keep out of direct sunlight.*

**PRESERVING** Herbs can be dried in three ways. The traditional method is to tie them in small bunches so that air can circulate freely around the herbage, then hang them upside down in a warm, airy spot for a few days.

The modern alternative is to dry them in the dark on racks. Stretch muslin over a frame (alternatively use metal drying racks) and place leaves, still on the stem, on these. Spread out well in a single layer. Place another layer of muslin on top to keep off any dust and place the trays in a warm, dark place – either an airing cupboard, or the plate warming drawer of an oven, with the door left ajar is ideal. Check if they are ready after 24 hours. When dry, the leaves will feel dry and be brittle to the touch. They should still be green; if they have turned brown the heat was too intense and the flavour will have been lost. Store immediately after cooling in glass jars, preferably dark in colour but otherwise in the dark, to retain strength. Flowerheads should be dried in the same way. Remove as much stalk as possible and handle very carefully as they disintegrate easily.

It is also possible to dry herbs in a microwave. Lay out on a double layer of kitchen paper, place a second double layer of paper over the top and using the lowest setting on the microwave check every minute, turning the sandwich each time. They should be ready in 2-4 minutes.

Some herbs, in particular basil, parsley, chives, chervil, dill and tarragon, are difficult to dry successfully and are better frozen. Chop parsley and chives and store in small bags or add a little water and freeze in ice cube containers. Chervil, fennel, dill and tarragon can be left as small sprays and packed in plastic bags. Basil leaves are best picked off the stem and stored in the freezer in small bags.

# ANGELICA

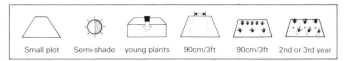

| | | | | | |
|---|---|---|---|---|---|
| Small plot | Semi-shade | young plants | 90cm/3ft | 90cm/3ft | 2nd or 3rd year |

Angelica is a lovely herb for the back of the garden, where it can act as a windbreak for more delicate herbs. Clusters of small greenish white flowers appear on the tops of the stems in the second year of growth.

**GROWING** It is easiest to buy your first angelica plant growing in a container and put it into a rich moist soil, in a partially shaded position, in spring. Once your plant is established, you can start to use the leaves, although for full flavour and scent you should wait until the second year. The seed which falls from the plant in the late summer of the second year will germinate early the following spring to provide a mass of seedlings growing round the old plant. Angelica can grow to 1.8m/6ft.

**HARVESTING** Gather leaves and flower stems in late spring and early summer. Cut off the flowerheads as they appear in summer, leaving one or two to set to seed.

**POSSIBLE PROBLEMS** Watch for leaf-mining caterpillars and remove affected leaves as soon as seen.

**USES** Candied angelica is well known as a cake decoration and can be easily made at home. Cut the young hollow stems into 5cm/2in lengths and boil them in a heavy sugar syrup until transparent and tender. Strain and allow the stems to dry completely before storing in screw-topped jars. They impart a delicious flavour when cooked with rhubarb or gooseberries.

# BALM

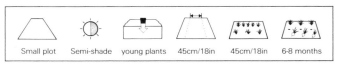

| | | | | | |
|---|---|---|---|---|---|
| Small plot | Semi-shade | young plants | 45cm/18in | 45cm/18in | 6-8 months |

Also known as Lemon Balm and Bee Balm, the leaves of this bushy plant carry a strong lemon fragrance; the flowers, insignificant in appearance, contain a lot of nectar and are very attractive to bees. A shorter form of balm, with yellow-variegated leaves, is more ornamental.

**GROWING** The scent of lemon balm will be strongest if it is grown in a fairly rich, moist soil. A sunny position is preferred. A plant bought from a herb nursery or garden centre and put in the garden in spring, can be increased in the autumn by root division.

**HARVESTING** Pick leaves as required after flowering throughout the summer.

**POSSIBLE PROBLEMS** Lemon balm spreads fairly rapidly so cut it back periodically to keep it a compact shape.

**USES** The chopped leaves, fresh or dried, can be used in recipes wherever a hint of lemon is called for. Try lemon balm in stuffings for lamb or pork, and cover a chicken with the leaves before roasting. Add to fruit drinks, wine cups, ice creams, fruit and vegetable salads, and to stewed fruit of all kinds. Melissa tea, made with the crushed leaves, is a refreshing drink sweetened with a little honey and taken hot or cold.

■ PRESERVING TIP

*Although angelica usually flowers in the second year it can take up to 4 or 5 years. After flowering the plant will die. If you want it to last for a further year remove the flower heads as soon as they appear. After harvesting large stalks for candied angelica remove the leaves and dry separately. Place on a rack in the dark in a warm, well-ventilated spot. They should then remain a bright green and retain their scent making them ideal for adding to pot pourri.*

■ GARDENER'S TIP

*Lemon balm, like mint, can quickly take over a herb bed so contain the roots by growing this plant in a container. If you prefer to grow balm in a herb or flower bed, plant it in a pot or bucket and sink this into the soil.*

# BASIL

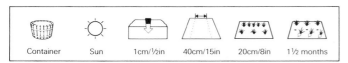

| Container | Sun | 1cm/½in | 40cm/15in | 20cm/8in | 1½ months |
|---|---|---|---|---|---|

There are two kinds of basil plants, sweet and bush. They are both treated as annuals in temperate climates. Sweet basil has largish, shiny, dark green leaves and bush basil has lots of small, pale green leaves and is good for growing in pots.

**GROWING** Basil has to be grown from seed or purchased as a pot plant. Sow seed in a rich, well-drained soil in a sunny, sheltered position out of doors after the danger of frost is over. Alternatively, sow in pots indoors. Plant out seedlings in summer and pinch out the flowerheads as they appear, allowing one plant or stem to flower and set seed for next year's plants. The compact habit of bush basil makes it ideal for container growing, where it will provide more leaves for use over a longer growing period.

**HARVESTING** The leaves are ready for picking about six weeks after the seedlings are planted out.

**POSSIBLE PROBLEMS** To avoid danger of damping-off disease, do not sow seed too thickly or over-water.

**USES** Basil is one of the best herbs to add to tomatoes and eggs, mushrooms and pasta dishes. It has a strong flavour, which tends to increase when the leaves are cooked. Fresh leaves are good in green salads and in oil and vinegar dressings. Add a tiny amount to butter sauces to accompany fish.

# BAY

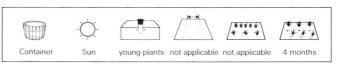

| Container | Sun | young plants | not applicable | not applicable | 4 months |
|---|---|---|---|---|---|

Bay, or sweet bay, forms a shrub-like evergreen tree. The glossy dark green leaves have a leathery texture; small yellow flowers bloom in early summer and are followed by purplish black berries. Bay is a good plant for container cultivation, when it can be trained into a pyramid, or a round-headed standard.

**GROWING** Good soil or compost, drainage and sun are essential, also shelter from cold winds. Bay will die quickly in a wet soil. It is easiest to buy a small bay plant from a herb nursery. Do not disturb the rootball when taking it out of its pot. Dig a hole large enough to accommodate the roots. Put the plant in the hole and gently fill in with soil, firming it down as you go. Tread round the plant to secure against wind. If grown in a pot or tub, bay can be taken indoors in a severe winter.

**HARVESTING** Once bay is established, the fully matured leaves can be picked for use. Pick and dry some leaves during the growing season for winter use, rather than pick them from the bush all the year round.

**POSSIBLE PROBLEMS** Scrape off any brown scale insects appearing on the undersides of leaves or on stems.

**USES** Add a bay leaf to the water when poaching fish; use a leaf in marinades. Bay leaves add their spicy flavour to meat and vegetables, soups and stews. Store a leaf or two in a jar of rice for a delicious flavour.

## ■ COOK'S TIP

*The famous Italian sauce Pesto is made from basil leaves and is delicious with fresh pasta. Use it, too, to enhance the flavour of minestrone. Place about 12 leaves, torn into small pieces, in a food processor with 3 garlic cloves and 100g/4oz Parmesan cheese. Slowly add to this 2 tablespoons olive oil until the mixture has a thick cream-like consistency. This sauce can be kept for a few days in the refrigerator or for some weeks in the freezer.*

## ■ COOK'S TIP

*A bay leaf is an essential part of the well-known culinary flavouring bouquet garni. This should also include 2 sprigs of parsley, 1 of thyme and 1 of marjoram. Tie together and use to flavour sauces, stews and casseroles.*

# BERGAMOT

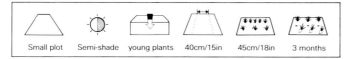

| Small plot | Semi-shade | young plants | 40cm/15in | 45cm/18in | 3 months |
|---|---|---|---|---|---|

One of the many varieties of bergamot, the *Monarda didyma* is also called bee balm because bees are so attracted by its scent. A perennial plant, bergamot is highly ornamental, producing vivid red flowers in early summer.

**GROWING** Plant bergamot in spring or autumn in a sunny moist spot. Some shade will be accepted. Clumps are prettiest as the flowers of single plants get lost amongst others in the border. After planting, put peat or leaf mould round the plants to keep the roots moist. The plants grow to 45cm-1m/1-3ft high, but they die down in winter, so use a stake to mark their position. Bergamot is easily increased by dividing the clumps in spring. To obtain bigger and better flowers for display, cut off all the flowerheads in the first season. The following year there will be a lovely show of much larger flowers.

**HARVESTING** Pick flowers and leaves in summer.

**POSSIBLE PROBLEMS** In early spring, watch for caterpillars and snails, which attack the new leaves.

**USES** Bergamot leaves and flowers dry well, retaining their scent and flavour, and make a delicious tea. A few dried crushed leaves mixed in with Indian tea adds a delicate flavour. Chopped leaves and flowers add flavour and colour to green salads, fruit and wine cups. Add leaves and flowers to fresh fruit salads and jellies.

# BORAGE

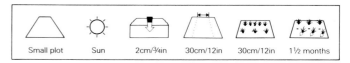

| Small plot | Sun | 2cm/¾in | 30cm/12in | 30cm/12in | 1½ months |
|---|---|---|---|---|---|

Borage is a tall, hairy-leaved annual with vivid blue star-shaped flowers. It is a strong-growing plant and continues to bloom for many months of the year. Both flowers and leaves have a fresh cucumber flavour.

**GROWING** Sow borage seeds in spring where they are to flower. Any soil and site will be suitable. Young plants should be thinned to leave at least 30cm/1ft between them. In a windy spot, it is best to stake the plants, because the many-branched fleshy stems become top heavy and after a downpour of rain or high winds will be found lying on the ground.

**HARVESTING** Seeds germinate quickly and the plants are fully grown in five to six weeks. Borage leaves are always used freshly picked.

**POSSIBLE PROBLEMS** Borage is not recommended for the small herb garden. It seeds itself freely, so keep it in check, or seedlings will come up all over the garden.

**USES** Pick only the young tender leaves, with a few fresh flowers and add them to green salads.

Candied borage flowers make a pretty decoration on cakes and ice creams and floating in a fruit salad. Dip the flowers first in beaten egg white, making sure they are completely covered, then into fine sugar. Leave the flowers to dry and harden on a nylon sieve. Candied in this way the flowers are for immediate use only.

---

■ COOK'S TIP

*Tea made from bergamot is soothing and was very popular with America's Oswego Indians. North Americans, when refusing to use British tea at the time of the Boston Tea Party, also took to drinking it. To make a cup of tea, fill the cup to be used, with cold water and pour into a saucepan. Bring to the boil, then add a teaspoonful of dried leaves and flowers, reduce heat and simmer gently for 5-6 minutes. The resulting tea is a rich wine red.*

---

■ ORGANIC TIP

*Borage is sometimes known as beebread because, like many other herbs, its scent and bright star-like blue flowers are very attractive to bees. Plant close to fruit or vegetables that require pollination.*

# CARAWAY

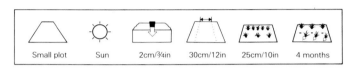

| Small plot | Sun | 2cm/¾in | 30cm/12in | 25cm/10in | 4 months |

Caraway is a feathery-leaved biennial plant grown mainly for the warm and spicy flavour of its fresh ripe seed, although the roots can be eaten too. Small white flowers are followed by the fruit in the second year.

**GROWING** Caraway can be sown in its flowering position in late spring or autumn. A well-drained soil and sunny place are important. Thin the seedlings to 25cm/10in apart. The plants reach their full height of 60cm/2ft in the second year. Once the seedheads have formed, keep a close watch to see when the seeds are ripe. To make sure no seeds are lost, cover the seedheads with fine muslin secured lightly round the stem.

**HARVESTING** When fully ripe, cut off the seedheads with long stems, tie the stems together and place the heads in a paper bag. Hang the bunches upside down so that when fully dried the seeds will fall into the bag. Dig up the roots for eating after harvesting the seeds.

**POSSIBLE PROBLEMS** As caraway takes over a year to flower and seed it is best to sow seeds as soon as they are ripe. Hoe around young plants to keep weeds at bay.

**USES** Caraway seeds can be used to flavour pork and liver, and vegetables such as cabbage, cauliflower and potatoes. The roots can be boiled and eaten like carrots with a parsley sauce. Use, too, in baking cakes, biscuits and buns, and sprinkle on Irish potato cakes.

# CHAMOMILE

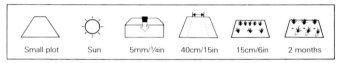

| Small plot | Sun | 5mm/¼in | 40cm/15in | 15cm/6in | 2 months |

There are two kinds of chamomile: *Matricaria chamomilla*, the true annual chamomile, and the Roman perennial chamomile, *Anthemis nobilis*, used for making lawns. Both are strongly aromatic. The true chamomile has white daisy-like flowers from late spring to mid autumn and fine needle-like leaves on a plant about 15cm/6in tall. Each plant produces many flowers, the only part of the herb which is used. Chamomile plants have for centuries been considered the physician of other plants and necessary for healthy life in the organic garden.

**GROWING** Very easy to grow from seed, chamomile prefers a dry, sunny position. Sow seed in early spring where it is to flower and keep seeds watered until the leaves appear. Thin the plants to 15cm/6in apart.

**HARVESTING** Flowers will appear eight weeks from sowing, and should be picked as soon as they open. The flowers can be used fresh or dried. Dry on nylon netting in an airing cupboard and store the flowers in glass screw-topped jars.

**POSSIBLE PROBLEMS** Mix sand with the tiny seeds to make sowing more even.

**USES** Chamomile makes a soothing tea for stomach upsets and indigestion, and with a spoonful of honey added, is a pleasant tonic or pick-me-up.

---

▩ PRESERVING TIP

*Caraway seeds add spicy fragrance to pot pourri and help to retain the scent of other herbs used in the mixture. Dry, then crush, the seeds before adding them to the other ingredients.*

▩ HEALTH TIP

*A relaxing bath additive, chamomile will perfume the water and help to cleanse the skin. Use a square of muslin tied with ribbon to form a bag to hold the flowers and tie the bag by length of ribbon to the hot tap so it lies in the water as the bath*

*fills. If you have fair hair use chamomile to lighten and condition it. Add a small cup of flowers to 150ml/¼ pint purified water. Pour boiling water over the flowers for a facial steam bath.*

## CHERVIL

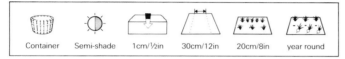

| Container | Semi-shade | 1cm/½in | 30cm/12in | 20cm/8in | year round |

Chervil is an annual with lacy foliage and clusters of little white flowers, which appear from early to late summer. The flavour is sweet and aromatic, reminiscent of aniseed, and the leaves are best used fresh.

**GROWING** Chervil seeds germinate so quickly that with successive sowings it is possible to have a supply of fresh leaves almost all the year round. From early spring to late summer, sow seed where the plants are to grow, in well-drained garden soil in partial shade. When they are large enough, thin the seedlings to 20cm/8in apart. Remove flowers when they appear. The plants die down in winter but will come up very early in spring, long before many other herbs appear. Chervil can also be grown in window boxes and containers.

**HARVESTING** Chervil leaves can be used when the plant is about 10cm/4in high.

**POSSIBLE PROBLEMS** Leaves wilt quickly and the flavour is soon lost. Avoid sowing chervil where it will be in the summer sun a few weeks after germinating, or it will bolt and die quickly, especially if dry.

**USES** The chopped fresh leaves are at their most delicious in chervil soup. Add to butter sauces to go with delicate vegetables and to green salads. As a garnish, use chervil generously over pork or veal chops and beef steaks. Sprinkle over glazed carrots and peas.

### ■ GARDENER'S TIP

*Pick leaves, especially in the early stages, from the outside of the plant so the plant continues to grow from the centre. If chervil is not permitted to flower, but instead cut almost back to the ground, it will continue to produce leaves until heavy frost occur.*

## CHIVES

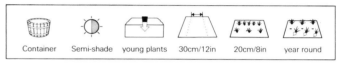

| Container | Semi-shade | young plants | 30cm/12in | 20cm/8in | year round |

A clump of chives is essential in the herb garden. The neat growing habit of chives makes them good edging plants in the herb bed, and if one or two clumps are left to bloom, their bright mauve pompom flowers provide a splash of colour.

**GROWING** Chives do best in a rich, damp soil and in sun or partial shade. They can be grown from seed sown in spring but germination is slow. It is quicker to divide clumps of established bulbs in spring or autumn. Grow several clumps of chives in order to have a succession of new growth and use the plants in rotation. Remove the flowers when they appear to keep the flavour in the leaves. Cover with cloches in autumn through winter, or dig up a small clump in autumn and transfer it to a pot to take indoors, where it will continue growing in the warmth. In spring throw out the exhausted plant.

**HARVESTING** Make sure new plants are well established before picking the leaves.

**POSSIBLE PROBLEMS** Do not allow the plants to dry out. At intervals during the growing season, feed them with a liquid fertilizer.

**USES** Chives chopped finely add a delicate onion flavour to soups, sauces and salad dressings. Blend chives with cream cheese or butter to use as a topping for baked potatoes and use to perk up fish and egg dishes.

### ■ FREEZER TIP

*Chives thrive when cut constantly. Use scissors to do this. This is not a suitable herb to dry, instead chop up leaves into short lengths of about 5mm/¼in and freeze with a little water in ice cube containers.*

# DILL

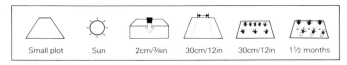

| | | | | | |
|---|---|---|---|---|---|
| Small plot | Sun | 2cm/¾in | 30cm/12in | 30cm/12in | 1½ months |

A decorative herb, dill looks at its best when a number of plants are clumped together in the herb bed. The needle-like leaves, and tiny yellow flowers from early to late summer, make it difficult to distinguish from fennel. Both the aromatic leaves and seeds are used.

**GROWING** Sow seed where it is to grow, in a well-drained soil and a sunny position. Cover the seed with a light sprinkling of soil. Make successive sowings from mid spring to early summer for a continuous supply of leaves. Stake the plant if the site is windy. Cut off the flowers of some of the plants as they appear so you can pick and use the leaves. Other plants can be left to go to seed. As soon as the flower-heads are brown, the seeds are ripe. The whole plant should then be cut down and the seed drying completed indoors.

**HARVESTING** Leaves can be used from six weeks after germination.

**POSSIBLE PROBLEMS** Watch for aphids.

**USES** Dill leaves make a particularly good sauce to go with fish. Add chopped leaves to green and raw vegetables, especially cucumber, and sprinkle over grilled lamb chops. Use whole or ground dill seed in lamb stews, herb butters, bean soups and in pickled baby cucumbers. Dill seed tea is good for the digestion and will also help you to sleep.

## ▪ PRESERVING TIP

*Leave the seeds on the plant until they start to turn brown, usually in late summer, and then harvest. If left to ripen completely on the plant they can easily fall to the ground and be lost. Cut off the stems that hold the seedheads and tie a few together with elastic bands to form small bunches. Hang upside down in a dry, airy shed. Place a cotton cloth spread out in a bowl below to catch the falling seeds. Store seeds in a tightly sealed container.*

# FENNEL

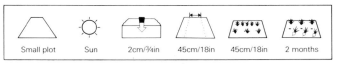

| | | | | | |
|---|---|---|---|---|---|
| Small plot | Sun | 2cm/¾in | 45cm/18in | 45cm/18in | 2 months |

Fennel is highly ornamental and grows up to 1.5m/5ft high. Tiny yellow flowers come in mid/late summer. The bluish-green needle-like leaves, the sweeter aniseed flavour, and the size of the plant help to distinguish it from dill. The seeds, which are dried for use, are oval in shape and have a much stronger flavour than the leaf.

**GROWING** Sow the seed in spring, in well-drained good garden soil and in a sunny position. If seed is not required, remove flower stems as they appear. Otherwise, leave some flowers on the plants to go to seed.

**HARVESTING** The seeds are ready to harvest when hard and a grey-green colour. Cut off the heads and complete the drying indoors.

**POSSIBLE PROBLEMS** Staking may be needed for this tall plant. Keep weeds under control; water fennel well in dry weather.

**USES** Seeds or leaves give an excellent flavour when added to the water for poached or boiled fish. Use the chopped leaves in fish sauces, or as a garnish to counteract the oiliness of rich fish. Add leaves to salads and raw or cooked vegetables, and try finely chopped leaves sprinkled over buttered new potatoes. Seeds can be used whole or ground to flavour bread, savoury biscuits, soups and sweet pickles. Fennel tea, made with leaves or seeds, is good for the digestion.

## ▪ GARDENER'S TIP

*If the seeds of fennel are required for culinary purposes it is important to sow seeds under cover in early or mid spring, then transplant them to the spot where they are to be grown. This early start allows time for the seeds to ripen.*

# HORSERADISH

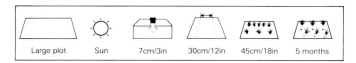

| | | | | | |
|---|---|---|---|---|---|
| Large plot | Sun | 7cm/3in | 30cm/12in | 45cm/18in | 5 months |

Horseradish is a hardy perennial with large floppy leaves growing from the base of the plant. The flowers are white on a single stem but they do not appear every season. The large thick roots are used sparingly, because of their hot flavour.

**GROWING** Plant 7-cm/3-in long root cuttings in a rich, moist soil in early spring, 30cm/1ft apart, just covered with soil. An open sunny place is best. These will establish to produce new plants. Lift all the plants in autumn, cut and store the larger roots in sand for winter use, and retain the smaller roots, also in sand, for planting the following spring. This ensures a constant supply of the best quality roots.

**HARVESTING** Established roots can be dug up as required, but the flavour is improved by cold weather.

**POSSIBLE PROBLEMS** The roots can become a great invader, so grow horseradish where it can be confined.

**USES** Horseradish is primarily used as a condiment, grated into cream, and makes a pleasant change from mustard. It is a superb accompaniment to roast or boiled beef. Add grated raw root to coleslaw and uncooked vegetable chutneys. Horseradish sauce helps in the digestion of rich smoked fish, such as eel, mackerel or herring. Horseradish paste made with cream cheese makes a tasty sandwich filling.

# HYSSOP

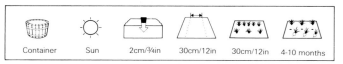

| | | | | | |
|---|---|---|---|---|---|
| Container | Sun | 2cm/¾in | 30cm/12in | 30cm/12in | 4-10 months |

A hardy evergreen perennial with a long flowering season, hyssop is a good herb to grow in garden or pot. It has woody stems and small pointed leaves which are pleasantly pungent. Hyssop flowers grow in long spikes of either blue or deep pink and have a heavy fragrant scent; they are loved by bees and butterflies. Hyssop leaves, the part used, have a slightly bitter taste, between rosemary and lavender.

**GROWING** Sow seed in spring in well-drained soil and a sunny position. You can increase the number of plants by taking stem cuttings 5cm/2in long in mid/late spring; they soon take root. Hyssop also reseeds itself and the seedlings come true to form. It grows to about 60cm/2ft. After three or four years, the plants become too woody and need replacing.

**HARVESTING** Remove the leaves for drying when the flower buds first appear and before flowering. Lay out in a warm and well-ventilated spot until brittle to the touch.

**POSSIBLE PROBLEMS** Cut hyssop back after the flowers have died to maintain a neat shape.

**USES** The faintly minty taste of hyssop leaves gives an unusual tang to green salads and vegetable soups. Hyssop is traditionally added to cranberries, stewed peaches or apricots, and to fruit drinks, tarts and pies. An infusion of hyssop makes a good cough syrup.

---

## ▓ GARDENER'S TIP

*For replanting in early spring, use roots of pencil thickness and plant in holes made with a dibber at an angle of 45° with the thick end uppermost. Seed can also be sown in early spring and the plants thinned to 30cm/12in apart.*

## ▓ ORGANIC TIP

*To help relieve colds and coughs make hyssop tea. Place 2 to 3 tsp dried flowers in a tea pot and pour over boiling water. Leave to infuse for about 8 minutes. A cup of this liquid can be drunk hot or cold, three times a day. To dry the flowers remove from the plant* *before the sun shines on it and when the flowers first appear, as this is when the volatile oils are strongest. Spread out on foil and dry slowly at the lowest oven setting with the door ajar.*

# LOVAGE

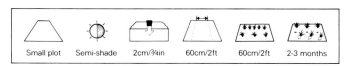

| | | | | | |
|---|---|---|---|---|---|
| Small plot | Semi-shade | 2cm/¾in | 60cm/2ft | 60cm/2ft | 2-3 months |

Lovage is a vigorous, handsome perennial. Greenish yellow flowers are followed by oblong deep brown seeds. All parts of the plant can be used for flavouring and have a pleasant yeasty taste, rather like celery.

**GROWING** Lovage grows well in a moist soil in either sun or partial shade. It can be raised from seed sown in early autumn in pots or seed boxes filled with compost. Cover the boxes with wire netting to stop the birds eating the seed, and leave the boxes in a sheltered place. In the spring, plant out the seedlings. In a good year, lovage will seed itself and in spring the seedlings appear near the parent plant. It can grow up to 2m/6ft tall. Towards the end of the season, leave one or two flowerheads to go to seed.

**HARVESTING** During the summer, when leaves are needed for cooking, freezing and drying, keep cutting off the flowerheads as they appear.

**POSSIBLE PROBLEMS** As lovage seeds only have germination power for a short period, harvest when they are just ripe on the plant, then immediately sow them.

**USES** Lovage soup is delicious and can be made from fresh or dried leaves. Chopped fresh leaves, young stalks or lovage seeds can be added to meat stews in place of celery. Use lovage leaves with boiled ham, in salads and with haricot beans.

# MARIGOLD

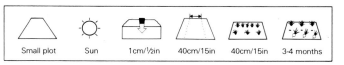

| | | | | | |
|---|---|---|---|---|---|
| Small plot | Sun | 1cm/½in | 40cm/15in | 40cm/15in | 3-4 months |

The cottage garden marigold, *Calendula officinalis*, or pot marigold, has long been popular as a flavouring.

**GROWING** Sow seed in early spring for summer flowering or in early autumn for late spring flowering the following year. A light, rich soil is best but marigolds do well even on poor soils. Water well and thin the plants when the seedlings are large enough to handle. Pinch out the growing points to encourage bushy growth. Keep weeds down until the plants are large enough to suppress them. Marigolds reach about 30cm/12in in height and can be grown in pots as well as in the border.,

**HARVESTING** Pick flowers for use when they are fully open. If you keep removing the flowerheads new blossoms will be produced for months.

**POSSIBLE PROBLEMS** Caterpillars eat the stems and leaves. Leaves may be spotted with smut in wet weather.

**USES** Use the petals, fresh or dried, to add a delicate colour and aroma to savoury rice, egg and cheese dishes. The fresh petals bring brightness and nutrition to a green salad.

■ PRESERVING TIP

*Use young leaves, still on their stalks, and dry at the oven's lowest temperature with the door ajar. Allow 1-2 hours for small quantities. When dry, the leaves will be brittle. Rub them off the stalks, keep in airtight containers in the dark. You can also dry herbs in the microwave. In this case sandwich small quantities between layers of kitchen paper. Use a low setting, check each minute and turn the sandwich over. Drying will usually take 2-4 minutes.*

■ PRESERVING TIP

*Petals for drying should be gathered when the flowers are fully opened and perfect. They are as vivid when dry as when in full bloom. Add to a pot-pourri mixture or use in cooking in place of saffron.*

# MARJORAM

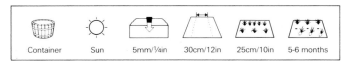

| Container | Sun | 5mm/¼in | 30cm/12in | 25cm/10in | 5-6 months |

Of the three forms of marjoram, the sweet, or knotted, annual marjoram has by far the best flavour for cooking. It is sweet and spicy but mild compared to the others. Wild marjoram is sometimes called oregano, from its Italian name; a perennial, it has the strongest spiciest taste of the three. The flavour of pot marjoram is not so pronounced as in the other marjorams. Combining the flavour of wild and sweet marjoram is a perennial named Daphne ffiske: the result is the best flavour with the growing habits of the perennial.

**GROWING** *Sweet* (knotted) *marjoram:* sow the fine seed mixed with sand under glass in early spring. Plant out seedlings in light, rich soil and a sunny, sheltered position. *Pot Marjoram:* propagate by seed sown in early spring or by rooted cuttings taken in autumn or spring. Ideal for growing in containers and indoors. *Wild marjoram:* easy to grow from seed sown in spring or by division of roots taken in spring or autumn. *Daphne ffiske:* grow in a pot either outside or indoors where it can be in the sun.

**HARVESTING** Marjoram leaves can be easily dried; gather sprigs just before the flowers appear.

**USES** The annual or the new perennial marjorams can be used sparingly in meat dishes and in salads. Marjoram adds good flavour to potatoes and pulses.

# MINT

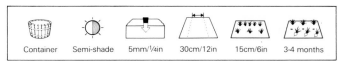

| Container | Semi-shade | 5mm/¼in | 30cm/12in | 15cm/6in | 3-4 months |

Common or garden mint (spearmint) is probably one of the oldest culinary herbs to be used in the Mediterranean region, and the best known of the mints. The long spikes of lilac flowers are a hit with bees. Peppermint and apple mint have the same growing requirements and are also enjoyed for their distinctive flavours.

**GROWING** In spring, sow mint seed in pots or boxes filled with compost and cover them with a piece of glass and newspaper until the seeds germinate. When the seedlings are large enough, set them out in the herb bed. Moisture and partial shade are the chief requirements. Spearmint grows to a height of about 30cm/12in, and is the best mint for window box and container growing, so long as the soil is kept moist.

**HARVESTING** Pick a few leaves from each plant as required. Cut right back in early summer to encourage a second crop in the autumn.

**POSSIBLE PROBLEMS** Mint is an invasive grower; in a small herb bed the plants can be restricted by surrounding them with old roofing slates sunk into the ground to a depth of 15-20cm/6-8in. The fungus disease rust can infect them, and such plants are best destroyed.

**USES** As well as using to make mint sauce and adding to the cooking water for peas and new potatoes, try mint with other young vegetables.

■ GARDENER'S TIP

*To divide roots of pot or wild marjoram, lift the plant out of the soil and pull it into two separate sections at the centre. Break off young shoots from the outer sides, cut the leaves back to 2.5cm/1in from the roots and replant.*

■ PRESERVING TIP

*Mint can be stored in a box of compost to provide fresh winter supplies. Dig up a clump of mint and remove some of the sprigs with roots, then replant the rest. In a wooden box put a layer of moist compost, lay the sprigs on their sides in the compost and*

*cover with more compost. Remove, cut and wash when required. Spearmint also dries well (see lovage for directions). In the Middle East dried mint is used in preference to fresh mint.*

# PARSLEY

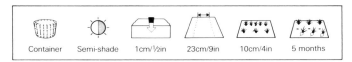

| Container | Semi-shade | 1cm/½in | 23cm/9in | 10cm/4in | 5 months |

The curly-leaved variety of parsley is the most widely used, perhaps because it makes an attractive garnish, but French, or flat-leaved parsley has more flavour. Parsley is a good plant for edging the herb garden, and ideal for container growing outside or indoors.

**GROWING** Though parsley is a hardy biennial, flowering in the second year of growth, it is usually treated as an annual and new seed is sown every year. Parsley does best in moist, slightly heavy soils and a shady position. Seed can be sown outdoors from early spring onwards, but if left until late spring, will germinate within ten days because of the increased warmth of the soil. Otherwise it can take three to five weeks. A second sowing in early mid summer will provide leaves through the winter. Thin the seedlings to 20cm/8in apart. Plants will sometimes grow on for two or three years. To ensure a long life for the plants, cut off all flowering heads in the second year.

**HARVESTING** Take only a few leaves at a time from curly-leaved parsley plants or you can affect growth.

**POSSIBLE PROBLEMS** Water well in dry weather to prevent bolting, and infestation by aphids.

**USES** Apart from its traditional use as a garnish, fresh chopped parsley is a good seasoning herb to add to meats, casseroles, soups, vegetables, stuffings, salads and eggs. Parsley is full of vitamins.

■ ORGANIC TIP

*Allow one parsley plant to flower and go to seed. This will provide you with continuous plants as parsley self-seeds. Cut the flower stems off all other plants to extend the period when leaves will be produced. Parsley, especially the curly-leaved*

*variety, is not hardy in a severe winter so protect plants with cloches. This will also extend the season when you can cut fresh parsley.*

# ROSEMARY

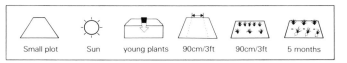

| Small plot | Sun | young plants | 90cm/3ft | 90cm/3ft | 5 months |

A strongly aromatic evergreen shrub, rosemary's small, narrow, grey-green leaves and blue flowers in late spring make it an ornamental addition to the herb garden. Eventually it grows up to 1.2m/4ft high. A dwarf variety is a neat alternative for a small garden or pot.

**GROWING** It is a slow process to produce rosemary from seed; it is best to start by buying a plant from a herb nursery or garden centre. In April, set the plant in a dry sunny spot towards the back of the herb garden. Increase the stock of plants by 5-7.5cm/2-3in cuttings of new shoot tips taken with or without a heel between mid spring and late summer. Place them in sandy compost and a warm, shaded place. In the autumn, cut back half the year's growth on a mature plant.

**HARVESTING** Although it is a slow-growing shrub, once the plant is established you can begin to use the leaves. Late summer is the best time to harvest for drying.

**POSSIBLE PROBLEMS** Protect young rosemary plants from frost in winter. Put a good layer of straw or leaves around the plant and surround it with wire netting.

**USES** Rosemary has a strong, spicy, sweet flavour which combines well in both sweet and savoury dishes. Add it, fresh or dried, to roast lamb and to beef or chicken casserole. Sprinkle it over potatoes when roasting and use it with other vegetables.

■ COOK'S TIP

*Make a herbal oil to add to salad dressings and marinades. To 600ml/1 pint green olive oil add 2 branches rosemary, 2 sprigs thyme, a few black peppercorns and a peeled and cut garlic clove. Seal and leave for two weeks.*

## SAGE

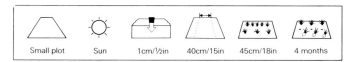

| Small plot | Sun | 1cm/½in | 40cm/15in | 45cm/18in | 4 months |
|---|---|---|---|---|---|

Garden sage is a strongly flavoured, small evergreen shrub. Varieties of sage, which have the same flavour, include Tricolor, with variegated leaves of white, green and purple-red, Icterina, with yellow-edged leaves, and purple-flushed Purpurascens.

**GROWING** Sage grows in any soil, provided it is well drained and in a sunny place. It can be grown successfully from seed sown in the early spring under glass and transplanted in late spring into the open ground. Alternatively, take cuttings from an established plant in late spring and put straight into the open ground. Plants should be 40-45cm/16-18in apart. When plants become leggy, pinch out the growing tips or cut the plants right back. Because sage plants become very woody over the seasons, renew every three or four years.

**HARVESTING** Garden sage produces leaves through the year which can be cut when needed. Decorative sages are not usually hardy so pot and bring indoors for the winter.

**POSSIBLE PROBLEMS** Stem cuttings or layering of side shoots are the only ways to increase the number of purple sage plants because its seed does not grow true to form but reverts to green-leaved sage.

**USES** Sage is most often used with roast pork but is also good with duck and sprinkled on to meat stews.

## ■ GARDENER'S TIP

*To increase by layering make a slanting cut in the underside of a thick stem. Dab the cut into rooting powder and bend the stem at this point, pushing it into the ground. Hold in place with a peg until rooted , then cut off from the main plant.*

## SALAD BURNET

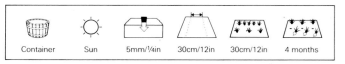

| Container | Sun | 5mm/¼in | 30cm/12in | 30cm/12in | 4 months |
|---|---|---|---|---|---|

Salad burnet forms a flat rosette of leaves on the ground, from which slender flowering stems grow up to 30cm/12in high. It is a hardy perennial and will stay green through a mild winter. The small, round red flowerheads bloom for three months in the summer.

**GROWING** You can buy the first plant from a herb nursery or grow salad burnet from seed. Set your plant in a sunny spot and renew the herb every year. In late winter or early spring, sow seed in boxes filled with a mixture of sand and compost. When the seedlings are large enough, prick them out into pots or seed boxes. Gradually harden off the plants and in late spring set them in their flowering positions, 30cm/12in apart. Salad burnet self-sows freely. To keep the flavour of the herb in the leaves, cut off the flowering heads as they appear.

**HARVESTING** Start to harvest leaves when the first flower shoots appear and cut when required. Cut the plant back periodically to 10-12.5cm/4-5in to ensure a continuing supply of young leaves.

**POSSIBLE PROBLEMS** This wild herb is easy to grow and should cause no problems. Do not try to transplant.

**USES** Mainly a salad herb as its name suggests, burnet leaves are at their best when used fresh. Add them to green and raw vegetable salads. Burnet vinegar has a delicious flavour, useful in making French dressing.

## ■ COOK'S TIP

*To make salad burnet vinegar, heat 450ml/¾pint of vinegar to boiling point then pour this over ½ cup of salad burnet leaves which have previously been chopped, crushed and put in a heat-proof bowl (not metal). Pound the leaves in the vinegar* *then leave to cool. Pour the herbal vinegar mixture into a tall storage or jam jar, cork and shake every few days for two weeks. Strain and rebottle adding a few fresh leaves. Include basil and borage for extra flavour.*

# SORREL

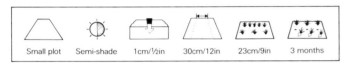

| | | | | | |
|---|---|---|---|---|---|
| Small plot | Semi-shade | 1cm/½in | 30cm/12in | 23cm/9in | 3 months |

Sorrel is a herbaceous perennial plant, dying down to ground level in autumn. The leaves are fleshy, light green and rather rounded; the tiny pink-red flowers that appear in early to mid summer should be removed.

**GROWING** A moist, fertile soil, such as a well-broken-down clay, gives good leaf size and succulence. Put in young plants in spring or autumn, 23cm/9in apart. Sun is preferred but sorrel will grow in shade.

**HARVESTING** Cut one or two leaves from each plant when individual plants have formed a group of more than five leaves, usually about three months after plants start to grow. Continue to harvest as required until the plants die back in autumn.

**POSSIBLE PROBLEMS** Soup recipes recommend 450g/1lb of leaves at a time, so a large harvest is needed. Whether you include this unusual herb in the kitchen garden depends upon how much space you want to devote to its cultivation.

**USES** Sorrel makes the famous and delicious sorrel soup, so popular in France, with a pleasantly sour flavour. It goes well with salads, and other vegetables, if used in moderation.

# SUMMER SAVORY

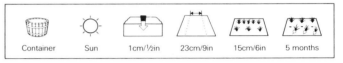

| | | | | | |
|---|---|---|---|---|---|
| Container | Sun | 1cm/½in | 23cm/9in | 15cm/6in | 5 months |

An attractive herb, summer savory is a bushy, low-growing annual, with tiny lilac flowers continuing from mid summer to early autumn. The long, narrow leaves have a spicy flavour. Summer savory is an excellent plant to grow in a pot or window box. Another form of savory is the perennial winter savory. Although it is easy to grow, its flavour is not so delicate as that of summer savory.

**GROWING** Summer savory should be grown in a light, rich soil and a sunny position. Sow seeds in their flowering position in late spring and thin the plants to 15cm/6in apart.

**HARVESTING** Summer savory is best used when fresh, but it dries well and the plant should be harvested for drying when it is in full flower.

**POSSIBLE PROBLEMS** Problems in germination are probably due to too thick a covering on the seeds which germinate by light. Seeds also need damp conditions during sowing but fully grown plants are not normally sensitive to dry conditions.

**USES** As a seasoning herb, use summer savory with meats, fish and eggs. Add to all kinds of beans and sprinkle on to vegetable soup and meat broth. Put fresh sprigs into wine vinegar and leave to permeate. Use the vinegar to make a tasty French dressing.

## ■ FREEZING TIP

*Build up a supply of sorrel leaves in the freezer until you have enough for soup-making. Wash, pat dry then place in plastic bags. If you want to preserve large quantities of sorrel it is best to blanch the leaves before freezing.*

## ■ PRESERVING TIP

*Well dried, summer savory will keep its flavour for a long time. Place cut sprigs on a frame and cover with net. Allow plenty of surrounding air flow. Place in a dark shed or cupboard where the temperature will not rise above 35C/95F. When leaves are dry* *they feel crisp but should retain their green colour. Reject any that turn brown. This happens when the drying temperature is too high. Rub leaves off the stalks and place these in an airtight container in the dark.*

## SWEET CICELY

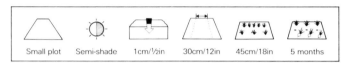

| | | | | | |
|---|---|---|---|---|---|
| Small plot | Semi-shade | 1cm/½in | 30cm/12in | 45cm/18in | 5 months |

Sweet Cicely is an ornamental perennial growing about 60cm/2ft high. Cut off the flowers that appear in late spring to retain the full aniseed flavour in the leaves. Let one or two remain to set seed. The seeds are long and jet black.

**GROWING** Easily grown, Sweet Cicely prefers a moist, deep soil and a little shade. Plant it in spring or autumn. Sweet Cicely self-seeds readily if the flowerheads are not cut off, so once you have purchased your first plant, you will have no problem in increasing the number. In the autumn, cut the large stems off at the base of the plant and leave the herb to die right down. Seed sown in autumn will produce seedlings the following spring.

**HARVESTING** Gather the leaves throughout the summer months and collect the seeds on any remaining flowerheads as they ripen.

**POSSIBLE PROBLEMS** Sweet Cicely's taproots go down very deeply, so be careful about where it is planted; the mature herb, once over a year old, cannot be moved to another part of the garden successfully.

**USES** Add finely chopped leaves when cooking gooseberries or rhubarb. Sweet Cicely reduces the acidity of tart fruits and less sugar is needed. It gives a delicious flavour when cooked with vegetables, too – particularly cabbage and swede.

## TANSY

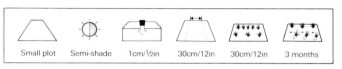

| | | | | | |
|---|---|---|---|---|---|
| Small plot | Semi-shade | 1cm/½in | 30cm/12in | 30cm/12in | 3 months |

A hardy perennial, 30-60cm/1-2ft tall with feathery leaves, tansy's yellow flowers appear in clusters from mid summer to early autumn. The common name comes from *Athanaton* – immortal – possibly because it lasts so long in flower, and its popular name, buttons, exactly describes the flower shape. Tansy has a curious, strong odour, not unpleasant and rather like camphor.

**GROWING** Tansy is easily grown from seed and is not fussy about either soil or situation. Alternatively, it can be grown by dividing the creeping roots. If cultivating by division, plant 30cm/1ft apart. The plant dies down in autumn.

**HARVESTING** Tansy has a bitter taste so use with care, cutting leaves as required. Dry for winter use.

**POSSIBLE PROBLEMS** This attractive herb can become invasive, so take care that it does not take up more of the herb garden than you would like it to.

**USES** Tansy can take the place of mint in sauce served with lamb and can be used in omelette and pancakes. Tansy cakes and tansy sauce were very popular in Elizabethan times and later.

### ■ DECORATIVE TIP

*To make a herb tuzzie muzzie start with a flowering herb in the centre, surround this with circles of herbs, mixing leaf shapes and colours. Tie each circle in place. Border with Sweet Cicely leaves and finally tie with a ribbon.*

### ■ ORGANIC TIP

*Tansy leaves with their medicinal smell can be used to keep away ants, fleas and flies. Keep a few fresh leaves in a food cupboard to repel ants, or in a pet bed to put off fleas. Add these very decorative frilled leaves to a flower arrangement to keep away flies. Pennyroyal is also disliked by ants. Cut a few leaves and rub these over the point where the ants enter the house and they will not cross the area.*

## TARRAGON

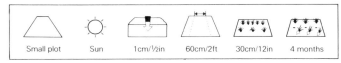

| Small plot | Sun | 1cm/½in | 60cm/2ft | 30cm/12in | 4 months |

French tarragon, *Artemisia dracunculus*, with its distinctive, slightly sweet-flavoured leaves, is one of the best culinary herbs for savoury cooking and no herb collection should be without it. It is a delicately bushy perennial plant, growing to 60-90cm/2-3ft. The Russian variety, *A. dracunculoides*, is inferior in flavour.

**GROWING** Tarragon needs a sunny, well-drained position in good garden soil. It will need feeding during the growing season to reach its full flavour. As tarragon does not set seed in temperate climates, propagate by taking cuttings of rooted shoots. Start by growing three or four plants set 30cm/12in apart in spring or autumn. Cut down plants in late autumn and protect from frost by covering them with leaves or straw.

**HARVESTING** Once the plant is established, leaves can be picked for use in the kitchen.

**POSSIBLE PROBLEMS** To keep it growing vigorously and prevent any risk of disease, tarragon should be divided every four years and replanted in fresh soil in the early spring.

**USES** Make tarragon vinegar by steeping the fresh herb in white wine vinegar. Use it when making French dressing. Add tarragon to roast meat, poultry dishes and fish. It is delicious in light buttery sauces to serve with mild-flavoured vegetables like marrow and artichokes.

### ■ GARDENER'S TIP

*To take a cutting, cut off the top 10cm/4in from a healthy stem with plenty of leaves. Remove the lower leaves, dip the cutting into water then rooting powder and place in moist cutting compost. Keep out of direct sunlight.*

## THYME

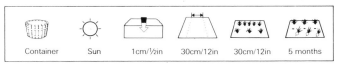

| Container | Sun | 1cm/½in | 30cm/12in | 30cm/12in | 5 months |

There are a large number of thymes that can be grown for their scent and as decorative plants, but for cooking the best flavours come from the common or garden thyme, *Thymus vulgaris*, and lemon thyme, *T. citriodorus*. Garden thyme is an evergreen shrubby perennial. Whorls of little mauve flowers bloom from early summer to late summer. Lemon thyme has a rather more trailing habit of growth. Thyme is a good container plant and can be used throughout the winter months.

**GROWING** Grow thyme in a dry sunny place in light, well-drained soil. Raise plants from seed sown in spring where they are to flower and thin the seedlings to 30cm/12in apart. Common thyme grows easily from seed. Lemon thyme is best bought as a plant. Thyme is easily increased from cuttings of shoot tips in summer.

**HARVESTING** Harvest thyme for drying when it is in full flower.

**POSSIBLE PROBLEMS** Cover the plants with leaves or straw in winter to protect from frost.

**USES** Use a little fresh chopped or dried thyme in stuffings and try finely chopped fresh leaves on potato purée, glazed carrots and other vegetables. Its fragrant leaves are an essential ingredient in bouquet garni, the seasoning posy used in all good cooking. Add sparingly to meats and fish, soups, stews and herb sauces.

### ■ GARDENER'S TIP

*To keep plants bushy and avoid woody stems, remove the growing tips regularly. To do this, pinch out the tiny new leaves between your thumb and index finger. Take cuttings in the same way as for tarragon.*

# SOFT FRUIT

Soft fruits have a long life, and because propagation is generally very easy, provide their own offspring so that you can continue to enjoy berries from new plants when the parents are exhausted. From raspberries and strawberries sweet enough to be served just as they are to refreshingly tart gooseberries, soft fruits offer a marvellous range of flavours. Strawberries alone among soft fruits cannot be frozen – all can be made into delectable jams and jellies. The high vitamin, mineral and fibre content of these fruits makes a useful contribution to a healthy diet.

**GROWING REQUIREMENTS**  Because they occupy the ground for so long, as a general rule fruits need deep, well-drained but moisture-retentive, fertile soil. If your garden soil falls short of the ideal, it is well worth putting some effort into improving it by deep digging and incorporating as much bulky organic material as you can obtain.

During their life, fruit bushes need regular feeding and watering. This seems like stating the obvious, but it is easy to forget how important it is to nourish the permanent features of your garden in a busy summer making sure your lettuces don't bolt and earthing up your potatoes. A dressing of general purpose fertilizer worked in in spring is needed by many fruits.

The blueberry is an example of an unusual soft fruit that needs relatively little attention. If time is one of the commodities you are short of, it is worth growing a fruit like this.

If you have a large, sunny enclosed garden and plenty of time at your disposal, you can grow a whole range of fruits that thrive in a temperate climate.

Long hours of sunshine are crucial to ripening tender subjects like peaches, but not all fruits are so demanding. Only gardens in warm districts can support late-ripening apple varieties and dessert gooseberries, for example, but those in cooler zones will have successful results by choosing early-ripening varieties of all species. In between is the vast majority of varieties specially raised to do well almost anywhere.

**PRUNING AND TRAINING**  As with tree fruits, fruit bushes need pruning from time to time and for the same reasons. The main purpose of pruning is to keep the plant at an acceptable size and compact shape. This in turn encourages the formation of healthy fruits that are easy to harvest. A neglected bush with overcrowded and tangled stems will be prone to diseases and disorders, while what few fruits there are will be difficult to get at. For all pruning operations it is essential to have good equipment kept in perfect condition. A pair of secateurs is indispensable. Training systems make the most of every inch of space. In a tiny garden, grow gooseberries, apples and pears as cordons, with strawberries in a barrel.

***Black currants***  Black currants bear their fruit on two-year-old wood. To make sure the bushes have a healthy proportion of new (light) and old (dark) wood, prune established bushes every winter, taking out completely about one third of the old wood. Make a clean cut 2.5cm/1in from the nearest break. Leave behind and untouched as much of the new wood as you can; misplaced or diseased wood should of course be cut out.

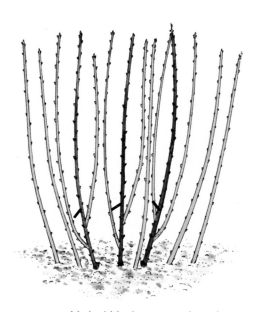

*In winter, prune established black currant plants by removing one-third of the old wood.*

If you inherit some neglected black currant bushes, revitalize them by pruning away all the old wood (which will be at the centre of the bush); and any broken or misplaced branches, old or new. Feed and water the bush carefully to help it back to productivity.

*Red and white currants* Unlike black currants, which shoot up from beneath the soil, red and white currant bushes sit on a short leg from which, ideally, 8 lateral branches radiate. If you are starting with cuttings, nick out with a sharp knife all but the top 4 buds before planting in late autumn. One year later 4 branches will have started to develop on a sturdy 10cm/4in stem. Transplant to the permanent growing site. Prune each branch by half, cutting to an outward pointing bud. By pruning the leaders in this way you will strengthen the plant, direct its habit of growth, furnish healthy new shoots and increase productivity. Repeat for the next 3 seasons, choosing suitably placed laterals to form further main branches up to 8. In the first growing season laterals will be produced from the main branches. Prune back any laterals not needed for new leaders to encourage the formation of fruiting spurs. In the winter, prune the leaders by about one third, and at the same time shorten the side shoots to 2.5cm/1in. Sublaterals will be produced in subsequent years from the original cutback shoots, and these too should be cut back to 2.5cm/1in.

Although not essential, summer pruning of the laterals carried by the fruiting bush is an aid to fruitfulness. Cut back the side shoots as soon as the first fruits begin to colour, leaving about 10cm/4in. Cut back the same side shoots to 2.5cm/1in in the winter.

*Gooseberries* Gooseberry bushes are pruned in the same way as red and white currants, in order to achieve the same basic shape of strong branches radiating from a central stem. The difference is that bushes raised from cuttings are usually left in the nursery bed for 2 years, rather than one, to build up their strength. When pruning the bushes, cut back to an inward or upward rather than an outward pointing bud, in an attempt to prevent the branches from dropping. The summer pruning suggested for red currants is well worth doing for gooseberries.

Gooseberries can easily be grown as cordons, in which case pruning is rather different. For a single cordon, choose a single sturdy shoot on a newly planted 1-year-old and remove all the others flush with the stem. Tie the shoot to a cane for support. This cane should be firmly secured in the ground as the cordon will need it permanently. For a double cordon keep 2 shoots 23cm/9in above the ground and for a triple cordon keep 3 at the same height. Train the 2 shoots of a cordon horizontally on supporting wires until they are 15cm/6in long and then train them upwards. With a triple cordon, train the central shoot upwards and the 2 side shoots as for a double cordon. Every winter cut back the leaders of all cordons to two thirds of the new growth, and all side shoots to 3 buds.

*Blackberries* Most varieties of blackberry have biennial stems, which die after fruiting and are then replaced by the young canes, but the fruiting rods of some of the more vigorous varieties are perennial. It is useful to know this, because if there are not enough young canes produced in a particular year the old rods

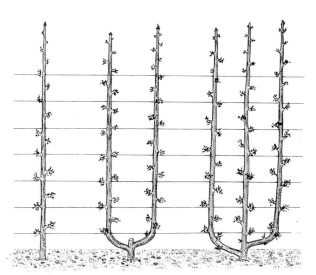

*Cut back main branches of red currant to strengthen and cut back sideshoots near junction with main branches.*

*Single and multiple cordon systems of training, which are suitable for gooseberries and red currants.*

*Train blackberries to keep fruiting and young canes apart. Weaving is an efficient and decorative system: cut out old wood after fruiting. Weave in young replacement canes.*

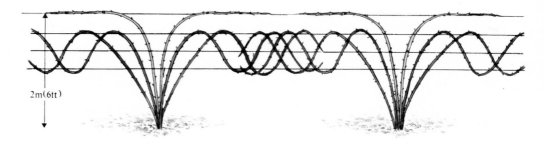

2m(6ft)

*An alternative way of raining blackberries is the one-way system. Train fruiting and young wood of adjacent bushes to left and right (the old wood in one direction and the new wood in the opposite direction).*

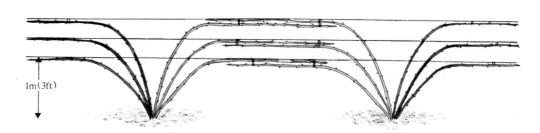

1m(3ft)

can be retained for another season. All that is necessary, apart from any repositioning required, is to prune the laterals which carried the fruits back to 2.5cm/1in. An effective method of training blackberries to keep fruiting and young canes apart, is to weave the rods along the bottom of four wires – wearing thick gloves – then tie in the young cane as it develops during the summer and train it along the top wire. After fruiting, cut out the old wood and weave in the young replacement canes as illustrated at the top of this page. If this training method seems too tricky, train fruiting canes in one direction and young canes in the opposite direction, as illustrated beneath weaving.

*Loganberries* Pruning loganberries is simplicity itself, consisting of the complete removal of the fruited wood and the training in its place of the young cane. Gloves should be worn when handling loganberry canes. It is when pruning that the value of the thornless variety is particularly appreciated.

A fan system of training is ideal for loganberries: spread the fruiting canes on to the top wire, taking care to maintain a wide central area through which the young cane is trained initially, on to the top wire. After fruiting, prune by removing the fruited wood completely and tie in the young cane in its place. This training method is illustrated below.

As an alternative, the one-way system shown above for training blackberries, keeps the canes in their separate age groups, protecting the young canes from any risk of catching cane spot disease from the older wood, and avoids double handling but at the expense of unoccupied training space.

*Raspberries* For heavy and regular cropping, raspberries should be grown against posts and wires. Space each post about 3m/10ft apart, and standing 2m/6ft 6in out of the ground. Three wires should then be stapled to the posts, one at the top, the bottom one 60cm/2ft from the ground and the other mid-way

*Using the fan system of training loganberries, tie young canes (light wood) on to the top wire, spreading the fruiting canes (dark wood) across the lower wires.*

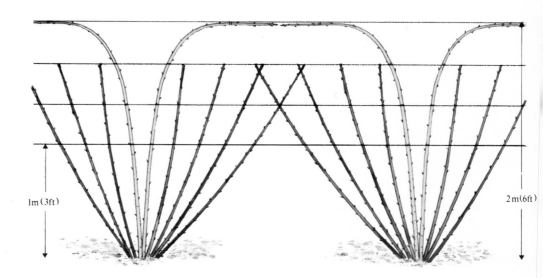

1m(3ft)

2m(6ft)

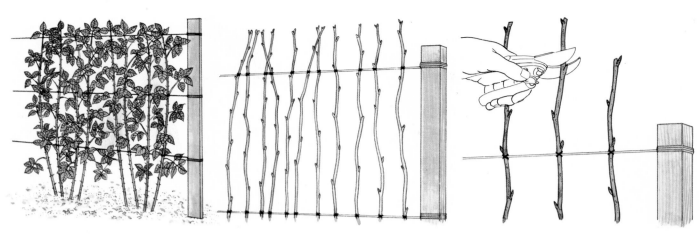

*Adopt a support system for raspberries: place wires at 2m/6ft, 1.2m/4ft, 60cm/2ft.*

*In the autumn tie in new canes at each level after cutting back old canes.*

*In spring, prune unripened tips. During the growing season pull out unwanted suckers.*

between the two. In early spring, prune the tip of each cane. Pull out weak surplus suckers during the growing season. Once fruiting is over, cut out the old canes and tie the new canes to the supporting wires.

**PROTECTING YOUR CROPS**  There are two kinds of protection available for fruit. One is protection from predators, which almost always means birds; and the other is protection from the elements – winds that rock the bushes and lash the berries and frosts that nip fruitfulness in the bud. Means of protection are also used to extend the season.

If you have a large garden and like to grow a lot of soft fruit, the ideal form of protection from predators, particularly birds, is a walk-in fruit cage. Most of us cannot accommodate such large structures and must resort to other means. Strong plastic netting can be draped over individual plants, though it should not be of so fine a mesh that pollinating insects cannot find their way through it. A number of scaring devices have been developed by exasperated gardeners, ranging from scarecrows, strips of fluttering plastic or glittering paper tied to the branches and tape-recorded frightening sounds.

The soft fruit crop which benefits most from protection from frost is strawberries, which because they are low-growing can be covered with cloches or a polythene tunnel and encouraged to fruit in early spring. Perpetual strawberries can be persuaded to fruit late into the autumn if placed under cover in early autumn.

**PESTS AND DISEASES**  A pest is an animal – usually an insect – which is harmful to plants at some stage in its life cycle, for example as larva or caterpillar.

Generally speaking the substances used to combat pests are insecticides.

Diseases occur when plants are invaded by bacteria and fungi. Many troubles are caused by viruses, against which there are no chemical controls. As most diseases are caused by fungi the materials used to control them can be referred to as fungicides. Fungi are more difficult to control than insects.

Many of the things that go wrong with plants are the result of poor environment – not enough nutrition, for example. These disorders can usually be traced to neglect by the gardener. The first step in pest and disease control is to grow good plants that are living in fertile soil, correctly watered and kept free of competing weeds.

Always start with healthy plants bought from a reputable nursery, and in the case of such fruits as black currants, make sure you begin with plants certified free of virus diseases. While crop rotation is a discipline for the vegetable garden, the principle also applies to strawberries, which must not be grown on the same bed for two or three seasons after the original plants are exhausted. Never propagate from diseased stock, only from vigorous, healthy plants.

Prevention is better than cure. Spray in advance against inevitable troubles such as infestation by aphids. Prune at the correct time, making clean cuts that heal quickly without admitting disease. Whatever insecticides and fungicides you use, make sure you keep them in a safe place where they cannot be found by children. Always follow the manufacturer's instructions, and do not spray fruit immediately before picking it. Wash all fruits before use. A guide to control of pests and diseases is given on page 126.

SOFT FRUIT

# BLACKBERRY

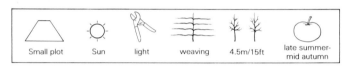

| Small plot | Sun | light | weaving | 4.5m/15ft | late summer-mid autumn |

The blackberry is very accommodating and tolerant of adverse site and soil conditions.

**GROWING** Although the blackberry will grow and crop in poor soil and in shady positions, it does best in soil in which large quantities of farmyard manure or composted vegetation or other moisture-retaining bulky organic matter have been incorporated, and on an open site. Spread out the roots of the new plant so that they occupy as large a feeding zone as possible. Cut the plant back to about 30cm/1ft. Depending on variety, plants should be spaced from 3-4.5m/10-15ft apart.

**PROPAGATION** In the wild, young canes arch over, and the tips root eventually. To increase your stock, copy nature: bury the tip of a selected young cane shallowly in mid summer, securing the parent cane to ensure that the tip is properly anchored and keep moist. During the following winter or spring, the new rooted shoot can be detached, lifted and planted.

**HARVESTING** Blackberries should crop heavily each autumn, indefinitely. Leave fruit for eating fresh on the plant until ripe and sweet. Pick fruit for jams and pies just as the berries turn black.

**POSSIBLE PROBLEMS** Always plant healthy plants: never start with weak, scarred or cankered canes.

# BLUEBERRY

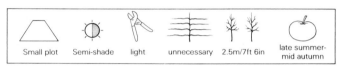

| Small plot | Semi-shade | light | unnecessary | 2.5m/7ft 6in | late summer-mid autumn |

Blueberries are a favourite in the USA where they feature in a popular pie as well as being stewed with sugar. The flavour of the small, blue-black berries is pleasantly sharp.

**GROWING** An acid soil is essential for success, so if rhododendrons thrive in your garden, blueberries should do well. You can raise plants from cuttings like black currants – otherwise set out young plants from the nursery in mid autumn. The mature bushes can reach a height and spread of 2m/6ft 6in and are heavy croppers. The only pruning required is to remove overcrowded branches and cut the whole bush back occasionally to keep the shape neat. Do not let the soil dry out – mulch with peat once a year. Keep competing weeds under control while the bush is establishing itself.

**HARVESTING** Pick the strings of berries when fully ripe and use immediately or freeze.

**POSSIBLE PROBLEMS** Usually trouble-free.

**VARIETIES** Bluecrop.

■ GARDENER'S TIP

*An effective method of training blackberries to keep fruiting and young canes apart, is to weave the rods along the bottom of four wires – wearing thick gloves – then tie in the young cane as it develops during the summer and train it along the top wire. After fruiting, cut out the old wood and weave in the young replacement canes. If this seems too tricky, train fruiting and young canes to right and left.*

■ GARDENER'S TIP

*You will need more than one plant as blueberries are not self-fertile and plants will take at least 3 years before they fruit but will then crop well for a number of years. High bush blueberries make an ornamental addition to the flower garden.*

# BOYSENBERRY

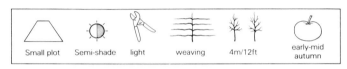

| Small plot | Semi-shade | light | weaving | 4m/12ft | early-mid autumn |

If you are interested in unusual fruits, the boysenberry is a rewarding subject. A hybrid of uncertain parentage, though certainly including members of the blackberry family, the fruits have a sweet-sharp flavour. The plants resist drought well.

**GROWING** Treat the boysenberry as a vigorous blackberry. Any soil will do as long as it is dug over before planting and a bucketful of well-rotted compost worked in. Set out young plants in the autumn and cut back to 30cm/12in. A system of horizontal wires makes it easy to control what would otherwise be a rampant bush. Tie fruiting canes in a fan shape on the lower wires. As new, light-wooded canes grow up, keep them out of the way on the top wires. After fruiting, cut the old wood right back and replace with the new canes. An alternative method which accommodates longer fruiting canes is to weave them in and out of the wires – wearing stout gloves to combat the thorns.

**HARVESTING** Pick the berries when they part easily from the bush. Use immediately in cooked desserts and conserves or freeze.

**POSSIBLE PROBLEMS** Cane spot fungus may damage the stems. Spray with bordeaux mixture just before and just after flowering.

**SUITABLE VARIETIES** No named varieties.

## ■ COOK'S TIP

*If you grow these and other fruiting canes organically there should be no reason to wash the fruit before serving or freezing. As they grow well above the ground they do not get mud spattered and washing will inevitably result in some loss of flavour. Eat fresh with a little honey and yogurt or make into ice cream, put in a pie or turn into jam.*

# GOOSEBERRY

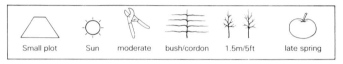

| Small plot | Sun | moderate | bush/cordon | 1.5m/5ft | late spring |

Most varieties of gooseberry are picked while green, for stewing; but some are so sweet when fully ripe they can be eaten straight from the bush.

**GROWING** Full sun is best, on a site sheltered from the wind. Deeply cultivated, fertile soil from which all perennial weeds have been cleared is best. Since gooseberries share red and white currants' need for potash, it makes sense to grow them together. A bush on a short stem makes it easier to weed and pick the fruit between the prickles. Plant healthy 2-year-old bushes between mid autumn and early spring, first incorporating a little sulphate of potash into the soil. Plant to the same depth as in the nursery. Pruning is important to achieve the desired shape. After planting, cut back new growth on 6-8 shoots by half, on the rest to 1 bud from the base. Thereafter, in summer cut back the side shoots to 10cm/4in and in winter cut them again, back to 2-3 buds. At the same time cut back the leading shoots by half and to an inward or upward pointing bud. Water well. Gooseberries can also be grown as cordons.

**HARVESTING** Fruits picked small and green can be stewed; use mid-season fruits for jam and preserves. Late ripening fruits can be eaten raw.

**POSSIBLE PROBLEMS** Aphids. Remove gooseberry sawfly larvae from the leaves by hand.

## ■ GARDENER'S TIP

*Gooseberries flower early, so if there are few available bees pollinate the flowers by hand, using an artist's paint brush to transfer the pollen from one flower to another.*

# LOGANBERRY

| | | | | | |
|---|---|---|---|---|---|
| Small plot | Sun | light | fan | 2.5m/7ft 6in | mid-late summer |

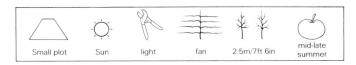

Although the loganberry is not as easy to grow as its relatives, the raspberry and blackberry, it is a worthwhile addition to the fruit garden for its special flavour.

**GROWING** Loganberries do best in soil in which large quantities of farmyard manure or composted vegetation or other moisture-retaining bulky organic matter have been incorporated, and on an open site. Spread out the roots of the new plant so that they occupy as large a feeding zone as possible and if planting more than one, space the plants about 2.5m/7ft 6in apart. A fan system of training is ideal: spread the fruiting canes across three lower wires and tie the young canes on to the top wire, taking care to maintain a wide central area through which the young cane is trained initially. A thornless variety is available: if this is not chosen, gloves should be worn when handling loganberry canes. After fruiting, prune by removing the fruited wood completely and tie in the young cane in its place.

**HARVESTING** Pick when the full colour has formed. Ripe berries are easily crushed, so pick with care.

**POSSIBLE PROBLEMS** Because of proneness to cane spot, propagation is not recommended; training loganberries so that the young canes are either above or to one side of the fruiting canes avoids any fungus on the older wood being carried in raindrops on to new growth.

# RASPBERRY

| | | | | | |
|---|---|---|---|---|---|
| Small plot | Sun | light | support | 60cm/2ft | mid summer-early autumn |

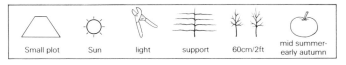

One considerable advantage the raspberry has over all hardy fruits except the strawberry, is the ability to come into full bearing quickly, if the plants are well grown.

**GROWING** For best results, incorporate large quantities of farmyard manure or composted vegetation, or other moisture-retaining bulky organic matter before planting. Spread the roots out and plant the canes shallowly in a sheltered place when the soil is reasonably dry, spacing them 60cm/2ft apart. Late autumn is the best time. Pruning begins on planting, the aim being to prevent the formation of fruit (on summer fruiting varieties) in the first year: cut each cane back to about 25cm/10in above ground level. In early spring, prune the tip of each cane. Pull out weak surplus suckers during the growing season, wearing a protective glove. Once fruiting is over, cut out the old canes and tie the new canes to supporting wires.

**HARVESTING** Autumn-fruiting varieties fruit on the current year's canes, while summer-fruiting varieties produce their fruit on the previous year's canes.

**POSSIBLE PROBLEMS** Bad drainage can lead to the death of canes, so avoid waterlogging in the winter months. Weeds that appear should be pulled up or gently hoed away. The raspberry beetle gives rise to maggoty fruits. Dust the fruitlets with derris or spray with malathion as soon as the first pink fruits are seen.

---

■ COOK'S TIP

*One of the most delicious fruit vinegars is made with raspberries but loganberries are just as suitable to tint and add taste to white wine vinegar. One-third fill a glass jar with the fruit then top up with the vinegar. Use a glass or cork stopper. Place the jar on a sunny window sill and shake daily for two weeks. Leave a little longer in cooler weather. Strain the now pink vinegar into a clean bottle and seal with a cork stopper.*

---

■ GARDENER'S TIP

*Raspberries are carried on side-shoots which are readily severed by a summer's gale, so plant them near a protective tree or shrub, as long as these produce only thin shade. Plant the canes in a relatively weed-free part of the garden.*

# ALPINE STRAWBERRY

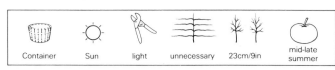

| | | | | | |
|---|---|---|---|---|---|
| Container | Sun | light | unnecessary | 23cm/9in | mid-late summer |

Alpine strawberries are small and grown on bushy plants that do not produce runners. While they are usually treated as summer strawberries, alpines are particularly suitable for growing in barrels. Large earthenware pots may also be used. These are the best strawberries for making jam as they are high in pectin.

**GROWING** Specially constructed strawberry towers are available, but old barrels are perfectly adequate and blend in nicely with the garden. They are sold with 5-cm/2-in holes bored in them 23cm/9in apart. Plant in late summer to fruit the following summer. Place drainage material such as broken pots in the base and lay turves grass side down on top. Make a central drainage column of wire netting filled with similar material. Use a rich potting compost, such as John Innes No. 3. As you fill the barrel, put the plants in place just inside the holes. Stop the drainage core 15cm/6in short of the top. Fill with compost and set more plants 23cm/9in apart on the surface. Do not let the compost dry out.

**HARVESTING** Start picking as soon as the fruits begin to ripen, removing the berries with the calyx and a little stalk. After fruiting, cut the leaves back to 7.5cm/3in. Replace stock and compost after the third year.

**POSSIBLE PROBLEMS** Birds, slugs and aphids.

**VARIETIES** Baron Solemacher.

# EARLY STRAWBERRY

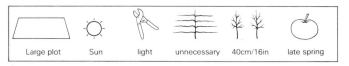

| | | | | | |
|---|---|---|---|---|---|
| Large plot | Sun | light | unnecessary | 40cm/16in | late spring |

Certain summer-fruiting varieties of strawberry can produce fruit in late spring if grown under protection.

**GROWING** A light, fertile, well-cultivated soil is essential. Double dig before planting, working in plenty of well-rotted organic manure, compost and peat. Set new plants out in late summer, taking care that the crowns are level with the surface of the soil. Water lightly to encourage the formation of plump crowns for the following year. In late winter, cover the rows. The ideal protection is a tunnel of barn cloches. As an alternative, use lengths of polythene sheeting stretched over wire hoops and secured to a stake at either end. As the plants come into flower, ventilate the rows by day to let pollinating insects in and to prevent the interior becoming overheated: remove every fifth cloche or raise the sides of the polythene. Do not let the plants dry out.

**HARVESTING** Inspect the plants daily from the end of spring and pick the berries as soon as they ripen. After fruiting, remove the cloches/polythene, trim back the foliage, remove runners and weeds. Let the plants fruit in summer in the normal way the following year.

**PROPAGATION** It is not advisable to propagate from plants that have been forced into early fruiting.

**POSSIBLE PROBLEMS** Slugs, aphids, grey mould.

---

■ GARDENER'S TIP

*To grow your own plants from seeds, sow the seeds in moist seed compost in autumn and overwinter in a cold frame. Alternatively, sow in trays in seed compost in early spring and keep at 17-21C/65-70F and covered until the seeds* *germinate. Prick out the seedlings when the first true leaves appear to 2.5cm/1in apart. Plant out at the end of spring. Spread bone meal on the soil shortly before planting, 2 handfuls per square metre/yard.*

---

■ GARDENER'S TIP

*Give further protection and warmth to early strawberries grown under cloches by placing black polythene over a bed raised towards the centre. Tuck the edges in under the soil at the sides. Plant through slits in the plastic.*

## PERPETUAL STRAWBERRY

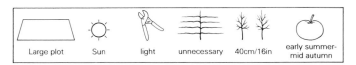

| Large plot | Sun | light | unnecessary | 40cm/16in | early summer-mid autumn |

## SUMMER STRAWBERRY

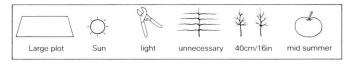

| Large plot | Sun | light | unnecessary | 40cm/16in | mid summer |

Also called remontant strawberries, these varieties differ from standard summer-fruiting types in that they bear flushes of fruits from early summer-mid autumn instead of a single crop in mid-summer. The disadvantage is that certified virus-free stock is not yet available so perpetuals must not be grown near summer-fruiting strawberries.

**GROWING** Plant in spring in deeply dug soil in which well-rotted organic compost has been incorporated. Set the plants in the soil so that the crowns are level with the surface: make planting holes with a mound in the centre and spread the roots out and around before covering them with fine soil. Firm in and water well. In the first year, remove the flowers that appear up till the end of spring. A light, early crop follows in 6 weeks, but the later crop will be much heavier. Feed during the summer with a general purpose fertilizer and keep weeds down. Protect the ripening fruits with clean straw or strawberry mats.

**HARVESTING** Pick the fruits as soon as they are ripe, a few at a time from each plant. Remove all dead and decaying leaves after fruiting. The second year's crop will be lighter. Replace plants in the third year.

**POSSIBLE PROBLEMS** Birds, slugs, aphids, grey mould. See summer and alpine strawberries.

Using different varieties stretches the strawberry season throughout the summer and beyond. Because strawberries are prone to virus diseases, the bed should not be used for strawberries again for 2 seasons after the crop is exhausted, which may be 4-5 years.

**GROWING** The best soil is light-medium, well drained and quick to warm up in spring. Work in plenty of manure, compost and peat before planting. Choose a site that is sunny by day and retains warmth at night. Buy in certified virus-free runners to plant in late summer or late spring. Set the plants so that the crown is level with the surface of the soil (see perpetual strawberries). Cover with soil, firm well and water in. A well-prepared bed will retain moisture, but in dry springs it may be necessary to water to plump up the berries. Stop watering after the fruits take colour. Remove all weeds, preferably by hand. If night frost is forecast, cover the rows lightly with straw or strips of black polythene and remove it by day. Cut out all runners unless – in the first year – you want to raise new stock from a limited number of plants.

**HARVESTING** Pick the berries on dry days, with the calyx and a little stem as soon as they are ripe. Clean up the bed and cut the plants right back after fruiting.

**POSSIBLE PROBLEMS** Protect from birds with netting.

## ■ ORGANIC TIP

*To stop birds harvesting the fruit before you do, upturn a series of glass bottles and push the necks in the soil. Light glinting on the glass appears to deter the birds from approaching.*

## ■ ORGANIC TIP

*To help to deter slugs, place the ripening fruits on a bed of straw, carefully placed right underneath them. Do this as the strawberries begin to swell, not before, because it also exposes them to any frost and insulates them from the soil's warmth. The*

*straw will also help to keep the strawberries clean. To deter grey mould do not over-water or add more than 2 handfuls of fertilizer per sq m/sq yd. Cut off and burn infected shoots.*

# WINEBERRY

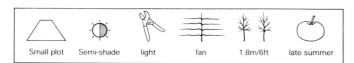

| | | | | | |
|---|---|---|---|---|---|
| Small plot | Semi-shade | light | fan | 1.8m/6ft | late summer |

Related to the blackberry, and sometimes called the Chinese blackberry, the wineberry produces beautiful fruits which are at first yellow then turn through orange to red. The whole plant is very ornamental, its long stems covered with red bristles.

**GROWING** Choose a sheltered site and dig in plenty of well-rotted manure. Plant in late autumn, spreading the roots out well and covering them with fine soil. Firm in and water well. Cut new plants back to about 25cm/10in above ground level so that they will not fruit in the first year, but build up a strong root system. Cover the rooting area with a mulch to conserve moisture and suppress weeds. Wineberries, like raspberries, benefit from a support system, as they reach 2m/6ft 6in in height. After fruiting, cut down old canes and tie the new canes into the wires. Pull out all weak suckers during the growing season, wearing thick gloves for protection. In spring, lightly prune back the unripened tips of the new canes.

**HARVESTING** Pick the berries as soon as they are deep red, plump and ripe. They can be served with sugar and cream, cooked in a summer pudding or made into jam.

**POSSIBLE PROBLEM** Dust the immature fruits with derris to deter raspberry beetle.

# BLACK CURRANT

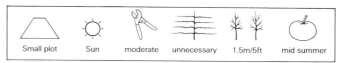

| | | | | | |
|---|---|---|---|---|---|
| Small plot | Sun | moderate | unnecessary | 1.5m/5ft | mid summer |

The unique flavour of black currants is delicious in desserts, ice cream, jam and syrup.

**GROWING** In the autumn, start with 1-year-old plants certified free from disease. Buy half the number needed to fill the plot, which should be in full sun and sheltered from strong winds. Black currants need rich, deep moisture-retentive soil. Dig planting holes large enough to spread the roots right out. Set the plants 2.5cm/1in deeper than they were in the nursery. Cover the roots with fine soil or potting compost and tread it firm. With secateurs, cut each shoot down to leave not more than 5cm/2in. This is essential to encourage strong basal shoots for the future. Use the cutting to start new bushes (see below). No fruit is borne in the first summer, only strong young shoots which carry the first crop in the next year. The first winter after fruiting, and every following winter, prune out one third of the old, dark wood, leaving the young golden wood intact. The best fruit is borne on 1-year-old wood.

**HARVESTING** Currants turn black in mid summer and are ripe 2 weeks later. Pick a whole truss if ripe, otherwise take individual berries.

**POSSIBLE PROBLEMS** Reversion is a virus disease that makes the bushes barren and distorts the leaves. Destroy affected plants and begin again with new stock.

■ GARDENER'S TIP

*The wineberry will grow best if fanned out against a wall or a fence. Its ornamental qualities will be highlighted too by this training system.*

■ GARDENER'S TIP

*To propagate black currants, discard the unripened tip of the cuttings and cut them into 25cm/10in lengths, cutting close to a bud at each end. Insert into the soil so that only 2 buds are showing, in groups of 3 set 20cm/8in apart in a triangle.*

*From these groups new composite bushes will form. In summer, give all the compost, lawn clippings and water you can spare as a weed-suppressing mulch.*

## RED CURRANT

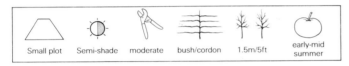

Small plot | Semi-shade | moderate | bush/cordon | 1.5m/5ft | early-mid summer

These gem-like fruits can be grown against a shaded wall if necessary.

**GROWING** Red currants like deeply dug, fertile, well-drained soil. Plant from late autumn-late winter, first incorporating a little sulphate of potash into the planting site. Buy 2-year-old bushes and plant to the same depth as in the nursery. While red currants can be trained as cordons to save space (see white currants), the ideal bush sits neatly on a short stem and carries 8 radiating branches. To achieve this, after planting cut the new growth on 6-8 strong shoots by half. Cut back other shoots to 1 bud from their base. Thereafter, prune twice a year. In early-mid summer, cut back all new side shoots to 5 leaves. Pull off suckers rising from the base of the bush. In winter, cut back the leading shoots by a half to an outward pointing bud. Cut the summer-pruned laterals back again to 2-3 buds. Water well in summer.

**HARVESTING** Pick red currants as soon as they are fully ripe and use straight away or freeze.

**PROPAGATION** Take hardwood cuttings in late autumn 30cm/12in long with a bud close to either end. Nick out all but the top 4 buds. Insert half-way in open ground. A small bush will be ready for transplanting in 12 months.

**POSSIBLE PROBLEMS** Tie strips of foil to the branches to scare off birds.

## WHITE CURRANT

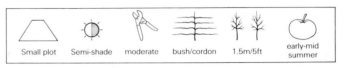

Small plot | Semi-shade | moderate | bush/cordon | 1.5m/5ft | early-mid summer

This unusual fruit is easy to grow and when fully ripe is very sweet. It is delicious in fruit salad.

**GROWING** Any well-drained, moisture-retentive soil is suitable, but like red currants, white currants need extra potash so work in a light dressing when digging over before planting between mid autumn and early spring. If space is at a premium, buy plants trained as cordons rather than bushes. Set 2-year-old plants in single rows 50cm/20in apart and support on wires between 5 × 5cm/2 × 2in stakes about 2m/6ft high. Prune in summer, cutting laterals back to 3-5 leaves. When the cordons reach 2m/6ft cut the new leader back to 4 leaves. In winter, cut the lateral shoots back to 1 bud. Before the leader reaches 2m/6ft, cut back new growth by up to 23cm/9in; after this point, remove new growth every winter.

**PROPAGATION** Take hardwood cuttings in late autumn, as for red currants.

**HARVESTING** Pick the fruits when fully ripe, either by the truss or individually. Use immediately or freeze.

**POSSIBLE PROBLEMS** White currants are relatively trouble-free. Scorching at the leaf edge is caused by a deficiency of potash. Aphids cause red blisters on the leaves. Spray with systemic insecticide just before flowering.

■ COOK'S TIP

*Red currants can be readily persuaded to part from their stems if the tines of a fork are used to isolate them. If the currants are to be frozen, leave them on the stalks. When solid, they will be very easy to remove.*

■ ORGANIC TIP

*If leaves brown at the edges this is a sign of potassium deficiency. Currants need extra potassium. To remedy, spray plants with liquid seaweed and apply rock potash, one handful to the square metre. For the organic gardener, rock potash is an invaluable source of potassium so apply in quantities as above in the spring. To deal with bad aphid infestations, spray with insecticidal soap and attract predators of aphids, as described on page 15.*

# TOP FRUIT

From the gardener's point of view, the endearing thing about fruit is its longevity. Fruit trees such as apples, pears and plums may take a few seasons' nurturing to start with, but they repay the effort with many years of productivity. To the cook, too, fruits are a delight. Not only is there a range of flavours, but textures vary as well, whether in a crisp green apple or a juicy, tender peach. Apples and pears can be stored, while plums can be made into most delicious jams.

**GROWING REQUIREMENTS** Because they occupy the ground for so long, as a general rule fruits need deep, well-drained but moisture-retentive, fertile soil. The best site is sunny and open but protected from strong winds, which can easily uproot young trees and lay dangerously chilly fingers on older ones. Most town gardens enjoy some shelter from wind provided by the house to which they are attached, but you can do more to create an advantageous micro-climate with permanent windbreaks formed by hedges and fences.

Space is an important factor. Very few modern gardens can accommodate a mature sweet cherry tree, for example; but even standard or half standard apple trees are fairly majestic, and if two are necessary for successful pollination a substantial area will be used up. It is for this reason that dwarf bush apples have been developed, while trees like the plum – in nature a large specimen – are not raised on their own roots but grafted on to a suitable rootstock (St Julien A) that will keep growth within manageable bounds.

For apples the most popular rootstock is M9, which makes a dwarf bush reaching 2-3m/6-10ft. Where soil is poorer the large M26, reaching 2.5-3.7m/8-12ft, can be used. The very dwarf M27 needs extra care and feeding. Pears are grown on Quince A or C rootstock, cherries on F12/1, and while many a domestic peach has been raised from the kernel, the finest trees are grown on St Julien A, which is also used for nectarines and apricots. One of the purposes of pruning and training, discussed in detail below, is to keep fruit trees and bushes to shape and at an appropriate size. Some

pruning is necessary for all the most important fruit crops.

During their life, fruit trees need regular feeding and watering. A dressing of general purpose fertilizer worked in in spring is needed by many fruits. An annual mulch of well-rotted organic manure or compost spread liberally over the rooting zone feeds the plant, conserves moisture and suppresses weeds. While peat is a useful mulch, environmentally concerned gardeners are looking for alternatives to plundering a non-renewable natural resource. Grass cuttings and fallen leaves are obvious candidates, but other fibrous materials that can be made available in commercial quantities are being researched. Remember too that while a carpet of grass beneath your budding apple may look charming, it is probably starving the tree.

**POLLINATION** In the case of apples, pears, plums and some other top fruits, your choice will be affected by the need to have varieties that will cross-pollinate. It may be, of course, that a neighbouring garden contains a tree that will perform this duty for you. If not, you will have to plant two trees or choose a variety that is 'self-pollinating (self-fertile). Even with self-fertile trees, pollination needs your assistance in simple ways: the flowers of plants protected by sheets of hessian, for example, are inaccessible to pollinating insects unless you remove the obstruction to their flight path. Do not use insecticidal sprays when the blossoms are open and the bees are at work, but earlier in the season, at the bud stage.

**PLANTING A TREE** The best time to plant fruit trees is between late autumn and early spring, the earlier the better. Order your trees in advance from a reputable nursery to make sure you get exactly what you want. Whether you are starting with a 1-year-old – a maiden – which you will prune to shape from the start, or – in the case of a fan-shaped tree – an older tree whose branches have been trained into the basic fan framework by the nursery, the planting method is the same. (See Greengage for fan training). Prepare the soil very thoroughly by digging deeply, breaking up the subsoil with a fork. Work in as much rotted compost, farmyard manure or peat as you can get. Positioning the young tree and firming it into place is much easier with two pairs of hands. Drive a stout stake 1.2m/4ft long into the ground so that 75cm/2ft 6in is showing above the surface. If you are planting more than one tree, use a stake for each one, spaced according to type. Maiden apples on M9 rootstock should be placed 3m/10ft apart; dwarf pyramids on M27 can be half this distance and cordons as close as 75cm/2ft 6in. A half-standard tree needs the extra support of a double-stake and cross-bar, using two posts each 2m/6ft 6in long. The tree is tied to the cross-bar and padded to prevent chafing.

Take out a wide shallow hole, without loosening the stake, and spread the roots out so that they can make rapid use of the largest amount of ground. Take care to keep the union, the swollen piece on the stem which marks the junction between root stock and variety, at least 10cm/4in above the ground. If you bury the union, the inherently vigorous scion will root and the weak system of the rootstock will be overpowered, resulting in a large unfruitful tree rather than the neat productive one you hoped for. Firm the soil over the roots so that the two are in close contact. If you can lay hands on used potting soil, add a large bucketful to each planting hole to get the young tree off to a good start. Tie each tree to its stake, using a broad tie which will not bite into the stem. Allow room for the tree

trunk to expand rapidly without being choked. Place the tie as high on the stake as possible. If you are planting on a windy site, position the tree and stake so that the stake is on the side from which the strongest wind is likely, to avoid chafing. Prune immediately (see below). Over the winter cover the root area with composted material 5cm/2in deep to conserve moisture and suppress weeds.

**PRUNING** Left to themselves, fruit trees become overcrowded, diseased and pest-ridden, carrying small fruits on exhausted branches. On the other hand, excessive pruning can lead to too much growth and to light crops of poor quality. All pruning has a purpose. The main objectives are to: admit light and air; train the tree to an acceptable shape and size; increase the size of the fruit; encourage or control growth, whichever the tree demands; assist establishment after transplanting; remove diseased and broken parts; and finally, but importantly, to strengthen the branch structure.

The pruning of apple trees provides a good example of what is needed and is described and illustrated on this page and page 113. Other trees may vary slightly in their individual requirements.

***The young tree*** The most common form is the open-centre bush tree. A one-year-old maiden tree without side shoots must be pruned as soon as possible after planting to compensate for the roots which are inevitably lost in transplanting. Cut the stem back to a height of 60cm/2ft, no more, making a clean cut just

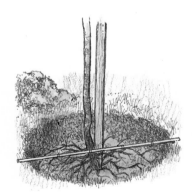

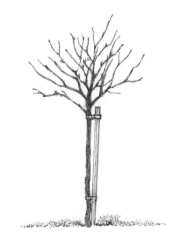

*Work plenty of well-rotted garden compost or manure into the bottom of the hole, and also into the earth that has been dug out. In addition, a light dressing of Growmore will be beneficial. Tread the soil well in as you fill in the hole.*

**Planting a tree**
*Dig out a hole large enough to accommodate the spread-out root system or the root ball. The depth should be sufficient to allow the soil mark on the stem to be level with the ground. Drive in the stake before planting to avoid damage to the roots.*

*The filling-in process is repeated until the hole is full and all the soil has been replaced. Use tree ties to steady the trunk against the stake. Lean this at a slight angle into the prevailing wind in an exposed site.*

above a bud. The buds below the cut will grow outward in the first summer. You need 3 or 4 evenly spaced shoots, none of which grows towards the stake. Rub out unwanted or misplaced buds.

In the first winter after planting, cut back the branches which have formed from the chosen buds. If they are thick and strong, cut them back by half, but if they look weak and spindly, cut back by two-thirds. Prune to an outward pointing bud. This degree of pruning seems ruthless, but it is necessary in order to direct, strengthen and increase the numbers of the branches and their side shoots. During the second summer, water and manure the young tree, spraying at appropriate times to deter pests and prevent disease. Replace the tie that secures the tree to the stake if it has become too tight. The head will now have taken shape, with perhaps 6 to 8 strong and well-placed branches with a number of side shoots.

In the second winter, each of the main (primary) branches will have shoots at the end called leaders. They should be pruned only if it is necessary to strengthen the branch; to change its direction; to provide it with new side shoots or to remove diseased or overcrowded branches.

If it is necessary to do so for any of these purposes the leaders should be shortened again by about one third, two thirds if growth is weak, each to an outward pointing bud.

The side shoots are called laterals. Those growing to the outside may be left unpruned to form fruit buds. Those growing inwards should be pruned back to about 7.5cm/3in or removed entirely if there is overcrowding.

At the end of the third growing season look again at the leaders. Use your previous experience about the extent of cutting back, knowing that weak shoots should be pruned harder than strong shoots.

Follow a similar procedure with maiden laterals – leave alone those which are well placed and shorten or remove the others. You must also deal with last year's maidens, now burgeoning two-year-olds. Leave alone those which are well placed and not competing with the primary branches. Those for which there is no room for further extension should be cut back to the topmost fruit bud. Two-year-old budded laterals should fruit in the following summer.

The cut-back laterals of an earlier year may be pruned to any obvious fruit bud. If no fruit bud has appeared, the extension shoots should be pruned to 2.5cm/1in.

Although there are more complicated procedures undertaken by experts, amateur gardeners can be confident of success by following the rules given about leaders and laterals. These apply to apples, pears, plums and Morello cherries.

**TRAINING** The most convenient and successful form of tree is the open-centre bush described above or the open-centre half-standard or full standard, which are identical except for size.

An interesting variant on this form is the central leader tree, a development which makes it possible to train fruit trees into compact shapes such as the cordon, spindlebush and dwarf pyramid. Cordons are a very useful shape for small gardens as they can be planted as close together as 75cm/2ft 6in. The trees

Right *First winter: before pruning and after, selected leaders reduced by two-thirds.*

Far Right *Second winter: reduce leaders by two-thirds, cut laterals back to about 3 buds.*

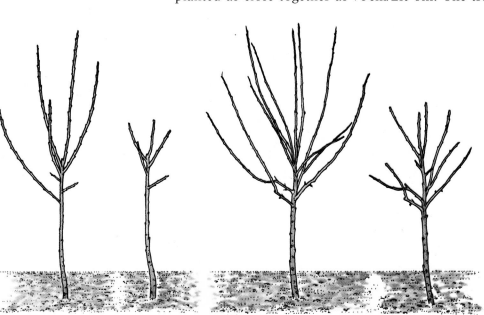

will be supported by a system of horizontal wires attached to posts firmly secured in the ground. The topmost wire should be 1.5m/5ft from the ground, with 3 further wires at 30cm/12in intervals below it. Plant in the same way as any 1-year-old tree. Attach a bamboo cane 2.4m/8ft long to the wires at an angle of 45 degrees. Tie the stem of the tree to the cane, using a soft twine so that the tree is not damaged. No pruning is needed until mid summer, and the same procedure is followed every year, cutting back the mature growth which is characterized by dark leaves and which is woody at the base. Prune back to 3 leaves from the cluster at the base. On the laterals there will be mature side shoots. These should be cut back to 1 leaf from the cluster at the base. Do not cut back the central leader.

When the leader reaches the top wire, remove the supporting cane. You can bend the stem to a more acute angle, gradually lowering it over a few seasons until it is 35 degrees from the ground. If you try to bend it lower than this the stem will break. When the tree cannot be lowered any further, prune the leader annually in late spring, cutting back new growth just above a bud to 1cm/½in.

The dwarf pyramid is a shape particularly useful for plums, and is described under dessert plums in the book. Shown in the illustrations below are the pruning cuts for the second year and for the mature tree.

For pruning fruit trees a heavy-bladed knife is very useful in addition to secateurs. A pruning saw is invaluable for dealing with older trees. Sharp blades help you make the clean cuts which are essential if the wound is to heal quickly.

**PROTECTING YOUR CROPS** Fruit trees grown in the open cannot be protected from wind and frost except when they are small enough to be draped with netting or have the bottom of the stem swathed in straw. Those grown against a wall, however, receive a good measure of protection from the wall, and can be covered with sheets of light netting or hessian, which should not touch the tree, on frosty nights.

Protection from birds is a perennial problem. Various scaring devices have been attempted. A resident cat is useful!

**PESTS AND DISEASES** Like soft fruits, tree fruits are subject to a number of pests and diseases, and to physiological disorders caused by adverse conditions or neglect. A brief guide to the control of common pests and diseases is given on page 126, with a spraying programme designed to protect apples.

Biological rather than chemical control is very useful in the greenhouse, where infesting white fly can be reduced by bringing in the parasitic insect *Encarsia formosa*, which eats them. A non-chemical way of attacking the codling moth larvae is to tie loose bands of sacking or corrugated cardboard around the trunks of susceptible trees in mid summer, before the larvae start their destructive journey up the trunk. Burn the sacking or cardboard in mid autumn. Similarly, trap the wingless females of the winter moth using greasebands placed on the trunks in autumn.

Preventing trouble in this, and other ways, is always better than cure: observe the rules of garden hygiene given at the end of the general introduction, on page 15.

Far Left *Retain central axis, removing competing and unnecessary shoots on 2-year-old pyramid.* Centre *Remove upward growing shoots on mature pyramid.* Below *Greasebands trap the wingless female winter moths.*

## EARLY-SEASON APPLE

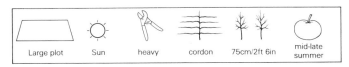

| Large plot | Sun | heavy | cordon | 75cm/2ft 6in | mid-late summer |

The first apples to ripen are ready for picking in mid summer. Their skin is usually very pale yellow, sometimes with a reddish stripe, and the flesh soft, juicy and slightly acid. The flavour is not as good as that of varieties ripening in late summer. Early-ripening apples do not store well.

**GROWING** Irrespective of fruiting time, apple trees should be planted from late summer to early spring, the earlier the better. A slightly acid soil is best, well prepared by digging thoroughly. Break up the subsoil with a fork and work in ample quantities of well-rotted manure or compost. Choose self-pollinating or complementary varieties and plant as described on page 112. Dwarf bushes, pyramids or cordons are best for small gardens. Over winter, cover the rooting zone with a 5-cm/2-in layer of composted material to conserve moisture and suppress emergent weeds. For prunning see page 113. Apples need an annual mulch or manure and should never be allowed to dry out. Apply a general purpose fertilizer each spring.

**HARVESTING** Remove surplus fruits in early summer if pollination is over-successful, taking off the smallest fruits and any that are distorted or diseased. The fruits are ready to pick when they part readily from the tree when lifted to the horizontal. Pick gently to avoid bruising.

**POSSIBLE PROBLEMS** Aphids; codling moth caterpillar.

## MID-SEASON APPLE

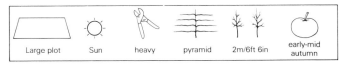

| Large plot | Sun | heavy | pyramid | 2m/6ft 6in | early-mid autumn |

By choosing to grow apples that ripen in the period from early-mid autumn, you can include some of the most delicious varieties, among them James Grieve, Ellison's Orange, Devonshire Quarrenden and Discovery.

**GROWING** Start with 1-year-old trees – 'maidens' – if you are going for a dwarf bush or cordon. With a fan-trained tree it is best to buy one from the nursery with the basic framework of branches already formed. Plant from late autumn to early spring, as early as possible, in slightly acid soil. Prepare the site well by digging deeply and incorporating plenty of well-rotted organic compost. For planting, see page 112. Spread a thick moisture-retaining mulch over the rooting zone. For pruning, see page 113. Water well, give an annual mulch of manure and top dress with general purpose fertilizer each spring.

**HARVESTING** When the fruits begin to ripen, start by picking the outermost apples with the brightest colour, leaving the remainder to flush and put on more weight. Mid-season apples store well. Keep healthy specimens only in a cool, moist clean place. Place in polythene bags and inspect regularly for signs of rotting.

**POSSIBLE PROBLEMS** Aphids; codling moth caterpillar; scab; mildew.

---

### ▦ DECORATIVE TIP

*In a small garden plant festooned trees in pots. These are grown on Pixy rootstock and the branches are trained to curve downwards by tying them, when they are young and supple, in summer to the stem or a lower branch.*

---

### ▦ ORGANIC TIP

*Use a pheromone trap to keep down the numbers of codling moth caterpillars, see page 118. Apple scab is a fungus which can flourish in wet weather. It appears as olive green blotches on leaves and small black or brown scabs on fruit and new shoots. Remove any infected leaves and shoots. Clear away fallen leaves that harbour spores. Apple aphids cause curled leaves and fruit distortion. Spray with insecticidal soap. Encourage bluetits in winter.*

# LATE-SEASON APPLE

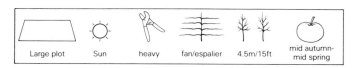

| Large plot | Sun | heavy | fan/espalier | 4.5m/15ft | mid autumn-mid spring |

The late season for apples is very long, extending from mid autumn right through to mid or even late spring, according to varieties. Those known as Reinettes, Pearmains and Pippins ripen in mid to late autumn, as well as the Russets. They are smaller than mid-season types, but the flavour is more aromatic and intense. All of these apples store very well. At the turn of the year, the choice of these varieties widens to include some with a long history, like Blenheim's Orange and the connoisseur's favourite, Ashmead's Kernel. The very late apples, those ripening late winter-early spring, need good soil and a long ripening season; these, like the old Cornish Gilliflower or the newcomer Golden Delicious, are best confined to warm districts.

**GROWING**  Choose a prime site for late-season apples; if you want fan-trained apples on a sunny wall, these are the ones that merit such special treatment. Prepare the planting site with particular care, as the soil near a wall dries out more quickly. After planting (see page 112), apply a moisture-retentive mulch and keep the trees well watered and nourished throughout their life. Keep weeds under control.

**HARVESTING**  Pick the outermost fruits first. Store undamaged fruits only in a cool, clean, moist place.

**POSSIBLE PROBLEMS**  Mildew; scab; codling moth.

■ GARDENER'S TIP

*When planting against a wall position trees at least 30cm/12in away from the wall so that roots can obtain sufficient water. Water each well initially. A little water merely encourages surface roots which suffer in dry weather.*

# COOKING APPLE

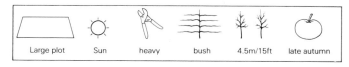

| Large plot | Sun | heavy | bush | 4.5m/15ft | late autumn |

While many dessert apples can also be cooked, there are a number of varieties with such a high acid content that they are always cooked before eating.

**GROWING**  The best known cooking apple, Bramley's Seedling, is the finest flavoured cooker with the best texture. It makes a very large tree, however, and needs the company of others in order to pollinate successfully. Choose from two other cooking varieties, Emneth Early or Grenadier (late summer-early autumn) or the dessert apple Worcester Pearmain (late summer-early autumn). Plant in late autumn, first preparing the site by deep digging and incorporating plenty of well-rotted organic manure or compost. After planting (see page 112), apply a thick moisture-retentive mulch. Water well, give an annual mulch of manure and top dress with a general purpose fertilizer each spring. Keep weeds under control. For pruning see page 113.

**HARVESTING**  The fruits are ready when they part easily from the tree when lifted to the horizontal. Pick carefully to avoid bruising. Store undamaged fruits only in a cool, moist, clean place.

**POSSIBLE PROBLEMS**  As well as the usual pests and diseases affecting apples, Bramley's Seedling is susceptible to frost damage.

**OTHER VARIETIES**  Woolbrook Russet; Crimson Bramley's Seedling.

■ PRESERVING TIP

*When picking apples for storage select only those in perfect condition and place them in a cloth-lined container as you pick to avoid damage. Make a couple of small ventilation holes in each polythene bag you store them in.*

# CRAB APPLE

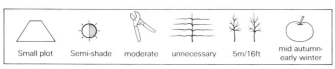

| | | | | | |
|---|---|---|---|---|---|
| Small plot | Semi-shade | moderate | unnecessary | 5m/16ft | mid autumn-early winter |

All apple trees are beautiful in blossom, but even lovelier is the crab apple, which carries a riot of flowers in spring. The wild crab, *Malus pumila*, is the parent of all cultivated apples. Crab apples are hybrids of this species and bear small fruits, round or conical in shape and golden, red or yellow flushed with pink in colour. They are used to make a delicious jelly.

**GROWING** Crab apples make compact trees if grown as standards on 1.2-2m/4-6ft stems, the exception being *M. baccata*, which may reach 15m/50ft in height. For best results plant 2 cross-pollinating varieties. They like fertile, well-cultivated slightly acid soils. Plant in autumn, giving the young trees the support of stakes. Cut the main stem back to 15cm/6in above the aimed-for height in early spring. A year later, cut back the resulting 3 or 4 shoots to 30cm/12in. Shoots appearing on the stem below these branches should be pinched back to 3 or 4 leaves. Remove them after 3 or 4 years when the trunk has thickened. Feed with annual mulches of well-rotted compost in mid spring until the tree is established.

**HARVESTING** Pick the fruits for use as soon as they part easily from the tree. They will stand on the tree for weeks if necessary.

**POSSIBLE PROBLEMS** Aphids are the most destructive pest. Any of the usual apple diseases may occur.

# SWEET CHERRY

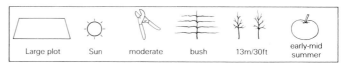

| | | | | | |
|---|---|---|---|---|---|
| Large plot | Sun | moderate | bush | 13m/30ft | early-mid summer |

Sweet cherries belong to the same family as the plum. The long-established type F 12/1 makes a very large tree, too big for most domestic gardens. Some gardeners have been successful growing it in a submerged pot to restrict the naturally vigorous growth. Because pollination is tricky it is essential to plant 2 compatible trees.

**GROWING** Give your cherries the choicest site and the best soil available in terms of depth, drainage and texture. Buy standards of certified virus-free stock with the head already formed and plant in autumn. Stake the young tree, firm in and water well. Apply a thick mulch over the rooting zone. Every spring, work in a top dressing of a general purpose fertilizer. Pruning is only necessary to assist the formation of a full head and to remove diseased or damaged branches in summer.

**HARVESTING** You will need a tall ladder to reach the whole tree. Ideally, wait until the fruits are completely ripe – in practice you may have to pick a little early to beat the birds. Use immediately. The crop potential from 2 trees is enormous.

**POSSIBLE PROBLEMS** Blackfly can quickly damage the foliage and the growing points of young shoots. Spray with malathion before the blossoms open. Birds are the worst pest. Fruits split after heavy rains.

---

■ COOK'S TIP

*To make crab apple jelly, wash and quarter 2kg/4¼lb crab apples, put in a saucepan and cover with cold water. Add the rind of two lemons. Bring to the boil then simmer for about 1 hour until the apples are well cooked. Pour into a jelly bag and*

*leave to strain overnight. Add 450g/1lb sugar for every 600ml/1pt juice and place back in a pan. Heat gently, stirring to dissolve the sugar. When the sugar has dissolved. Boil fast until setting point is reached, then cool and pour into jars.*

---

■ GARDENER'S TIP

*In a small garden, grow sweet cherries against a south-facing wall. If you only want one sweet cherry, Stella is self-fertile, or grow a sweet and a Morello cherry that flower at the same time: so that the Morello can fertilize the sweet cherry.*

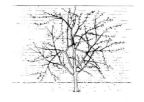

## Morello Cherry

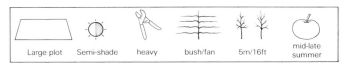

| | | | | | |
|---|---|---|---|---|---|
| Large plot | Semi-shade | heavy | bush/fan | 5m/16ft | mid-late summer |

The Morello cherry is a self-fertile tree quite distinct from the demanding sweet cherry – smaller, hardier and with sharper tasting fruits. Hybrids between the Morello and sweet cherries are called Dukes. The term Acid or Sour is used to describe the group as a whole. These cherries can be used to make delicious pies or jam.

**GROWING** Morellos are easy to grow and will even survive the rigours of a shady wall. Care is still needed when planting: dig over the planting site and incorporate plenty of well-rotted compost, manure or peat. Make a shallow planting hole, drive in a stake and arrange the young tree – a 1-year-old is best – with the roots carefully spread out. Cover with fine soil, firm well and water in. Attach the tree to the stake. Spread a thick layer of moisture-retaining mulch over the rooting area. Prune as for bush apples. Once the tree is established, simply remove crossing branches as well as cutting back to old wood on 3 selected branches annually in late spring to maintain a compact shape. Give copious top dressings of well-rotted manure and keep weeds well under control.

**HARVESTING** Remove fruits by the stalk when fully ripe.

**POSSIBLE PROBLEMS** Spray with malathion before blossom to deter blackfly. Birds are a pest. Cut out branches affected with silver leaf.

## Fig

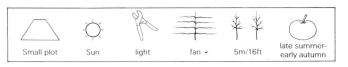

| | | | | | |
|---|---|---|---|---|---|
| Small plot | Sun | light | fan | 5m/16ft | late summer-early autumn |

These small, pear-shaped fruits, usually deep purple when ripe, are borne on handsome trees.

**GROWING** Figs are natives of warm countries. In cool climates they do best trained as fans against a sunny wall, as a bush if the site is sheltered, or in pots in a greenhouse. Well-drained but moisture-retentive soil is essential, and soil that is too rich will encourage the formation of soft shoots that are vulnerable to frost. Restricting the roots helps the tree to maintain its vigour; protected plants do very well in 23-25-cm/9-10-in pots. If grown outside, make a planting hole 1m/3ft deep and line it with bricks, placing drainage material in the base. Mix 250g/8oz sterilized bonemeal with the soil before replacing it. Plant in spring; if training a fan, have the supporting wires in place beforehand. Pruning consists of removing over-strong or misplaced shoots, either as they form or at the end of the summer. Where necessary, tie in young growths for next year's fruiting. Pull off any suckers that develop. Do not let the soil dry out in summer, especially near a wall. Spread a layer of moisture-retaining mulch over the rooting area in spring. Protect the shoots from frost with a wrapping of straw.

**HARVESTING** Wait until the fruits are fully ripe and soft before picking. The skin is delicate and splits easily.

**POSSIBLE PROBLEMS** Relatively trouble free.

### ■ ORGANIC TIP

*Use a codling moth trap hung among your fruit trees to lure male moths on to a sticky base from which they can't escape to breed. The trap lures the male with pheromone, used by the female to attract a mate. One kit protects up to five trees.*

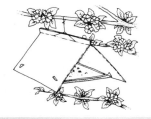

### ■ GARDENER'S TIP

*A fig tree will bear two crops a year but outdoors in this climate only one of these will ripen and this is the second set of fruits which are pea-sized at the beginning of winter. These overwinter, provided they are not caught by frost, to ripen in the following year. Remove the fruit which form earlier in the year in autumn. Our summer is not long enough for these to ripen. This allows all the plant's energy to go into the young fruit.*

# BLACK GRAPE

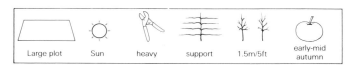

| Large plot | Sun | heavy | support | 1.5m/5ft | early-mid autumn |

Most of the black grapes which ripen well in cooler climates are best for wine, but Tereshkova is suitable as a table grape.

**GROWING** Choose a site open to the sun but sheltered from wind: a south-facing wall is ideal. Make windbreaks from netting or hedges if necessary. Any well-drained soil will do, though very heavy clays will need refining with compost or peat. Magnesium deficiency causes yellow veining on older leaves: correct this with agricultural Epsom salts. Put up the supporting posts and wires for the vines before planting. Set 2-m/6-ft posts into the ground 3m/10ft apart. Fix the lowest wire 45cm/18in from the ground. At 22cm/8½in above it set 2 wires 2.5cm/1in apart horizontally, then another double strand 30cm/12in above the second. These 2 wires are separated horizontally by spacer bars 30cm/12in long attached to the posts. Fix a final set of double wires exactly like the third 30cm/12in above it. On this system the branches are carried upwards and outwards, admitting light and air to foliage and fruit. Set out 1-year-old plants in spring, next to the posts, in holes filled with composted vegetation, peat or potting soil. Water well until the vines are rooting freely. Keep them supplied with a balanced fertilizer.

**HARVESTING** Fruit is borne the second year.

**POSSIBLE PROBLEMS** High humidity causes mildew.

# WHITE GRAPE

| Large plot | Sun | heavy | support | 1.5m/5ft | early-mid autumn |

The choice of white grape varieties suitable for growing in cooler climates is wider than for black types. For growing, see black grapes.

**PRUNING AND TRAINING** After planting, cut back each new plant to 2-3 buds. When they start into growth, select the strongest, rubbing out the others, and tie it to the post to grow vertically. At the end of the season, cut back the single canes to 60cm/2ft from the ground. The next year, 3 shoots will emerge close behind the cut. Let them grow upwards, slipping them between the wires at the second level. At the end of the season, tie 2 canes to the bottom wire, one going left and the other right. Cut the middle cane right back to 3 buds from its origin. In year 3 the horizontal canes will bear flowers and fruit on upward growing laterals: secure these to the widely spaced double wires. When the flowers appear, remove weak laterals, leaving the remainder 20cm/8in apart. Stop the fruiting laterals at the top wire. Let the 3 new central growths grow upwards. After the harvest, remove the fruited canes from the bottom wire and replace them with 2 of the new canes. Cut the central cane right back to 3 new buds.

**THINNING** After fruit set remove some berries from the heart of the bunch with long-bladed scissors.

**HARVESTING** Remove ripe bunches with scissors.

---

■ PRESERVING TIP

*Try making grape juice wine. After crushing the grapes check the amount of sugar they contain with a hydrometer and decide whether you wish to add extra sugar or not. If you intend adding sugar dissolve this in a little hot water then, cooled, include with the crushed grapes. Add the yeast, cover and leave to ferment for ten days, stir each day. Squeeze out the pulp, strain the juice and make the wine following a home winemaking book.*

---

■ ORGANIC TIP

*Powdery mildew appears as grey powder on leaves and grapes. Downy mildew appears on leaf undersides. Mulching and watering help to prevent both. Spray with a copper fungicide like Bordeaux mixture.*

## COOKING PEAR

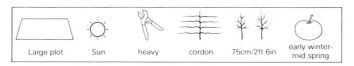

| Large plot | Sun | heavy | cordon | 75cm/2ft 6in | early winter–mid spring |

While all dessert pears can be used for cooking if you wish, there are a few varieties which are used exclusively for this purpose. Stew them slowly in syrup. Ripening as they do in mid winter, cooking pears fill a gap in the gardener's calendar.

**GROWING** Cooking pears have the same requirements as dessert varieties: a slightly acid, deeply dug soil to which a fertilizer containing magnesium and potash is added before planting. Stake the young tree, taking care not to bury the union between rootstock and variety, and spread a thick layer of a moisture-retaining mulch over the rooting zone. Pears must not be allowed to dry out or to become waterlogged, and can take copious amounts of well-rotted organic manure both before planting and afterwards as mulches. Prune as for apples. In some years, following a frost-free spring, too many fruits may be set: the result will be small fruits and an exhausted tree, so thin in mid summer.

**HARVESTING** Check regularly to make sure you pick the pears just before they are completely ripe. Use immediately or store healthy fruits only in a cool, moist place until needed.

**POSSIBLE PROBLEMS** Birds, aphids and wasps are the worst pests. If pear scab is troublesome, spray with captan or benlate before the blossoms open.

## DESSERT PEAR

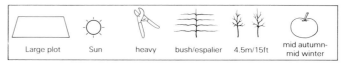

| Large plot | Sun | heavy | bush/espalier | 4.5m/15ft | mid autumn–mid winter |

If pears are grown on Quince A or C rootstock they are compact enough for the average garden. Two open-centre bush trees that will cross-pollinate should be set 3m/10ft apart for best results.

**GROWING** Pears dislike lime, so shallow chalky soils are unsuitable. Choose the most sheltered site in the garden, while avoiding shade and competition from other trees. Before planting in the autumn, break up the sub-soil and work in large quantities of well-rotted manure or compost. Add a potash and magnesium fertilizer. Make a planting hole, drive in a stake as for an apple tree and arrange the tree with the roots spread out, taking care not to bury the union between rootstock and variety. Cover with fine soil, firm well and water in. Fix the tree to the stake and spread a thick mulch of rotted garden compost or other moisture-retaining material over the rooting zone. The initial pruning of a 3-year-old bush will have been done in the nursery. A 1-year-old will need pruning as for apples.

**HARVESTING** Pick pears just before they ripen: if the fruits part easily from the branch when lifted to the horizontal, they are ready. Keep in a cool, moist place.

**POSSIBLE PROBLEMS** Bullfinches eat the buds. Birds and aphids damage shoots. Pear scab is a fungus disease occurring in wet districts.

■ ORGANIC TIP

*Trap wasps before they attack the fruit by making a tasty concoction they can't resist. Half-fill a jar with jam and water or cider, cover the top with paper or polythene in which there is a smallish hole and tie a trap in each tree.*

■ GARDENER'S TIP

*Choose the variety Conference if space is limited, as it will set its own pollen. Doyenne du Comice has the finest flavour of all pears. Pears can be trained as cordons, fans and espaliers on walls.*

# APRICOT

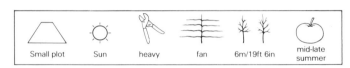

Small plot | Sun | heavy | fan | 6m/19ft 6in | mid-late summer

Apricots have been grown since the 16th century and can still be raised successfully even in cooler areas.

**GROWING** Apricots are best grown trained as fans on a south or west-facing wall. Prepare the ground thoroughly before planting in mid autumn by digging deeply and incorporating plenty of well-rotted organic manure or compost. Fix the supporting wires to the wall in advance, with brackets at the top from which to hang protective netting on frosty nights. Buy young trees on St Julien A rootstock with the framework of branches already formed in the nursery. Dig a shallow planting hole and spread the roots. Cover with fine soil, firm in and water well. Spread a thick mulch over the rooting zone. Fix the ribs on canes to the wires. Pruning is as for a fan-trained peach, except that apricots fruit on spurs as well as on young shoots. If there is space on an established tree you can encourage spurs to form by shortening sideshoots in mid summer. Water regularly in summer and put down a moisture-retaining mulch. Apricots are self-pollinating. If you put netting up at night, remove it by day to let insects in to do their work.

**HARVESTING** Twist off the fruits when ripe without bruising the flesh. They can be eaten raw or cooked.

**POSSIBLE PROBLEMS** Frost damage; cut out dead branches and paint the wound.

## ■ COOK'S TIP

*Ripe fruit are deeper in colour and taste delicious picked from the tree and eaten raw, straight away. They also make a wonderful addition to a lamb or pork casserole. As a pudding poach them in honey syrup flavoured with lemon juice or vanilla. Glazed apricot tart is a favourite on the continent. Add slices of apricot to creamy Greek yogurt plus a little orange juice and some honey. Place in a glass bowl and decorate with chopped almonds.*

# NECTARINE

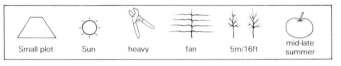

Small plot | Sun | heavy | fan | 5m/16ft | mid-late summer

The nectarine is a smooth-skinned peach. It has become very popular, but because it is not as hardy as the true peach should only be grown in warmer districts, preferably fan-trained on a sunny wall.

**GROWING** Soil should be well drained, deeply dug and moisture retentive. Plant in mid autumn, first working plenty of well-rotted organic material into the soil. Buy a young tree with the basic framework for fan-training already formed in the nursery. Fix the supporting horizontal wires to the wall before planting, and attach brackets at the top to hold a sheet of light hessian or plastic netting, which can be hung in front of – not touching – the tree on frosty nights. Remove the protective fabric by day to admit the light and warmth of the sun as well as pollinating insects. If these are few, use a tuft of cotton wool to speed things up. Nectarines are self-pollinating but flowering early as they do is a disadvantage. For pruning, see fan-trained peaches. Thin the fruits in mid summer to stand 20cm/8in apart. If the crop is too heavy the fruits will be all stone and no flesh, and the tree will be exhausted.

**HARVESTING** Pick the fruits when the flesh at the stalk yields to light pressure. Hold in the palm, twist off gently.

**POSSIBLE PROBLEMS** Frost damage; peach leaf curl; aphids; red spider mite.

## ■ GARDENER'S TIP

*Use a support system of wires and nails to tie branches in to protect them from wind damage. Make up a frame of horizontal wires, about 45cm/18in apart, held stretched taut away from the wall with vine eyes or wall ties.*

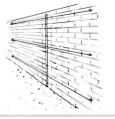

## PEACH

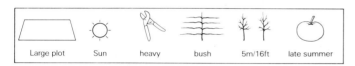

| Large plot | Sun | heavy | bush | 5m/16ft | late summer |

Peaches can be grown successfully in cooler climates in the open as long as you avoid obvious frost pockets or windswept sites. Early flowering exposes peach blossom to frosts; another disadvantage is that fewer insects are around and you may have to assist pollination with a tuft of cotton wool. All varieties, except Hale's Early, are self-pollinating.

**GROWING** Soil should be deep and well-drained but retentive of summer moisture. A pH level of 6.2 is about right. Buy a 1-year-old tree from a reputable nursery for planting in mid autumn. Incorporate plenty of well-rotted organic compost or manure into the soil. Take out a shallow planting hole, spread the roots out wide and attach the tree to a stake. Cover with fine soil, firm well and water in. Cut the tree back to 60cm/2ft and reduce the branches by two thirds. Apply a moisture-retaining mulch over the rooting zone. Subsequent pruning is as for bush apples, except that each spring it is necessary to prevent established trees from carrying all the fruit at the ends of the branches by cutting 3 chosen branches back to old wood. Water well and give an annual mulch. In heavy-cropping years thin out badly placed and damaged fruits to leave the remainder 20cm/8in apart.

**HARVESTING** Fruits ripen over a 6-week period.

**POSSIBLE PROBLEMS** Peach leaf curl; Aphids.

## FAN-TRAINED PEACH

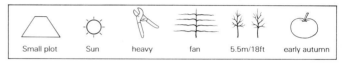

| Small plot | Sun | heavy | fan | 5.5m/18ft | early autumn |

The protection of a sunny wall allows you to fan-train late-ripening peaches like Bellegarde.

**GROWING** Soil should be deep, well drained and moisture retentive. It dries out much quicker near a wall, so water regularly. Buy the tree with the basic framework of branches formed in the nursery and fix the supporting horizontal wires to the wall before planting in mid autumn. Drape protective fabric from brackets in front of the tree on frosty nights and remove it by day. Pruning of an established fan is dictated by the fact that peaches fruit on the previous year's growth. Wood that has fruited does not fruit again and must be cut out at the end of the season, along with any damaged branches, so that a replacement shoot can be tied in. Spring-pruning encourages the production of these shoots. First, rub out any shoots pointing straight out or into the wall. From those remaining, leave healthy shoots at 15cm/6in apart on the ribs and one on the end. These will grow on as laterals. The next spring, growth buds will appear at the base of each lateral. Allow one to grow on as a replacement, and remove the others when they reach 5-7.5cm/2-3in. In the summer the laterals bear fruit – let the tips grow on but pinch out any sideshoots.

**HARVESTING** Lift off the ripe fruits in the palm of your hand.

**POSSIBLE PROBLEMS** Blackfly; peach leaf curl.

### ■ ORGANIC TIP

A pH tester is an inexpensive and valuable piece of equipment with which to test how acid or alkaline your soil is. Once you know this you can adjust a too-acid soil by adding small amounts of lime in the spring before you sow or plant (not at the same time as manure though). A soil which is chalky and too high in lime needs to be deeply dug and to have lots of manure and compost added to increase the acidity.

### ■ GARDENER'S TIP

Protect trees from frost by covering them with hessian. Place canes around the plant to stop the fabric touching the blossoms. Remove covers when temperatures rise to admit pollinating insects.

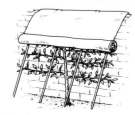

# PEACHES UNDER GLASS

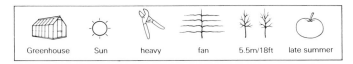

| Greenhouse | Sun | heavy | fan | 5.5m/18ft | late summer |

Growing peaches in a glasshouse is a great luxury, since ideally the house should be devoted to the tree. Choose the variety Peregrine, which is dependably self-fertile.

**GROWING** Peaches grown under glass should be trained in a fan shape. The tree is best planted in a border 60cm/2ft wide and trained up the span on one side of the house. Make sure the roots have a minimum depth of 45cm/18in of well drained loam. The procedures for fan-training (see Peaches against a wall) must be assiduously carried out, and will be necessary at earlier stages of the year thanks to the protected environment. Keep the border well watered, especially in summer, and ventilate the house well during the day. The winter night temperature need not be more than 4C/40F, but not less than 10C/50F in summer. It is essential to hand-pollinate the flowers. As soon as the fruits set, spray the tree lightly every day with clear water to keep the foliage bright and the fruits swelling.

**HARVESTING** Pick the ripe fruits very gently, lifting them in the palm of the hand.

**POSSIBLE PROBLEMS** Dryness at the roots is the most important cause of failure. In these conditions glasshouse red spider mite can thrive and cause great damage.

# QUINCE

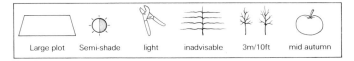

| Large plot | Semi-shade | light | inadvisable | 3m/10ft | mid autumn |

The quince is a handsome tree, bearing flowers like apple blossom in spring. It has yellow pear-shaped fruits that are slightly acid and with a pungent aroma when ripe. They are used for making a delicious golden jelly.

**GROWING** Quinces need shelter and a certain degree of warmth. In cold districts it is possible to grow them as fans against a sunny wall, but in practice the trees dislike being trained. Unlike other tree fruits, quince – which is self-pollinating – is grown on its own roots, so you do not have to worry about choosing a suitable rootstock. In fact if there is a healthy tree growing in your area, a sturdy sucker can be detached in the winter and easily started into growth. Otherwise, start with a 2-year-old tree and plant in autumn in any fertile soil. Quinces may be planted near water. Give a generous mulch after planting and every subsequent spring until the tree is established. Keep down weeds. Pull off suckers and otherwise prune only to remove diseased, damaged or overcrowded branches.

**HARVESTING** Leave the fruits on the tree until late autumn. Store in a cool but frost-proof shed and pick over for use as they ripen. Apples and pears kept in store with quinces will inevitably pick up their stronger aroma so it is best to keep them separate.

**POSSIBLE PROBLEMS** Birds and aphids.

## ▦ ORGANIC TIP

*To prune, rub out any shoots pointing straight out. Leave healthy shoots at 15cm/6in apart on the ribs and one on the end to grow on as laterals. The next spring, growth buds will appear at the base of each lateral. Allow one to grow on.*

## ▦ ORGANIC TIP

*Make delicious quince jelly. Simmer 1.75kg/4lb peeled, cored and chopped quinces in 600ml/1pt water until tender, then pour into a jelly bag. Leave overnight to drain through, add 1 tablespoon lemon juice, and 400g/14oz sugar to every*

*600ml/1pt liquid. Stir until the sugar dissolves, then boil briskly until setting point is reached.*

# DAMSON

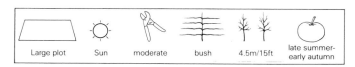

| Large plot | Sun | moderate | bush | 4.5m/15ft | late summer-early autumn |

Related to plums, but smaller and invariably deep purple in colour, damsons are usually used for jam or in preserves.

**GROWING** While damsons like the fertile, deep and slightly acid soil necessary for plums, they can cope better with heavy rainfall and high wind (particularly the variety Farleigh Damson). Start with a 2 to 3-year-old half-standard tree on St Julien A rootstock. Plant in autumn and double-stake as for cooking plums. Take care not to bury the union between rootstock and variety. Prune as for cooking plums, and remove any suckers that shoot from the base by scraping away the soil and pulling them away: if you cut suckers off they grow back even stronger. In heavy-cropping years, thin the fruits in early summer to take the weight off the branches, leaving the remaining fruits as evenly spaced as possible.

**HARVESTING** Pick the ripe fruits and make jam or bottle them immediately.

**POSSIBLE PROBLEMS** Birds, wasps and aphids are the major pests. Inspect for silver leaf: cut off and burn affected branches.

**VARIETIES** Farleigh Damson (pollinated by Czar or Golden Transparent Gage plums); Merryweather (self-fertile).

# GREENGAGE

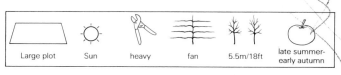

| Large plot | Sun | heavy | fan | 5.5m/18ft | late summer-early autumn |

As greengages are not completely hardy, most are trained as fans against a sunny wall.

**GROWING** A deeply cultivated, fertile and slightly acid soil is best. Incorporate plenty of well-rotted organic manure before planting in the autumn. If you are planting in the open, stake the young tree as described for cooking plums. For a fan-trained tree, choose St Julien A rootstock. Before planting, fix the supporting horizontal wires to the wall spaced 30cm/12in apart. Start with a 1-year-old tree and prune it back to 60cm/2ft. The 2 buds at the top will produce shoots which will make the first ribs of the fan, one left, one right. In the summer, when they have reached 23-30cm/9-12in, tie the shoots to canes and attach the canes to the wires at an angle of 45°. Follow a system of early spring pruning and summer training, selecting 3 evenly spaced shoots from each rib to start with until over the years you have built up 32 evenly spaced ribs. Always use canes to train the extension growth. They can be removed when the growth is woody. Do not allow any shoots to grow strongly upwards.

**HARVESTING** Let greengages ripen on the tree as long as possible, then pick them by the stalk to prevent bruising. Use immediately.

**POSSIBLE PROBLEMS** Bullfinches; aphids.

---

■ GARDENER'S TIP

*If necessary, thin the damsons when the stones have just formed by pulling off some of the fruit. Repeat if necessary when the fruits have expanded. Leave a final spacing of about 5cm/2in between the fruit.*

■ COOK'S TIP

*Make tasty fruit crumble with greengages instead of apples. Stone 675g/1½lb ripe greengages and arrange in an ovenproof dish. Sprinkle with sugar to taste. Rub 75g/3oz butter into 175g/6oz flour until the mixture resembles fine breadcrumbs, then* *add 75g/3oz sugar. Sprinkle over the fruit and bake at 200C/400F/gas 6 for 40 minutes. To freeze, leave unbaked and cover with clear film before putting in the freezer.*

# COOKING PLUM

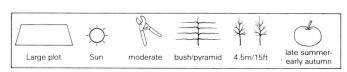

| Large plot | Sun | moderate | bush/pyramid | 4.5m/15ft | late summer-early autumn |

Plum varieties, such as Czar and Marjorie's Seedling with a relatively low sugar content are suitable for preserving, jam-making or for use in cooked desserts. The popular Victoria can be used for cooking and for eating raw.

**GROWING** As long as the soil is fertile and slightly acid, most plums tolerate heavier, wetter (but not waterlogged) conditions than apples or pears. Dig in plenty of well-rotted organic manure, compost or peat before planting in the autumn. Buy a 2 or 3-year-old half standard tree of a self-fertile variety on St Julien A rootstock or on Pixie for a dwarf pyramid. Make a wide, shallow planting hole. Drive in a double stake using 2 posts 2m/6ft 6in long, connected by a 45-cm/18-in crossbar. Spread the roots out wide, cover with soil and firm well in. Do not bury the union between rootstock and variety. Attach the stem to the crossbar, padding it to prevent chafing. Cut back all branches to 60cm/2ft. Prune for the next 2 winters as for apples. Thereafter prune only in summer to remove diseased or crowded branches. Water well and apply a general purpose fertilizer in early spring. Mulch in summer to suppress weeds.

**HARVESTING** Pick the fruits as soon as ripe and use immediately or freeze. Plums cannot be stored.

**POSSIBLE PROBLEMS** Silver leaf (see tip). To avoid sharka disease, buy certified virus-free stock.

# DESSERT PLUM

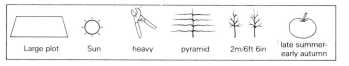

| Large plot | Sun | heavy | pyramid | 2m/6ft 6in | late summer-early autumn |

Dessert plums are those which develop a high sugar content and are delicious to eat raw.

**GROWING** Dessert plums have the same requirements as cooking varieties: a well-cultivated, fertile, slightly acid soil on a site not too exposed. The trees are vulnerable to strong winds since they bear a lot of fruit. Dwarf pyramid trees on Pixie rootstock are useful for small gardens, but must be trained to shape. Give the leader of the newly planted tree a stout 3m/10ft cane for support. In the mid spring after planting, cut the tree back to 1.5m/5ft. Reduce any sideshoots by half, but remove completely any close to the ground, up to 50cm/20in to give a short leg. Toward the end of summer, shorten the ends of the branches, not the central leader, to 20cm/8in, cutting any sideshoots to 10cm/4in. In each case, cut back to a downward pointing bud. Next mid spring, reduce the central leader by two thirds. Repeat the end of summer pruning annually; cut the central leader well back every mid spring until it reaches 3m/10ft. After that, prune the leader every late spring to within 2.5cm/1in of the previous year's cut.

**HARVESTING** Pick and use as soon as ripe.

**POSSIBLE PROBLEMS** Silver leaf; aphids; birds.

**VARIETIES** Early Transparent Gage; Victoria; Severn Cross (all self-fertile).

## ■ ORGANIC TIP

*Silver leaf gives the leaves a silvery appearance and shoots and branches die back, with a purplish stain produced on the dead wood. The fungus enters through wounds from pruning, so treat large wounds with Trichoderma powder. All dead growth needs to be removed back to 15cm/6in of healthy wood. Inoculate infected trees with Trichoderma pellets. Insert them in 5cm/2in holes in the trunk. Spray aphid-infected trees with insectidal soap.*

## ■ DECORATIVE TIP

*Some plums do well in pots and can be trained decoratively in a pyramid shape or in a row as single cordons growing at 45 degrees against a wall or fence. Cover plants with netting in the spring to protect the blossoms against frost.*

# FRUIT PESTS, PROBLEMS AND DISEASES

| Problem | Symptoms | Remedy |
|---|---|---|
| Aphids | Visible on shoots. Yellowing and distorted leaves. Sticky coating covered with sooty mould. | Wash off with soapy solution. Use tar oil to destroy over-wintering eggs. Spray with derris or malathion. |
| Big bud | Black currant buds become large and round and finally wither. | In winter, pick off enlarged buds to prevent spread of virus. Spray with lime sulphur. |
| Botrytis (grey mould) | Grey fluffy mould on stems, leaves, flowers and fruits. | Avoid overwatering. Remove affected parts. Spray with systemic fungicide. |
| Cane spot | Stems of raspberries and loganberries are covered with small purple spots in early summer. Spots enlarge to form white blisters. | Cut out affected canes. Spray with benomyl at 14-day intervals. |
| Canker | Bark of apple and pear trees shrinks in concentric rings. | Cut off damaged twigs. Cut out cankered bark. Coat wound with protective paint. |
| Capsid bug | Reddish spots and little holes in leaves. Fruits cracked and discoloured. | Keep garden free of debris. Spray apples and black currants in winter with malathion. |
| Codling moth | Grubs in apples, pears and plums in mid/late summer. | See spraying programme for apples. Trap larvae with corrugated cardboard bands round trunk in mid summer. |
| Damping off | Seedlings topple over as stems rot. | Sow thinly and do not overwater. |
| Die back | Branches of fruit trees die from the tips downwards, either from frost damage or fungal attack. | Cut off and burn affected part. Coat cuts with protective paint. |
| Flea beetle | Small yellow and black beetles puncture leaves with tiny holes. | Good garden hygiene will reduce the number of beetles hibernating in debris. A spray of derris may be used to protect young seedlings. |
| Leaf spot | Blotches on leaves of black currants and other plants. | Remove and burn affected leaves. Keep garden free of debris. Spray with fungicide. |
| Peach leaf curl | Rusty blisters on leaves of peaches, nectarines and apricots. Leaves fall prematurely. | Spray with lime sulphur or Bordeaux mixture in mid/late winter and again 14 days later. |
| Powdery mildew | Leaf surface and fruits covered with white powdery deposit. | Apply sulphur dust, benomyl or dinocap. Remove all diseased shoots in autumn. |
| Raspberry beetle | Small brown beetles damage flower buds of raspberry, blackberry and loganberry. Grubs eat berries. | Spray with derris as the flowers start to fall and again when berries begin to flush with colour. |
| Sawfly | Shows on apples as a ribbon scar on the surface with stickiness at entry hole. On gooseberries, leaves are reduced to skeletons. | Destroy fallen apples. Spray with malathion. |
| Scab | Affects leaves, twigs and fruits of apples and pears, discolouring and distorting. | See spraying programme for apples. |
| Slugs and snails | Eat stems, roots and leaves of a variety of plants. | Strew soot or sawdust around stems. Pick them up at night and drop into paraffin. Use metaldehyde bait. |
| Wasps | Attack soft-skinned or damaged fruits. | If damage is severe, catch wasps in jars of sweetened water. |

## SPRAYING PROGRAMME FOR APPLES

*(Do not spray open blossoms with insecticides: remember the busy bees.)*

| Timing | Materials | Control |
|---|---|---|
| Blossom buds showing but still green | Benlate and Malathion (or Rogor) | Scab<br>Mildew<br>Aphids<br>Caterpillars |
| Immediately after blossoming | Repeat spray 1 | as above |
| 14 days later | Benlate<br>Karathane | Scab<br>Mildew |
| Early summer | Benlate<br>Karathane<br>Malathion | Scab<br>Mildew<br>Codling moth |

# GLOSSARY

**Acid** Used to describe soil with a pH reading below 7.0. Because acid soils contain little lime, it is necessary to add lime in order to grow plants such as brassicas.

**Alkaline** Used to describe soil with a pH reading above 7.0. A slightly alkaline soil suits most plants.

**Annual** A plant that completes its life cycle in one growing season.

**Axil** The angle between the stem and a leaf, from which further growth arises.

**Biennial** A plant that needs two growing seasons to complete its life cycle, e.g. the herb angelica.

**Blanching** Excluding light from vegetables such as chicory and celery in order to whiten the stems or leaves and remove the bitter taste.

**Bolt** Running to seed prematurely. Lettuces and beetroot bolt if deprived of water in hot weather.

**Broadcast** To spread seed or fertilizer evenly over a wide area.

**Calyx** The outer protective part of a flower which persists at the top of the fruit, e.g. tomato, strawberry.

**Cane** The woody stem of raspberries, blackberries and loganberries.

**Catch crop** A quick-maturing crop grown between rows of slower-growing species or sown and harvested in the brief time between one crop being picked and the next being sown.

**Chlorosis** Deficiency of minerals in the soil causing the leaves to be pale.

**Clamp** A store for root vegetables made of a mound of soil and straw.

**Cloche** Glass or plastic covering to protect plants in the open in order to raise early crops.

**Cordon** A plant grown on a single main stem, achieved by strict pruning. Double and triple cordons have two and three stems respectively.

**Crown** The bottom of a perennial, e.g. rhubarb, from which roots and shoots arise.

**Curd** The heads of cauliflower and broccoli, made up of tightly packed flower-buds.

**Damping down** Watering the greenhouse or frame in warm weather to increase humidity.

**Drill** A straight furrow made in an outside bed to sow seeds.

**Earthing up** Drawing up soil around the stems to exclude light.

**Espalier** A type of tree trained with the support of wires, often against a wall. The main stem is vertical with pairs of branches extending horizontally at regular intervals.

**Fertilization** The fusion of the male and female elements of a plant (pollen and undeveloped seed) to form a mature seed.

**Festoon** A system by which tree branches are trained to curve downwards.

**Forcing** Bringing plants to fruit before their natural time.

**Fungicide** A substance used to eradicate fungal diseases.

**Germination** The first stage in the development of a plant from a seed.

**Half-hardy** Used to describe plants that require protection during the winter.

**Hardening off** Acclimatizing plants that have been grown under heated glass to outside conditions.

**Hardy** Description of plants that survive frost in the open.

**Haulm** The leafy stems of potato plants.

**Heeling in** Inserting shoots or roots of plants into the soil for a limited period to keep them moist until the time is right to put them in their permanent positions.

**Humus** The substance remaining when dead vegetable matter has broken down.

**Inorganic** A chemical substance, such as fertilizer, which does not contain carbon.

**Insecticide** A substance used for killing insects.

**Larva** The immature stage of some insects, such as caterpillars and grubs.

**Lateral** A stem or shoot that branches out from the leaf axil of a larger stem.

**Leader** The main stem of a tree that extends the system of branches.

**Lime** Calcium, a chemical that may be used to neutralize acid soils. Too much lime makes it impossible for some nutrients to be available to plants.

**Loam** Soil which is a compound of clay, silt, sand and humus. It is moisture-retentive and mineral-rich.

**Maiden** A one-year-old fruit tree.

**Mulch** A layer of organic matter spread on the soil surface to conserve moisture.

**Neutral** Used to describe soil with a pH reading between 6.5 and 7.0, which is neither acid nor alkaline.

**Organic** Used to describe substances that are the product of the decay of living organisms.

**Pan** A layer of hard soil that may form if soil is repeatedly worked to the same depth.

**Peat** Partially decayed organic matter. Sedge peat comes from the roots of sedges growing in bogs.

**Perennial** A plant that lives for an indefinite period.

**pH reading** The pH scale is used to measure the acidity or alkalinity of soil. The neutral point is 7.0; a reading above this denotes alkalinity and one below it denotes acidity.

**Pinching out** Removing the growing point of a stem to encourage bushy growth.

**Pollination** Transferring pollen grains (the male cells of a plant) on to the stigma of a flower.

**Pricking out** Planting out seedlings for the first time to larger trays or to a nursery bed.

**Propagation** Increasing plants.

**Pyramid** A type of tree, trained to have an outline like a pyramid.

**Root run** The soil area occupied by the roots of a plant.

**Rootstock** The name for the plant on to which another is grafted.

**Runner** An aerial stem which roots at the tip when it touches the soil, to make a new plant e.g. strawberry, blackberry.

**Scion** A shoot of a plant joined to the rootstock of another. Used to propagate fruit trees.

**Seedling** A young plant.

**Self-fertile** Used to describe a fruit tree that does not need a pollinator to set fruits.

**Self-sterile** Used to describe a fruit tree that needs a pollinator to set fruits.

**Spit** A spade's depth – about 25-30cm/10-12 inches.

**Spur** A small lateral branch on a fruit tree which bears flower buds.

**Stake** Support for top-heavy plants, from tomatoes to fruit trees.

**Sucker** A shoot that arises from below ground level.

**Tender** Used to describe any plant susceptible to damage by frost.

**Tilth** The surface layer of the soil, which is fine and crumbly.

**Truss** A cluster of fruits or flowers.

# INDEX